SYMBOLISM AND GROWTH

American Academy of Religion
Dissertation Series

edited by
Wendell Dietrich

Number 36

SYMBOLISM AND GROWTH
The Religious Thought of Horace Bushnell
by
David L. Smith

David L. Smith
Symbolism and Growth: The Religious Thought of Horace Bushnell

Scholars Press

Distributed by
Scholars Press
101 Salem Street
Chico, California 95926

SYMBOLISM AND GROWTH
The Religious Thought of Horace Bushnell

David L. Smith
Ph.D., 1979, University of Pennsylvania
Philadelphia, Pennsylvania

Library of Congress Cataloging in Publication Data

Smith, David Lester.
  Symbolism and growth.

  (American Academy of Religion dissertation series ;
no. 36)
  Originally presented as the author's thesis,
University of Pennsylvania, 1979.
  Bibliography: p.
  Includes index.
  1. Bushnell, Horace, 1802–1876. I. Title. II. Series:
American Academy of Religion. Dissertation series—
American Academy of Religion ; no. 36.
BX7260.B9S64   1980   230'.58   80-14600
ISBN 0-89130-409-6
ISBN 0-89130-410-X (pbk.)

Printed in the United States of America
1 2 3 4 5
Edwards Brothers, Inc.
Ann Arbor, Michigan 48106

CONTENTS

INTRODUCTION

The argument of this dissertation is that the religious
thought of Horace Bushnell (1802-1876) is modeled on a theory
of the power of symbolic expressions, linguistic and otherwise,
to facilitate human moral growth. We will refer to this seminal
theory throughout as Bushnell's theory of communication, not because we consider Bushnell a precursor of contemporary communication theory, but because the word "communication" pinpoints
Bushnell's preoccupation with the role of social interaction in
the formation of religious character, and because of its etymological links with other concepts that play crucial roles in
Bushnell's thought: "community" and "communion" above all. Our
argument will be made in two stages. First, we will offer a
brief account of the origins of Bushnell's theory of communication in his early life and intellectual milieu. Second, through
a detailed analysis of his works, we will show how his theory
of communication gave him a framework for understanding the
means and ends of the Christian redemptive economy.

A parallel aim of this study will be to show that Bushnell's
theory of communication reveals an inner unity in his thought
that has hitherto been unappreciated. The search for a "key"
to Bushnell is nothing new. Several commentators have claimed
to discover the "secret of Horace Bushnell" in such things as his
theory of language and his theory of divine immanence.[1] It is
our contention, however, that these interpretations stop short
of Bushnell's real depth. While they correctly identify major
themes in his work, they fail to discover Bushnell's crucial
contention that religion is an effective, transforming power
in the normative growth of the mind. This theory of Christianity
as a power that makes for moral and spiritual self-realization is
concentrated in Bushnell's theory of communication. It is with
the theory of communication, then, that we propose to begin.

By thus presenting Bushnell's work as a unified intellectual
project, we hope to do service to his reputation. We set out,
however, with a clear sense of the limitations of our material.
Bushnell is admittedly a minor figure in intellectual history,
one whose work has not worn well with time. In his own day,

Bushnell built a reputation as a religious radical, a minor
master of oratory and didactic prose, and a prophet of the
cultural and educational ideals of Protestant liberalism. Look-
ing at his writings today, we are not particularly surprised
that the reputation has not survived. Bushnell's thought may
have seemed radical to the provincial New England Calvinists who
wanted him tried for heresy in 1849, but his spirit seems tame
in historical perspective. We now file Bushnell away as a
cautious mediator between orthodoxy and transcendentalism, and
look to Emerson as the more truly adventurous mind of that
generation. Even if we did not continue to read Emerson for
his ideas, we would know him for his literary art. But no one
today would make high claims for Bushnell's language. As
William James put it long ago, Bushnell's occasionally fine
prose all too often verges on "mouthing."[2] Finally, the status
Bushnell still enjoys among historians as the "father of American
religious liberalism"[3] is ill-suited to inspire much enthusiasm.
American religious liberalism has generally been viewed by
scholars as a poor relation of the European original. Such an
offspring, reviled or ignored by the world, is hardly a credit
to its father.

The world finds little in Bushnell, in short, that sets
him apart from the painfully obvious limitations of his age.
Modern studies of his life and thought therefore use him most
often to illustrate the forces at work in a failed culture. For
example, Barbara Cross's biography portrays Bushnell as a personality "straitened by the dualism of power and failure" that
hobbled the emotional life of an ambitious young nation.[4]
Ann Douglas understands him as one of the well-meaning but
insidious forefathers of America's sentimental mass culture.[5]
And Donald Crosby studies his theory of language as an intellectual curiosity--a complex of ideas with a rich past but no
very distinguished future.[6] If, on the other hand, Bushnell
is studied for what he can contribute to specialized modern
fields of inquiry, his preoccupations and ours turn out to be
a bad match. Recent theological studies slight him because he
sacrificed critical rigor to a "literary" concern for the
inspirational quality of ideas, while studies of literary

culture lose patience with him because he was too theological.[7] Bushnell, in sum, is neither great enough to be contemporary nor attractive enough in context to be admired.

All of these estimates are just in their way. It is far easier to bury Bushnell than to praise him. It will be a major aim of this dissertation to show, however, that while previous studies have shown us some of Bushnell's shortcomings, they have failed to do justice to qualities in his work that still richly deserve and repay humanistic study. Over the years, Bushnell has exerted a persistent fascination over students who take the trouble to read him closely. Like Jonathan Edwards, he is a writer who inspires enthusiasm for reasons that are not immediately apparent. One senses that a system or vision of great power and cogency lies just below the surface of any given writing, even though the vision itself never quite appears. One feels that a radical reconsideration of the basic stuff of religion is in progress, even before one understands how it is being done. In the case of Edwards, that feeling has been vindicated. Scholars have done the spade-work required to uncover the special meanings Edwards attached to his terms, and to show how each contributes to a deeply original view of divine-human relations.[8] Bushnell's works have never been afforded the same respect, however. Commentators recount his ideas, but do not attempt to probe them for the inner structuring that gives the whole its significance and drive. Our aim, then, will be to explicate that inner structure, and so to show something of the vision of human existence that was the inspiring force behind Bushnell's entire intellectual project.

Bushnell's vision, as we have already indicated, took the form of a theory of communication, a theory of how one mind influences others through its expressions. Exposition of the details of the theory would be out of place in this introduction, but perhaps a few words are in order to help orient the reader to the role of that theory in the general context of Bushnell's religious thought.

Religion, according to Bushnell, is primarily a means of fostering normative human growth, or what he generally calls "moral" growth. The end of religion is to produce "character,"

ix

a state of psychological wholeness and moral integrity that
might be discussed today in terms of authenticity or self-
realization. The means by which religion reaches this end, in
turn, are expressive or communicative. It uses the doctrines,
symbols, and rites of its tradition as teaching tools--expressive
"vehicles"--whose primary function is to evoke or encourage
growth in the life of the spirit.

The theological implications of this view of the nature and
function of religious symbols are quite sweeping. It means,
above all, that God is not to be understood primarily as a trans-
cedent, metaphysical entity, but as a factor in human experience.
Likewise, it implies that the meaning or "truth" of religion's
words about God is not exhausted by the facts to which they
refer ostensively, but consists in the state of mind they elicit
from those who have come to understand them (just as the meaning
of a poem is not exhausted by the ostensive reference of its terms,
but consists, in part, in the quality of the reader's response).
As Bushnell put it:

> What [religious teachings] carry into our soul,
> feeling or perception, or awaken in it by ex-
> pression, is their only truth, and that is a
> simple internal state of the soul itself.[9]

The reality of God, we might say, is one with the power the idea
of God exerts on the human imagination.

This focus on the subjective meaning of religious symbols
would seem to make the divine-human relation a rather one-sided
affiar. But here another aspect of our characterization of
Bushnell's theory as one of communication becomes significant.
Bushnell was not only interested in the growth of the mind, but
in the role played by interpersonal relations in growth. Communication between persons, as Bushnell understood it, is what
makes human growth possible. His own life experience, together
with his observation of others in society, had convinced him that
all persons form their identities through their social inter-
actions--that "character" is passively received from other persons as well as actively developed from within. Society, he
said, is a medium in which persons "flow together" through
various channels of influence.[10]

Bushnell was so sure that persons thus "get their insides"
from the influence of other persons in community that he went

on to propose a curious corollary to the principle. Whenever a mind is morally influenced through its intercourse with the world, he held, communication can be said to occur; and where there is communication, there is a communicator. Every *impres*sion received by a mind is occasioned by a corresponding *ex*pression made by another mind. Thus, for example, if a book brings us noble thoughts, a noble mind must have been its author; if a sunset fills us with a sense of well-being and wonder, it must be because awesome moral qualities are expressed in it by the Author of nature; finally, if Scripture inspires a "divine" possibility of existence or encourages the development of Christlike moral character, it can only be because the mind it expresses is divine--is God. When Bushnell suggested, then, that the reality of God is one with the power the idea of God exerts on the imagination, he did not mean that God is a projection of human feelings or potentials. He meant rather that the divine life--expressed to mankind in nature, Scripture, and Christ--and the life-direction given to mankind by that expression are identical. God is that power of influence in the universe that makes for character; and conversely, whatever serves to nurture character in man can be viewed as an expression of the divine mind.

We will have much more to say about the theological implications of Bushnell's theory of communication in the body of the thesis. We will also discuss in some detail its specific premises, its possible intellectual sources, and its implications for a theory of language. It will be no part of our intention, however, to make a case for the contemporary relevance of Bushnell's theory or his theology as a whole. The theory is fraught with technical difficulties and the theology partakes of them. For example, an absolutely crucial premise of Bushnell's understanding of communication is that every symbolic expression of a mind is a direct and reliable index of its author's thoughts, feelings, and moral character. The premise was a commonplace of the philosophy and literary criticism of Bushnell's day.[11] Given our contemporary psychological sophistication, however--our sensitivity to the mind's resources for self-deception and conscious or unconscious fraud--Bushnell's

premise is hardly creditable today. We could not live with it;
Bushnell could not get along without it. Nevertheless, it is
a presupposition of this study that such discrepancies between
Bushnell's thought-world and our own pose no barrier to an ap-
preciative understanding of his thought. Our aim is to comprehend Bushnell's intellectual project in its essential integrity,
as one man's attempt to use the intellectual resources of his
age to meet his needs in personal, cultural, and professional
contexts. To see how such things have been done by persons in
the past, we hold, is a thing of abiding interest and value.
Humanistic scholarship has no higher end.

Our approach to Bushnell, then, is as follows. In the
first chapter, we will explore the origins of Bushnell's intellectual project in his own early life and in a pair of literary
traditions which were widely influential in Bushnell's New
England. The examination of his life will show his developing
sensitivity to the power of interpersonal communication in
moral and spiritual growth. The literary traditions, in turn,
will be shown to have provided him with possible models for
understanding how a person's expression of his own identity can
influence the growth of other persons. The first such model
was provided by religious typology in its peculiarly American
guise, culminating in the works of Jonathan Edwards. The second
emerges from a complex of metaphysical and aesthetic theories
associated with the Scottish "common sense" philosophy which dom-
inated educated American opinion in the early nineteenth century.
Unfortunately, we will be able to say very little about how much
of this material Bushnell knew at first hand. Bushnell almost
never recorded his intellectual debts; in his explicit pronounce-
ments, he generally insisted on his own originality. Nevertheless,
the parallels between Bushnell's understanding of interpersonal
communication and the traditions we will review are striking.
We will contend that it is at least appropriate to say that
these traditions represent a continuing conversation in New
England religious thought into which Bushnell entered, tenta-
tively and on his own terms, and in which he found his voice
as a writer.

In the first chapter, we will also touch on the vexed
question of the extent of romantic influences on Bushnell. The
position taken will be that while Bushnell was deeply informed
by what little he read of the writers generally classed as
romantics, he is far more fruitfully viewed as part of a more or
less indigenous American tradition of reflection on the role of
symbols in spiritual growth. He was not a great romantic writer
or thinker, but his achievement in context is such that he becomes a truly "representative man," an abiding example of a reflective mind drawing resources for growth from its inevitabili-
ties.

In Chapter II, we will look briefly at Bushnell's earliest
theological interests and examine his first attempts to approach
theological questions by way of a theory of interpersonal communication. We will concentrate on two documents: an unpublished
address on "Revelation" (1839) and a sermon titled "Unconscious
Influence" (1846). Both are relatively sketchy when compared
to his more mature works, but together they outline a position
on the meaning and religious relevance of expressive symbolism
from which he was never to deviate.

The following three chapters will illustrate Bushnell's
applications of the theory of communication to his developing
thought on divine-human relations. The first topic to which
Bushnell applied his views was Christian education. Seeking
an alternative to revivalism as an account of how a person becomes a Christian, Bushnell explored the implications of his
theory for the doctrine of grace. Bushnell held that a properly
supernatural grace could be communicated through the natural
channels of society and history--that Christian character could
be gradually acquired through exposure to representations of
the divine mind immanent in the life of the world. A similar
line of thought also lies behind a major work of his later years,
Nature and the Supernatural (1858). This book and the writings
on education show a common concern with nature and society as
influences over character, and so we will consider them together
in Chapter III.

Chapter IV will take up Bushnell's mature reflections on
language and symbolism, in which his ideas on the educative

power of communication achieved their sharpest definition. We will see how his theory of language shaped his ideas on the limits and proper business of theology and suggested a means of reconciling Calvinist orthodoxy and Unitarianism, the two major theological parties of his day.

Finally, Chapter V will analyze Bushnell's views on a theological topic that he (along with many other seminal thinkers of Protestant liberalism) viewed as an epitome of the Christian redemptive economy--the doctrine of the atonement. Bushnell rejected both orthodox satisfaction theories and Unitarian "moral" theories of the work of Christ in favor of a doctrine modeled on his own theory of communication. He hoped to encompass both orthodox language and Unitarian aims in a single theory of how the forms of God's self-revelation--Christ, nature, Scripture, and the theological formulas that translate them--all serve as vehicles for the communication of a divine character to mankind. The heart of Bushnell's religious vision is contained here. His faith in the utility of religious symbols as instruments for the education of character is a faith that life in the world gains value from the glimpses of a divine life granted to us by cultural traditions, and from the possibilities of present existence to which that vision witnesses. A discussion of Bushnell's doctrine of the atonement will thus be a fitting conclusion to our study.

NOTES

INTRODUCTION

[1]For the contention that language is the "key to Horace Bushnell," see Mary Bushnell Cheney, *The Life and Letters of Horace Bushnell* (1880; rpt. New York: Arno Press, 1969), p. 203. The point is also assumed in Donald Crosby, *Horace Bushnell's Theory of Language* (The Hague: Mouton & Co., 1975), and in dissertations by Foard, Baird, and Howell cited in the bibliography. For the contention that divine immanence is Bushnell's major theme, see Theodore Thornton Munger, "The Secret of Horace Bushnell," in *Bushnell Centenary* (Hartford: Hartford Press, The Case, Lockwood & Brainard Co., 1902), pp. 35-46. William Johnson, *Nature and the Supernatural in the Theology of Horace Bushnell* (Lund: cwk Gleerup, 1963), develops a similar thesis.

[2]William James, "Review of Bushnell's *Women's Suffrage* and J.S. Mill's *The Subjection of Women*," *North American Review*, CXIX (October 1869), p. 556.

[3]Sydney E. Ahlstrom, ed., *Theology in America* (Indianapolis: Bobbs-Merrill, 1967), p. 64.

[4]Barbara Cross, *Horace Bushnell* (Chicago: University of Chicago Press, 1958), p. 50 and throughout.

[5]Ann Douglas treats Bushnell frequently and very suggestively in *The Feminization of American Culture* (New York: Alfred A. Knopf, 1977).

[6]Crosby, *op. cit.*

[7]Theological condescension stands out in Johnson, *op. cit.*, p. 11. The best brief accounts of Bushnell's place in the context of American literature are R.W.B. Lewis, *The American Adam* (Chicago: University of Chicago Press, 1955), pp. 66-73; and Charles Feidelson, Jr., *Symbolism and American Literature* (Chicago: University of Chicago Press, 1953), pp. 151-57.

[8]Two of the most illuminating studies of Edwards in this regard are Perry Miller, *Jonathan Edwards* (New York: W. Sloane Associates, 1949); and Roland Delattre, *Beauty and Sensibility in the Thought of Jonathan Edwards* (New Haven: Yale University Press, 1968).

[9]Bushnell, *Christ in Theology* (Hartford: Brown and Parsons, 1851), p. 17.

[10]Bushnell, *Views of Christian Nurture* (1847; rpt. Delmar, New York: Scholars' Facsimiles and Reprints, 1975), p. 40.

[11]See Meyer H. Abrams, *The Mirror and the Lamp* (New York: Oxford University Press, 1953), pp. 226-62; and William Charvat, *The Origins of American Critical Thought 1810-1835* (Philadelphia: University of Pennsylvania Press, 1936). This concept and associated ideas will be treated more fully in Chapter I below.

CHAPTER I

THE ORIGINS OF BUSHNELL'S INTELLECTUAL PROJECT

Our argument in this dissertation is that Horace Bushnell modeled his religious thought on a theory of how human persons shape each other--for better or worse--through their social and linguistic interactions. In this chapter, we will look at some themes in Bushnell's early biography and in the intellectual life of his times that lie at the root of his particular understanding of interpersonal communication. His own formative experiences, we will show, gave him insights into the role of social relations in personal and spiritual growth. His times, in turn, gave him a vocabulary for understanding his experinces in terms of transactions with other minds, human and divine, expressed in nature and history. In subsequent chapters, we will look at the theory of communication he developed out of these materials in more detail, and examine its bearing on his theology.

1. Young Man Bushnell

Bushnell was born into a farming, wool carding and weaving family in rural Litchfield County, Connecticut, in 1802.[1] He was also, in a sense, born to the ministry, at least as far as his mother was concerned. As the saying went, she was "ambitious for the Kingdom of Christ," and ambitious for the education and social advancement of her sons.[2] Horace, the eldest son, thus learned very early in life that to be what he ought to be, he must enter college and thence the service of God. The case is strikingly similar to that of young St. Augustine and his Christian mother, Monica. The mother's prophecy that her son would one day stand by her on the rule of faith fixed a longing in the son's heart that resisted any other solution; the bonds of maternal love and nurture made the prophecy self-fulfilling: "Our hearts are restless till they rest in Thee."

But the young Bushnell *was* restless. In adolescence, he held aloof from the Calvinist doctrine in which he was trained wherever it failed to satisfy his reason.[3] He had a strong

1

emotional attachment to Christianity that never altered, as his daughter--his first biographer--was at pains to show.[4] But Bushnell in his teens was determined to deal with his inbred religious sentiments on his own terms, to master them intellectually or as he put it, "to dig out a religion by my head."[5] The attempt may or may not have been fully rebellious, but it indicates a young man in tension with the self-image to which he had been raised.

A similar ambivalence is apparent in Bushnell's protracted indecision over what career he should pursue.[6] When his first opportunity to enter college came up, he chose to stay on the family farm instead. When he finally went off to Yale in 1823, it was under the impetus of a resolve to join the Congregational church in which he had been raised and fulfil his duties as a Christian. But in the course of his years at Yale, his new learning and budding vanity as a scholar--his new feel for a world beyond home--drew his attention away from the ministry again. After graduation, he began to test out possibilities for a secular career. He taught school for six months in Norwich, Connecticut, but found the work odious. In February of 1828, he accepted a position as reporter and editorialist for a newly founded New York City newspaper, the *Journal of Commerce*. Here he won considerable success, but found it, again, "a terrible life." After ten months, he returned to Yale to study law, and quickly conceived a plan to go to Ohio, join a law office, and make his way in politics. At 27 years of age, then, it seemed that Bushnell was set on a career of overt public action--that his restlessness was about to find outlet in the nation's rapidly opening channels of power and progress.[7]

But at this point, his mother came on the scene again. Just as Bushnell had settled his plans to go West, he received an offer to stay at Yale as a tutor of undergraduates. He was about to turn the offer down when, on a trip home, he was swayed by his mother's wish that he stay in Connecticut and take the post. His decision to stay proved crucial, for as a tutor, the conflict between his inbred sympathies and his rational self-assertiveness assumed a powerful new form. His students and charges idolized him; the power of his personality was such that he was mirrored and imitated.[8] But Bushnell was disturbed

by the reflected image. His students took up his religious
reticence along with his moral earnestness. And Bushnell--now
perhaps seeing through the eyes of his mother, the eyes of a
nurturer--felt their lack of simple faith more keenly than he
did his own.

The crisis came during one of the religious awakenings
that periodically swept Connecticut throughout the 1820's and
1830's.[9] In the winter of 1831, all Yale seemed to be awash
with evangelical fervor--all except Bushnell and his charges.
The scene piqued Bushnell's sense of reponsibility terribly.
"I must get out of this woe," he said to a friend. "Here I am
what I am, and these young men hanging to me in their indif-
ference amidst this universal earnestness on every side."[10]
The situation forced Bushnell to reconsider his personal religious attitudes from the standpoint of an educator. Where he
alone was concerned, it had once seemed possible simply to
suspend his sentimental allegiance to Christianity, to hold
aloof from what he could not bring himself to reject outright.
But in 1831, he saw that to remain uncommitted was to communicate
nothing but a superficial indecision and confusion to others.
If he was going to make an impression with the sympathies and
values that lay deepest in him, he determined, he must own up
to them. And this meant that he must profess his Christianity
in an open and effective way.

We have two retrospective accounts of Bushnell's conversion
to an open profession of Christianity. First, an eye witness
recalled the following from a meeting of tutors during the
revival:

> On one occasion [Bushnell] came in, and throwing
> himself with an air of abandonment into a seat,
> and thrusting both hands through his black, bushy
> hair, cried out desperately, yet half-laughingly,
> "O men! What shall I do with these arrant doubts
> I have been nursing for years? When the preacher
> touches the Trinity and when logic shatters it to
> pieces, I am all at the four winds. But I am glad
> I have a heart as well as a head. My heart wants
> the Father; my heart wants the Son; my heart wants
> the Holy Ghost--and one just as much as the other.
> My heart says the Bible has a Trinity for me, and
> I mean to hold by my heart. I am glad a man can
> do it when there is no other mooring, and so I
> answer my own question--what shall I do? But
> that is all I can do yet."[11]

Second, Bushnell himself told a story in a late sermon that
seems to be based on his experience at Yale. He described a
young man at school, disturbed on finding that his accustomed
faith has dimmed to the vanishing point. In despair, the youth
asks himself:

> "Is there, then, no truth that I do believe?
> Yes, there is this one, now that I think of it:
> there is a distinction of right and wrong that
> I never doubted, and I see not how I can; I am
> even quite sure of it. . . . Here, then, . . .
> will I begin. If there is a God, as I rather
> hope there is, and very dimly believe, he is a
> right God. If I have lost him in wrong, perhaps
> I shall find him in right."[12]

The accounts differ in certain respects. In the first,
it is the "heart" that gives Bushnell his reasons for embracing
Christianity--reasons which the reason does not know. In the
second, it is an intuitive distinction of right and wrong, or
what he had been trained to call the universal moral sense of
mankind.[13] The common theme of the accounts is what interests
us most, however. Bushnell's conversion resolve was marked by
an increased willingness to entertain and act on his inward
wants and affections. Resistance to Christian belief had brought
him to despair; receptivity to it thus promised an energizing
release from a long-standing tension. And such proved to be
the case. By choosing Christianity, and choosing the ministry
along with it, he at last found himself with both a faith and a
vocation in harmony with his earliest training. As a student
at Yale Divinity School, he was able to consolidate his talents
around the affectional core of his personality. As he wrote in
later life:

> as I look back on the crisis here passed, it
> seems very much like the question whether I
> should finally *be*. No other calling but this
> ministry of Christ, I am obliged to feel, could
> have anywise filled my inspirations and
> allowed me to sufficiently be.[14]

The Congregational ministry at the time Bushnell entered
the field was not the most promising of careers, however. The
New England clergyman in the 1830's had lost most of the overt
political power he had once enjoyed. Direct financial dependence on his congregation in the wake of disestablishment
weakened his social leverage and practical independence.[15]
Nevertheless, a high opinion was commonly held of the "power

of the pulpit" to mold public sentiment through the word alone.
Through writing and rhetoric, the clergyman was supposed to ac-
quire an almost magical influence over the moral and spiritual
lives of his people.[16] Bushnell eagerly seized on this definition of his role, for it promised him a stage from which to
carry on the work he had begun at Yale--the education of Christain character in others by means of personal influence. It
was not political power that he sought after all, but exemplary
power, or what he came to call "moral power."[17] He was thus to
find a congenial sphere of action in the rapidly developing
Victorian "communications network" as a pulpit orator and independent writer.[18]

The educative power of personal influence is at best a
subtle and perhaps an illusory thing, however.[19] Bushnell himself seems to have entertained doubts about this understanding
of his role from the start. Early in his career, he vacillated
between confidence in the power of exemplary influence and a
suspicion that his chosen style unsuited him for a truly active
professional life. For instance, he recalled in 1853 that his
state of mind at the time he took his first and only church was
tentative and conditional:

> I did not really expect to remain in the
> ministry long. I thought if I could some-
> time be called to a professorship of moral
> philosophy, it would be a more satisfactory
> field of exertion.[20]

But in 1840, when Bushnell was offered the presidency of
Middlebury College, he turned it down after much anguished
deliberation.[21] The decision marked his willingness to stay
within the terms of his resolve, to live out the consequences
of the providence that he touched him in 1831.

2. The Intellectual Context

With this brief sketch of Bushnell's formative years in
mind, we now turn to examine the intellectual tradition which
gave him a framework for understanding his experience and a
key to its theological relevance. Our analysis of Bushnell's
life and thought up to this stage has brought out a pattern.
A concern with the unification of his own personality led him
to profess Christianity. Concurrently, he discovered the power

of his character to influence the growth of others; and subsequently, he sought to put this power to work in his ministry. What we propose to do now is to raise two questions about this pattern. First, we will ask how Bushnell could move as easily as he did from the experience of personal growth he achieved through receptivity to his Christian heritage and moral conscience to the conclusion that he had entered a new relation to the divine--that he had been redeemed, indeed, through receptivity to the forms of his own life in history. A suggestive though inconclusive answer will be found in an indigenous American tendency to interpret the relations between God, history, nature, and the self in terms of typological symbolism. Some typologists, we will show, understood redemption as receptivity to God's presence in history and experience in a manner very similar to Bushnell. Second, we will ask how Bushnell understood the personal power by which he sought to communicate divine life to others. Here, the answer will be found in some implications of the Scottish philosophy of common sense in which Bushnell was trained.

a. Typology and Divine-Human Relations

One of Bushnell's favorite Scriptural texts was II Cor. 3:18: "And we all, with open face, beholding the glory of the Lord are changed into that same image from glory unto glory." He quoted the verse frequently, always intending it as an epitome of the Christian redemptive scheme. By beholding God, he implied, we begin to take on his identity; by responding openly to his glory, we come to share in it. A strikingly similar understanding of the nature and means of Christian redemption developed out of American Puritan reflection on religious typology, culminating in the typological doctrines of Jonathan Edwards. This tradition has received considerable attention lately through the work of Sacvan Bercovitch, Ursula Brumm, Mason Lowance, and others.[22] Their work has already proved its power to cast new light on early American culture and history.[23] We draw on it here simply to call attention to an understanding of divine-human relations that virtually defines the Puritan heritage as received by Bushnell.

Typology, in its simplest form, is a mode of Biblical exegesis which affirms continuity between the Old Testament and the New. A "type" is an Old Testament figure or event which is seen somehow to foreshadow the life and work of Christ, who is the "anti-type" or fulfilment of the Old Testament history. The practice is as old as Christianity itself. Paul, for example, wrote in Romans 5:14 that Adam was "a type [*typos*] of the one who was to come."

Typology has a long and variegated history, complicated by its tendency to become confused with other modes of symbolic exegesis such as allegory, analogy, and tropology.[24] Nevertheless, typology reached the seventeenth century Puritans in a relatively pure form. Samuel Mather's influential compendium, *The Figures or Types of the Old Testament*, retained the strict, classical definition of a type. "A type," he wrote, "is some outward or sensible thing ordained of God under the Old Testament to represent and hold forth something of Christ in the New."[25] The important point for Mather was to distinguish typology from allegory. Unlike allegory, he held, a type has both feet firmly planted in Scriptual history.[26] A type makes no reference to present events or abstract spiritual truths. The typical relation, we might say, is a closed circuit of meaning. It gives the redemptive history a tight internal logic, with Christ as "the Truth and Substance and Scope of all."[27] In so doing, however, it isolates the redemptive history from the world beyond Scripture. Typology, strictly defined, is thus irrelevant to the interpretation of present history or the experience of the individual Christian.

As we shall see, however, the dominant trend in American Puritan literature was to expand the logic of typological reference to include events beyond the bounds of Scripture. There were two basic reasons for this, which Bercovitch has explored in some detail.[28] First was the Puritans' sense of the eschatological ultimacy of their mission to America. The founding of the Bay Colony was not just an event in secular history in the eyes of many of the Puritan founders; it was the beginning of the end of time. God's millennial Kingdom was to be born--soon--in New England. Consequently, the Puritans were not content to read Scripture in a way that isolated redemptive from secular history. Exegetes like John Cotton, Samuel Sewall, and Cotton Mather, to name only a few, expanded the logic of typology to include American experience within the circuit of Scriptual meaning--to make America the anti-type or referent of the redemptive plan. As Samuel Sewall put it, "The New Jerusalem [in America] is that which the Old and New Testament do ring of."[29] The voyage from England to America became the anti-type of Israel's crossing of the Red Sea. New England became New Israel. Ultimately, secular history and the workings of grace were correlated to the point where good standing in the civil order could be equated with sainthood.[30]

Second, the American Puritans used an expanded doctrine of typology to help solve a perennial problem in Calvinist devotional thought. The problem is how a human person--understood to be totally depraved in his self-nature--can either take steps to better his position before God or find assurance that he has been saved. The self is an unreliable agent in either case. It contains no resources for improvement, and has no internal touchstones by which to judge the things of God. Of course, Calvinism allowed that there are a few approved authorities by which the self can be regimented--e.g. Scripture and the Christian community. But these external aids cannot really make up the soul's basic deficiency. For in the last analysis, people cannot get away from themselves. Even the struggle to conform to an expression of God's will is an act of self-will. A person's acts are inescapably his own, and so partake of his depravity. The self is thus caught in a double bind. To right himself and find assurance, a person must leave his corrupt nature behind. But to do this he must act himself, according to his own desire and will. And where the self is involved, there can be no assurance of a good end. Even the self's flight into heteronomous authority is blocked by the fact that it is the hated self that wills and flees.[31]

Basically, there are two possible theological responses to this problem. Either one can say that mankind is indeed helpless and must wait for grace to break through the sphere of nature and transform his state, or one can seek ways to mitigate Calvin's sharp separation of nature and grace. In general, Puritan theologians took the latter course. The

attempt to bridge the gap between nature and the divine took
many forms.[32] Most interesting for our purposes are the schemes
by which the Puritans sought to relate the self-natures of
individual Christians to the redeemed selfhood of Christ by
means of the theory of the types.

One such attempt can be illustrated from the works of the
Puritan poet, Edward Taylor. Unlike his friend and contemporary,
Samuel Sewall, Taylor did not fuse nature and grace on the
assumption that America was the site of an imminent millennium.[33]
He did not believe that American experience was redemptive simply
because it was American. However, Taylor, like Sewall, used an
expanded definition of typological meaning. He kept Christ as
the central point of reference--the anti-type of all types--but
he held that everything in the world, present as well as past,
could be called a type if it somehow recalled Christ to the
Christian imagination by its intrinsic excellence. For Taylor,
every morning's sunrise was a type of Christ as truly as Moses
was. He saw Christ not only in the Old Testament prophecies,
but in

> The glory of the world slikt up in types,
> In all Choise things chosen to typify
> His glory upon whom the worke doth light.[34]

Taylor thus held that many features of present experience were
"typical"--i.e. shadows of which Christ was the substance. The
natural world was accordingly full of Christ, and valuable as
such.

> Thou givst thy Truth to them: thus true they bee.
>   They bring their Witness out for thee. Hereby
> Their Truth appeares emboxed indeed in thee,
> And thou the true Messiah Shin'st thereby.
> Hence Thou, and they make One another true
> And They, and Thou each others Glory Shew.[35]

Such a circuit of meaning between type and Christ is familiar
to us already from our discussion of Samuel Mather. In Taylor's
typology, however, the circuit is inclusive rather than exclu-
sive of nature and present experience. Grace informs nature
and nature reflects grace in such a way that one Christic identity circulates through all. This world is drawn directly into
the drama of redemption.

A similar approach to the Puritan devotional dilemma emerged
from the works of writers who simply equated American experience

as such with life in the City of God. The assumption that
American history was redemptive history made it possible to
assert that individual persons could participate in Christ
simply by virtue of their participation in the American setting
and society. Cotton Mather's biographies of outstanding Puritans in the *Magnalia Christi Americana* are classic illustrations
of how this assumption could be used to mediate Christ to the
individual Christian. Mather presented the lives of the Puritan
founders under the aspect of the typical figures of Scripture,
the Old Testament heroes prefiguring Christ, on the assumption
that the two groups shared an equal spiritual dignity. For
instance, as Bercovitch points out, John Winthrop became
Nehemias Americanus in Mather's account. Mather identified
Winthrop's life and achievements with those of Nehemiah, who
participated in Christ because of his status as a type. As
Nehemiah had his "truth" in the participation, then, so did
Winthrop. Winthrop's life was, in effect, Christ's substance
shadowed forth in the forms of American experience. Winthrop's
biography thus served as an immanent and "greatly imitable"
model of divinely approved identity. The gap between man and
Christ's otherness was bridged by a network of symbolic
identifications.[36]

The works of Edward Taylor and Cotton Mather thus illustrate
how a broadened understanding of typology could bring what
Bercovitch has called "Christic identity" to mankind's very
doorstep. The world could be understood as full of the glory
and truth of Christ, a shadow of which Christ himself was the
substance. But a problem remained: how did fallen man get
the ability to lay hold of the possibility of existence thus
communicated to him? How could the individual participate in the
redemptive identity that informed his environment and culture?
Plainly, for typology to do its appointed job of mitigating the
split between nature and the divine for the individual believer,
further assumptions concerning man's practical access to the
divine had to be called into play. Doctrines such as preparationism and Arminianism, Ramist philosophy, and the covenant
theology were all used in this connection to affirm that man
"by nature" has access to God--that God has appointed means for
mankind's edification and left him with enough innate good

sense to recognize and use them.[37] However, this sort of doctrinal tinkering with the Calvinist worldview put the proponents
of the New England Way on dangerous intellectual ground. Their
peculiar theory of the types was relatively non-controversial;
it simply had not become an issue in most Calvinist countries.
The quasi-Arminian theories by which they supplemented it,
however, were of the sort to which Calvinists everywhere were
hypersensitive, especially after the Synod of Dort. The affirma-
tion that mankind had innate means of access to redemption seemed
to deny both man's total depravity and God's absolute sovereignty--
the lynchpins of the Calvinist cosmos. The flaw in the typological solution of the devotional dilemma, in short, was that to
become a solution on the personal level, it had to flirt with
heresy.

The only American thinker to take real strides towards
solving this problem--and indeed, the first to define it
clearly--was Jonathan Edwards. Edwards shared the Puritan
vision of the redemptive destiny of America.[38] However, while
Edwards acknowledged the immanent possibility of hightened
religious experience promised in the typological interpretation
of creation, he disagreed with his predecessors over how that
promise could be realized in the lives of individual Christians.
Because the solution Edwards hit upon anticipated Bushnell's in
many respects, we will examine it in some detail.

Edwards began his public career with a vigorous reassertion
of the Puritan devotional dilemma--a blast against the popular
"Arminian" assumption that the gulf between man and God was not
really so wide as Calvin found it to be. By contrast, in "God
Glorified in Man's Dependence," Edwards put the case against
mankind in its starkest form: unaided persons can do nothing
to win God's favor. Human nature includes no seed of divine
identity which persons can make good by their own efforts.
Rather, God's own being monopolizes the means and ends of the
entire redemptive process. God, he wrote, is "the *cause* and
original" of all good; he is "the medium by which it is obtained
and conveyed;" and "he is the *good itself*, given and conveyed."[39]
Fallen man, as separate from God, has no entrée to this circle
unless God vouchsafe it to him. Hence, man depends on God,
both to will and to do.

Once Edwards had opened this gap between nature and grace, however, he needed some way to understand how it could be overcome for the elect. Of course the gap could only be crossed by grace, by an act of divine good pleasure. But the question remained, what is grace, and by what means is it communicated to mankind? Here is where Edwards made a significant contribution to the theory of the types. By conceiving divine-human relations on the model of the relations between type and antitype, he effectively extended the idea of a type's participation in Christ which his predecessors had already applied to nature and history to the understanding of individual Christian identity.

This move hinged on Edwards' particular theories of how God communicates himself, as the "good," to the soul of man--his understanding of grace. Specifically, Edwards distinguished two forms of the good: objective and inherent. The objective good is the goodness of extrinsic objects, those things which one enjoys as "possessions," external to one's self. The inherent good, on the other hand, is a quality of the soul itself which the perceiver acquires in response to the perceived good and which is identical with the divine nature. Edwards usually called this quality excellency, beauty, or joy.[40] Not all persons sense the inherent good. Because it is divine sensation, it is not inherently available to fallen man. If any persons do discover some measure of excellence or beauty in their own experience, then, it is a sufficient indication that "they are made excellent by a communication of God's excellency . . . . They are made partakers of the divine nature."[41] The experience of excellence in the soul, in short, is grace; and grace in the soul is God himself, or rather, an infinitely small fraction or "earnest" of him. Redeemed identity according to Edwards was thus divine identity in an immediate and proper sense.

Edwards' chief originality was his use of a quasi-Lockean epistemology to define the means of this participation of God in the soul of man. This aspect of Edwards' thought has often been discussed, so we will present it very briefly here. What God communicates to man--that in which grace consists--is a new sense, a "sense of the heart," by means of which the redeemed are made capable of knowing God as beauty or the inherent good.

As Miller says, somewhat cryptically, for Edwards, "Grace is
sensible."[42] Without this sense, man is blind to God's excellence and dead to any experience of him; his understanding can
be merely notional. With it, however, man acquires both 1) a
knowledge of God as valuable being, and 2) an inclination to do
his will. That is, 1) on the cognitive side, our knowledge of
God as excellence is immediate and sure because there is no
essential difference between the sensation and the object. Like
love or the taste of honey, God's nature is such that, qualita-
tively speaking, it *is* what it is experienced *as*, and can only
be known in this "sensible" way.[43] And as the sensation is
valuable, so is the object. God's value is intrinsic, then, in
the sense that it is immediately experienced as valuable.

2) On the moral side, there is no gap between having the sense
for God and doing his will, for the will "is as" one's "inclination"--the unitary tendency of the total self. And the "heart,"
in which the new sense resides, is virtually identical with the
inclination. As one's heart perceives, so one will be inclined
to do.[44]

Typology entered Edwards' scheme at this point as an illustration of his concept of grace as a new sense of the heart.
New Englanders were familiar with the promise of immanent
redemption held out by the vision of American life as life in
the New Israel. Their problem was simply to relate the assumed
redemptive quality of the environment to the sinful condition
of its inhabitants. Edwards' epistemology offered a novel
approach to the problem. Edwards held, in effect, that to
experience the typical significance of nature--to live fully in
the familiar promise--was already to participate in the redemptive reality for which the types stood. To perceive and experience the inherent good of nature as a type of God was
literally to be the good. To see the world as radiant with
grace was to be full of grace oneself. Conceiving grace as a
new sense of the heart, in short, Edwards made the state of
the soul correlative with one's way of seeing. The world to
natural perception was simply the natural world. But that
same world to the person transformed by grace became a communicative vehicle of the divine substance it shadowed forth.
Typology, in short, codified the way of seeing the natural

world made possible by the new Christian sense. Actually to
see God in the forms of the world, in the manner that the types
defined, was the objective correlative of grace in the soul.
We run ahead of our story, however. Let us back up and
examine Edwards' theory of the types in detail. Actually,
Edwards' doctrine of typology was inconsistent, as Lowance has
demonstrated.[45] At times, Edwards stuck close to Samuel Mather's
conservative definition, restricting the application of the term
to Old Testament prefigurations of Christ, as in his *History of
the Work of Redemption*. In a few crucial documents, however--
especially in his "Miscellanies" and in the fragments assembled
by Miller as *Images or Shadows of Divine Things*--he vastly
extended his application of the term, making all nature and
history a network of types of both the divine nature and the
redemptive activity of God in Christ. Edwards' broader definition is clearly presented in the following passage from the
"Miscellanies:"

> This may be observed concerning types in general,
> that not only the things of the Old Testament
> are typical; for this is but one part of the typo-
> logical world; the system of created things may
> be divided into two parts, the typical world, and
> and antitypical world. The inferior and carnal,
> i.e. the more external and transitory part of
> the universe, that part of it which is inchoative,
> imperfect, and subservient, is typical of the
> superior, more spiritual, perfect, and durable
> part of it, which is the end, and, as it were,
> the substance and consummation, of the other.
> Thus, the material and natural world is typical
> of the moral, spiritual and intelligent, or the
> City of God.[46]

Here, Edwards' types are not just events prefiguring other
events, but symbolic representations of ideas in the mind of
God, spiritual facts under material form. The significant source
for such a concept would seem to be Platonistic allegorical
exegesis and the cosmology of emanation.[47] What then remained
of the more limited connotations of "type" in this definition?
Very little, apart from the implication that nature has its
"truth" or reality in what it shadows forth of the spiritual
world, as the pure type has its truth in Christ. Further, the
idea that types are providentially ordained for man's edification
persisted in Edwards' usage. In the types, he wrote, "God
glorifies himself and instructs the minds he has made."[48]

Thus, Edwards' theory of the types transformed the received doctrine in the process of translating it into his system. Edwards' theory not only brought the types into the sphere of present experience; it correlated perceptual experience and the spiritual status of the perceiver. According to Edwards, that is, there was no gap between perceiving and being. Perception of the type *as* type was tantamount to participation in the reality it stood for. Just as his philosophy of grace made perception of the beauty of God dependent on the possession of a new principle of vision in in the soul, which was identical with the Spirit, so his theory of the types made the Christian's relation to God through the types inward, immediate, and spiritually informative.[49] The types quite literally communicate an experience of divinity to the perceiver. Thus as Miller writes, "the beauty of a type was exactly that, if it existed at all, it needed only to be seen, not argued."[50] Seeing, in this case, is believing.[51]

In sum, Edwards managed to give the same "typical" status to Christian identity that New England exegetes had previously accorded to nature and history. The relation between the Christian and God as pictured by Edwards mirrored the structure of the relation between type and anti-type. In each case, the two poles of the relation are ultimately of one substance. Identity circulates between them in an unbroken stream. Thus, what Edwards said of the relations between God and creatures recalls Edward Taylor's lines on the relations between the type and Christ. Taylor understood the relation between Christ and the types on the analogy of facing parallel mirrors, infinitely reflecting and reinforcing each other's image, so that "They, and Thou each others Glory Shew." Edwards wrote similarly of the divine-human relation:

> Here is both an emanation and a remanation.
> The refulgence shines upon and into the creature,
> and is reflected back to the luminary. The
> beams of glory come from God, and are something
> of God, and are refunded back again to their
> original. So that the whole is *of* God, and *in*
> God, and *to* God, and God is the beginning,
> middle, and end of this affair.[52]

In Edwards' thought, then, the understanding of Christian identity pioneered by the American Puritans through their extension

of typical status to present experience comes to characterize
the entire divine-human relation. The special status of the
Christian is defined relative to his receptivity to and similarity to the divine image expressed in the order of the world.
The extent to which Bushnell's own views on the nature of
Christian identity repeat this pattern will not be fully
apparent until we have discussed his works in greater detail.
We can, however, indicate the basic elements of the relation.
We have noted that Bushnell's conversion to an open profession
of Christianity involved increased receptivity to his own inbred
sympathies, the ties of his Christian upbringing. The new power
to "be" that this receptivity gave him was interpreted, in turn,
as an influx of divine energies, a closer communion with the
divine life mediated to him through his personal history and
through the vast network of "types, patterns, shadows, images,
ensamples" in nature.[53] Bushnell thus tended ever after to
think of the Christian as one who has a special sensitivity to
the expressions of the divine mind in nature and history. And
like Edwards, he held that the ground of this ability is the
Christian's intimacy with God. We understand the divine
significance of experience, he wrote, only if we have God
"imparting himself to our secret experience as the light of all
seeing, and molding us ever to that state of divine consciousness, which is, at once, the condition and principal substance
of knowlege."[54]

    That Bushnell was directly acquainted with Edwards' doc-
trine of the types is highly unlikely, since Edwards' manuscript
reflections on typology were unpublished in Bushnell's day.
We can say very little, in fact, about the extent to which
Bushnell was directly influenced by any of the materials reviewed in the section. Too little information exists about his
reading to make firm conclusions possible. Nevertheless, Bushnell's place in the history of New England theology and the
striking similarity between his preoccupations and those of the
tradition make a weak but suggestive conclusion possible. As
we hope to show in the sequel, Bushnell inherited the problems
of Puritan reflection and reconstructed solutions similar to
those we have been discussing out of the materials of his own
experience. Working not as a scholar, but out of his own

inclinations and interests, he took his place unconsciously
in America's intellectual mainstream.

b) Analogy and Interpersonal Communication

A second theme in Bushnell's conversion to an open profession of Christianity was his awareness of the power of
individual character to mold or influence the character of
others. His own experiences as a tutor at Yale gave rise to
the insight. But his subsequent use of the concept of influence
depended largely on the way he came to understand the dynamics
of interpersonal communication. In this section, we will
examine some of the ideas in Bushnell's thought-world that
shaped his understanding of how received expressions of
character can influence the growth of the mind.

Bushnell's first and most important premise in this regard
was that there exists an "analogy" between the acts and expressions of a person and his inward thought and moral character.
The idea that acts and artifacts express the mind of their
creator has roots at least as far back as Plato's speculations
on the character of the created world in the *Timaeus*.[55] But
Bushnell's special theory of an "analogy" between personality
and appearance, creator and creation, indicates that his most
important antecedents lay in one relatively specific tradition
of reflection. From the Renaissance on, nature has frequently
been characterized as God's book, a creation in which God is
present in the same sense that an author is present in his
works.[56] For nearly as long, the rhetorical category of
"analogy" has been an attractive device for conceiving the
mode of that presence.[57] There have been two primary schools
of thought on how to "read" nature with an eye to the analogy
of God in it. The most familiar held that nature is an elaborate system of graduated levels, a "great chain of being,"
each layer of which is formally similar or analogous to the one
above it in certain regular ways. By study of how the natural
orders "imply" each other, it was assumed, one could ultimately
learn how the whole system of nature is related to the divine
being that crowns it. John Milton gave the view in classic
form:

```
The scale of nature set
From center to circumference, whereon
In contemplation of created things
By steps we may ascend to God.[58]
```

As late as the nineteenth century, we find this scheme alive
in William Kirby's famous "Bridgewater Treatise," in which God,
"the great Instructor," is represented as ordering the world
by laws of analogy to provide mankind with clues to the divine
Original.[59]

There is another conception of the analogy of creation,
however, which is far more relevant to our story. The premise
of this second school is that the world is like its author
simply because the divine, the efficient cause of creation, has
communicated something of itself to its effects. The analogy
of creation here consists in directly perceivable traces or
intimations of the divine being in our experience. We need
not infer God's presence from his effects or "ascend the scale
of being" to reach him. We find him immediately expressed in
his creation as a person is expressed in his facial expression.
The "loco-descriptive" poetry of the eighteenth century is a
clear illustration of this principle at work. Its premise was
that a moral meaning is intended by the creator in natural
scenes and that this meaning can be perceived directly by the
poet's discerning eye.[60] A similar sensibility frequently
appears in Jonathan Edwards' *Images or Shadows of Divine Things*:
"The waves and billows of the sea in a storm, and the dire
cataracts that come of rivers, have a representation of the
terrible wrath of God and amazing misery of [them] that endure
it."[61] The conceit seems rather quaint to us, but Edwards'
thought-world gave it the force of reality. Nature is significant of the life of the spirit because it was created, and because creation speaks directly of the mind that made it.

This second approach to the analogy of creation got its
most influential expression in the English speaking world of
the eighteenth century through Scottish philosophy and aesthe-
tics--the philosophy that provided the framework for most
American philosophy and criticism in the early national period.[62]
Here, the specific assumption that nature expresses God's mind
was transformed into a general theory of creation. The moral
or aesthetic qualities of any created object, it was assumed,

belong most properly to the mind of the creator. As Thomas
Reid wrote,

> A great work is a work of great power, great
> wisdom, and great goodness, well contrived for
> some important end. But power, wisdom, and
> goodness are properly the attributes of mind
> only; they are ascribed to the work figuratively
> but are really inherent in the author. . . .[63]

Thus, we refer moral and intellectual qualities to works only
analogically, said Reid, as when we say that there is virtue
in an act rather than in the persons who acts.[64] As a general
rule, whatever is experienced of beauty or worth in the material
world refers us to the mind of a creator, divine or human,
whose qualities it expresses.[65]

From the idea that nature is an analogy of the mind of
God, then, we arrive at the idea that all created works are an
index of the character of their creator. This conclusion was
drawn quite bluntly by an American disciple of the Scottish
philosophy, Francis Wayland, in his "Discourse on the Philosophy
of Analogy" (1831). It is self-evident, he wrote, that "The
work of an intelligent and moral being must bear in all its
lineaments the traces of the character of its Author."[66] The
metaphor of authorship is here explicitly combined with the
metaphor of facial expression. The work is as intimately
connected with the author's subjectivity as his facial expression; it *is* his expression, "in all its lineaments," and is
immediately perceptible as such. Wayland and his predecessors
called this relation analogical. Today a more suggestive term
might be that the work is the "objective correlative" of the
creator's thoughts. In any case, the Scottish meaning is clear:
the significant content of created works and acts--that which
they convey or communicate--is a moment in the life of another
mind. Through such expressions we gain a window on worlds
that are otherwise invisible to us: the inwardness of other
persons and the being of God.

This way of conceiving the presence of the creator in his
creations raises an important question which will lead us
directly into Bushnell's theory of the dynamics of interpersonal
influence. Given that a person is directly represented in his
expressions, how can other persons read those expressions
accurately, so as to understand the inward experiences expressed?

Wayland's essay on analogy addressed just this problem, and
again, provides us with an epitome of contemporary thought on
the question. His radical interest was to apply the principles
of the analogy of creation to the logic of scientific discovery.
Why is it, he asked, that some scientists seem to know precisely
the right direction in which to search for new natural laws?
His answer: because some men have a greater sympathy with or
prior knowledge of the character of God, of whose mind the
natural order is an expression. To understand the work, he
implied, is to understand its author. To grasp a law of nature
is to "rethink God's thoughts." So, to have prior insight into
the creator's mind is to have a clue to the form of the work
that represents it. Say we have half of one of Raphael's
paintings before us, suggested Wayland. How would we know
where to draw the next line? Only by means of a profound insight into Raphael's "genius," an ability virtually to feel as
he felt, think as he thought, and share in the spirit of his
inspirations. Similarly, he concluded, the best scientists are
inevitably Christians, like Newton, whose closeness to and
sympathy with the divine mind allows them best to complete our
image of the world God has made. Knowing God, they know his
world.[67]

Wayland's conclusion regarding the logic of scientific
discovery is merely picturesque. What remains interesting in
his essay, however, is his underlying assumption that unless
we know something in advance about an author's character, we
are not likely to understand his expressions. Dugald Stewart,
a highly influential Scottish philosopher, reached a similar
conclusion in the context of a discussion of our ability to
read facial expressions. Stewart asked how it is possible,
given the invisibility or immateriality of other minds, that
we are able to infer emotions from appearances, and even to
feel the contagion of other peoples' emotions through the
medium of expression. His answer was that there must exist a
"psycho-moral sympathy" between persons, communicated through
the medium of the body. Stewart acknowledged that the ability
to interpret facial expressions has a learned component.
Nevertheless, he argued that some sort of intuitive sympathy
or pre-established harmony between the natures of the

communicating parties is absolutely essential to the process.
The link between inward feelings and outward expressions is
invisible to us in the case of all persons except ourselves.
We can observe how our own subjective states are expressed, and
assuming human uniformity, we can make inferences based on our
own experience about how another's expressions should be interpreted. But we could not even begin to learn what inner
quality another's smile, grimmace, or blank stare might mean
unless our own feelings and expressions were correlated in
similar or identical ways. Without some natural bridgehead
between minds, we would be forever strangers to each other.[68]

This bridgehead was secured, in turn, by the Scottish
philosophy's characteristic moral doctrine--that all human
beings have a common moral sense, an inborn homing instinct
for an absolute distinction between right and wrong and a
natural inclination to do what is right.[69] Because they have
this common moral make-up, people share certain subjective
experiences. A common texture of moral emotion and aspiration
is essential to their humanity. And because all persons pre-
sumably express their inner lives in similar ways, it is
possible for one person to use his own behavior as the key to
the interpretation of another's. The seeds of sympathy, sown
in the innate norms of the moral character, bear fruit in
inter-subjective understanding.

This doctrine of a common human moral nature also ensured
mankind's capacity to understand the mind of God. Mankind,
like nature, is God's creation, and so can be expected to bear,
"in all his lineaments," the traces of divine character. The
universal moral nature of man is therefore an index of the
moral being of God.[70] Ralph Waldo Emerson spoke as a disciple
of the Scottish philosophy when he wrote in an early journal
that the moral sense is "a rule coextensive and coeval with
Mind. It derives its existence from the eternal character of
the Deity, . . . and seems itself to imply and therefore to
prove his Existence."[71]

The Scottish understanding of creation as an expression
of the mind thus passed easily into a general theory of the
nature and means of inter-personal communication. Understanding,
as a communion of minds, is possible for two reasons:

1) because the works, acts, and expressions of a person, divine or human, are a direct reflection of his mind, and 2) because other persons can share his experiences, interpreting his expressions by reference to their own corresponding experiences and ways of expressing themselves.

From these premises, in turn, it was but a short step to the conclusion commonly drawn in eighteenth century literary theory that expression can be a medium of personal influence, a powerful tool of moral education and instruction. After all, said Stewart, the process of communication itself works through "those moral ties by which Heaven has been pleased to bind us together."[72] The author or orator, by expressing and evoking the highest, truest, and most universal sentiments of mankind can thus awaken his audience to their own normative selfhood. Ideally he will awaken them to their moral sense, to that in themselves which is most nearly akin to the image of God. In any case he will communicate himself, reproducing his character in the medium of his audience's own resources of response. If he is not a power for good, he will surely be a power for evil.[73]

Bushnell's discovery of the power of his character to shape the moral growth of his students at Yale did not take place in a vacuum, then. His own plaguing sense of responsibility for the moral impression he made on others found a rationale in a theory of the educative power of expressions and the means of their operation that pervaded the philosophy and literary theory of his age. He came to understand himself and his role as a minister not only from his personal experiences, but from the theoretical constructs that made those experiences intelligible to him. As in the case of Bushnell's understanding of divine-human relations, however, the extent of his intellectual debts to the tradition outlined here cannot be appraised until we take a close look at some of Bushnell's own writings on the subject. To this we will turn in the following chapter.

c) A Note on Romanticism

Before we go on, a word of caution is in order concerning an interpretive category frequently applied to Bushnell. Bushnell is often classed as a "romantic" theologian.[74]

But the question of the nature and degree of Bushnell's romanticism is difficult to resolve with any clarity. From one
point of view, Bushnell's romanticism is vibrant and pervasive.
That is, numerous parallels can be drawn between his ideas,
attitudes, and literary practice and those of writers generally
classed as romantic, especially Coleridge.[75] For instance,
Bushnell and the romantics all countered the Lockean split between mind and its objects with the theory that nature is
teleologically imbued with mind. Thus, along with Coleridge,
Bushnell regarded nature as "that eternal language which thy
God utters,"[76] and speculated broadly on the correspondent Logos
in mind and the world. For similar reasons, commentators often
point out "strong Kantian overtones" in Bushnell's work,[77] not
because Bushnell ever read Kant, but because of superficial
resemblances. Like Kant, he assumed that a noumenal world is
mediated to mankind through the forms and categories of the
mind--that mind is engaged in the construction of experience
and is implicated in all it perceives. In theology, in turn,
Bushnell shared the romantic or more generally liberal tendency
to put the religious affections at the beginning of theological
reflection. Like Schleiermacher, for instance, he held that
religion originates "where the living contact of man with the
world fashions itself as feeling."[78] All this amounts to
prima facie evidence for some sort of similarity between the
thought projects of Bushnell and the romantics. They did
similar things through their writings, and often for the same
reasons.

On the other hand, it is distressingly difficult to pin
down any specific lines of influence between Bushnell and
documents of romantic philosophy, critical theory, or even
literature at this early stage of his career. Later in life
he read Cousin and Neander in translation; snippets of
Schleiermacher, F. Schlegel, and Richard Roethe; the English
disciple of Schleiermacher, John Morell; and the American
Hegelian psychologist, Fredrick Rauch.[79] These, at least, he
mentions; some--Cousin and Schleiermacher in particular[80]--left
clear marks on a few of his published works. There is no evidence that he ever read Kant or any of the post-Kantian
idealists.[81]

The only indisputably romantic author that he read prior
to his graduation from divinity school was Coleridge.[82] Bushnell's debt to Coleridge is frequently stressed. Bushnell
himself once remarked that he owed more to Coleridge "than to
any extra-Scriptural author."[83] But while Coleridge certainly
played a galvanizing role in Bushnell's development, the nature
of Bushnell's "debt" is ambiguous.[84] For example, Coleridge
may well have called Bushnell's attention to the "analogy of
creation," the symbolic character of the universe. Coleridge
wrote in the *Aids to Reflection*:

> there is something in the human mind that makes
> it know (as soon as it is sufficiently awakened
> to reflect on its own thoughts and notices),
> that in all finite quantity there is an infinite,
> in all measure of time an eternal; that the
> latter are the basis, the substance, the true
> and abiding reality of the former. . . .[85]

Similar passages abound in Bushnell's earliest writings. He
noted, for example, that nature is "the expression or symbolic
language of God." Or again,

> matter is but an appointed alphabeth or language
> in which the Divine Spirit or power interprets
> itself to human spirits and through which they
> are able to hold a moral commerce with each
> other. . . .[86]

We have already seen, however, that such passages also reflect
eighteenth century views of nature as either a "type" or an
"analogy" of its creator's mind, expressive of his nature and
intentions. There was therefore a wide range of sources, of
which Coleridge was only one, from which Bushnell could have
derived his theory that God is analogically present in nature--
that the outward and physical world is expressive of an inward
and spiritual truth. Thus, while Bushnell's views on natural
symbolism were clearly similar to those of many romantics, the
likelihood seems to be not that he absorbed them from the
romantics proper, but that his ideas grew out of the same
soil as theirs.

There are many other parallels that might be drawn between the thought of Bushnell and Coleridge. But in nearly every
case, as in the above, we should refrain from singling Coleridge
out as Bushnell's source. Bushnell took what he "found" from
Coleridge--or in a favorite phrase of Bushnell's, itself

borrowed from Coleridge, he took what "found him." What struck
Bushnell, however, can usually be seen to depend on what his
experience and training prepared him to recognize. He did not
appropriate Coleridge or any other thinker systematically. What
he said of his reading habits should be sufficient warning
against all attempts to pin down his sources with certainty:

> It is very hard for me to read a book
> through. . . . [I]f it is really worth reading,
> it starts my mind off on some track of its own
> that I am more inclined to follow than to find
> out what the author has to say.[87]

Our suggestions in this chapter have all been made with this
caveat in mind.

NOTES

CHAPTER I

[1] Mary Bushnell Cheney, *Life and Letters of Horace Bushnell* (1880; rpt. New York: Arno Press, 1969), pp. 3ff. This work will be cited hereafter as *LL*.

[2] *Ibid.*, pp. 8-9. See also Bushnell's recollections quoted here, pp. 31-32.

[3] *Ibid.*, p. 32. Noah Porter reports a rumor that the teenage Bushnell was a member of an "infidel club" in a neighboring town, headed by a "hard headed Deist of the type of Paine." If true, the tale would fit nicely with Bushnell's hints at his early rationalism. See Noah Porter, "Horace Bushnell," *The New Englander*, XXXVI (1877), pp. 153-54.

[4] *LL*, pp. 15-23.

[5] *Ibid.*, p. 32.

[6] Bushnell's difficulties in selecting a career can be fruitfully compared with Emerson's. See Henry Nash Smith, "Emerson's Problem of Vocation," *New England Quarterly*, (March 1939), pp. 52-67.

[7] *LL*, pp. 35-55.

[8] *Ibid.*, pp. 53-54.

[9] See Charles Roy Keller, *The Second Great Awakening in Connecticut* (New Haven: Yale University Press, 1942).

[10] *LL*, p. 56.

[11] Robert McEwen, quoted in *ibid.*

[12] Bushnell, "The Dissolving of Doubts," *Sermons on Living Subjects* (New York: Scribner, Armstrong & Co., 1872).

[13] For a good survey of academic moral philosophy in Bushnell's America, see D.H. Meyer, *The Instructed Conscience* (Philadelphia: University of Pennsylvania Press, 1972). Bushnell seems to have been introduced to the doctrine of the moral sense through the works of Dugald Stewart. According to the Yale College catalogue for 1826, when Bushnell was a senior, "Stewart's Philosophy of Mind" was required reading for all fourth year students. The text used was probably an abridgement of Dugald Stewart's *Elements of the Philosophy of the Human Mind* such as that prepared by William Fissenden (Brattleborough, Vermont: 1808).

[14] *LL*, p. 33. See also Cheney's remarks in *ibid.*, pp. 59-60. Bushnell's statement that the ministry gave him a power to "be" is admittedly vague. Nevertheless, we can safely quess his meaning to be that the choice allowed him to live with

27

confidence and a clear conscience. This meaning emerges when Bushnell's statement here is contrasted with a remark made during a later period of depression and self-doubt, when he felt unable "to be or even half be anybody." See *LL*, p. 251.

[15]See Ann Douglas, *The Feminization of American Culture* (New York: Alfred A. Knopf, 1977), pp. 17-43.

[16]On the American preoccupation with pulpit oratory, see Barbara Cross, *Horace Bushnell* (Chicago: University of Chicago Press, 1958), pp. 85-92.

[17]This term, which was later to play a crucial role in Bushnell's theory of the atonement, first appeared in his earliest published sermon, "Duty Not Measured by Our Own Ability," which appears in *Sermons for the New Life* (New York: Charles Scribner, 1858). See pp. 297-99.

[18]See Daniel Walker Howe, "American Victorianism as a Culture," *American Quarterly*, XXVII (December 1975), pp. 529, 530-31.

[19]Ann Douglas argues throughout *The Feminization of American Culture* that the theory of influence, pervasive among both liberal clergy and woman writers of the period, was a blind alley with respect to the main currents of power in American life. Frustration haunted the works of its most successful proponents.

[20]Bushnell, "Twentieth Anniversary" (Hartford: Elihu Geer, 1853), p. 9.

[21]*LL*, pp. 95-97.

[22]Seminal works in this field include Sacvan Bercovitch, *The Puritan Origins of the American Self* (New Haven: Yale University Press, 1975); Ursula Brumm, *American Thought and Religious Typology* (New Brunswick, N.J.: Rutgers University Press, 1970); and the articles by Mason Lowance and others in *Typology and Early American Literature*, ed. Sacvan Bercovitch, (Amherst: The University of Massachusetts Press, 1972).

[23]Perry Miller's groundbreaking works--*The New England Mind: The Seventeenth Century* (New York: The Macmillan Co., 1939); and *The New England Mind: From Colony to Province* (Cambridge: Harvard University Press, 1953)--found the key to colonial thought in the Puritans' perception of "declension" from the ideals of the founders to the bugeoning confusion of eighteenth century life. The tendency of the new scholarship is to see in this history the growth of new strategies of national- and self-understanding--the development of a means of encompassing the paradoxes of Puritan belief and experience in a typological theory of the Christian self.

[24]On the early history of typological interpretation in Christian thought, see Erich Auerbach, "Figura," in *Scenes from the Drama of European Literature* (New York: Meridian Books, 1959), pp. 11-76; and Thomas M. Davis, "The Traditions

of Puritan Typology," in *Typology*, ed. Bercovitch, pp. 11-45.

[25]Samuel Mather, *The Figures and Types of the Old Testament* (2nd London edition, 1705; rpt. New York: Johnson Reprint Co., 1969), p. 52.

[26]Auerbach, *op. cit.*, p. 54, makes the point that this tight logic is what sets "type" apart from other rhetorical concepts. For another version of the distinction between type and allegory, see Miller's exerpt from Benjamin Keach's *Tropologia* (1681) in Miller, ed., *Images or Shadows of Divine Things by Jonathan Edwards* (New Haven: Yale University Press, 1948), pp. 142-43.

[27]Samuel Mather, quoted in Karl Keller, "'The World Slickt Up in Types:' Edward Taylor as a Version of Emerson," in *Typology*, ed. Bercovitch, p. 188.

[28]The major outlines of what follows were suggested by themes running throughout Bercovitch's *Puritan Origins*. My work has been to clarify those themes, with an eye to their relevance as background to Bushnell, and to illustrate them with materials drawn from my own research.

[29]Quoted in Karl Keller, *op. cit.*, p. 189.

[30]See Bercovitch, *Puritan Origins*, pp. 118-25. Moves to assimilate America to the City of God did not go uncriticized. Roger Williams, for instance, pointed out that the claim that American experience was anti-typical violated the principle that Christ alone fulfills the types. New England typological practice, Williams gibed, "wakes Moses from his unknown grave and denies Jesus yet to have seen the Earth." See Williams, *Complete Writings* (New York: Russell & Russell, 1963), vol. III, p. 416.

[31]Bercovitch, *Puritan Origins*, p. 18, refers to this problem as "the dilemma of Puritan identity."

[32]See Miller, *The New England Mind: The Seventeenth Century*, pp. 111-299.

[33]See Karl Keller, *op. cit.*, p. 180. For a full treatment of Taylor's life and thought, see Keller, *The Example of Edward Taylor* (Amherst: The University of Massachusetts Press, 1975), pp. 11-78.

[34]Edward Taylor, *The Poems of Edward Taylor*, ed. Donald E. Stanford (New Haven: Yale University Press, 1960), p. 83.

[35]*Ibid.*, p. 171.

[36]This way of building the bridge had the added advantage of using the hero as a buffer as well as a link between the self and Christ, thus guarding against antinomian extremes. See Bercovitch, *Puritan Origins*, pp. 26-27.

[37]The best available study of preparationism is Norman Pettit, *The Heart Prepared* (New Haven: Yale University Press,

1966). On the role of the covenant theology in Puritan thought about divine-human relations, the seminal work is Miller, "The Marrow of Puritan Divinity," in *Errand into the Wilderness* (Cambridge: The Belknap Press of Harvard University Press, 1956), pp. 48-98.

[38]See Edwards' comments in *Some Thoughts Concerning the Present Revival of Religion in New England*, in *The Works of President Edwards* (London 1817; rpt. New York: Burt Franklin, 1968), vol. VI, pp. 5-206.

[39]Edwards, "God Glorified in Man's Dependence," in *Jonathan Edwards*, ed. Clarence Faust and Thomas Johnson, American Century Series Edition (New York: Hill and Wang, 1962), p. 92. For a lucid discussion of this sermon and the motives behind it, see Perry Miller, *Jonathan Edwards* (New York: W. Sloane Associates, 1949), pp. 3-34.

[40]Edwards, in Faust and Johnson, eds., *op. cit.*, p. 98. For a discussion of Edwards' distinction, see Roland Delattre, *Beauty and Sensibility in the Thought of Jonathan Edwards* (New Haven: Yale University Press, 1968), pp. 4f., 62f., 80-84.

[41]Edwards, in Faust and Johnson, eds., *op. cit.*, p. 99.

[42]Miller, *Jonathan Edwards*, p. 325.

[43]Jonathan Edwards, *Religious Affections*, ed. John E. Smith, (New Haven: Yale University Press, 1959), pp. 234-36, 233.

[44]John E. Smith, ed., *Religious Affections*, p. 13.

[45]Mason Lowance, "'Images or Shadows of Divine Things' in the Thought of Jonathan Edwards," in *Typology*, ed. Bercovitch, p. 221.

[46]Quoted in *ibid.*, pp. 218-19.

[47]Edwards here draws on a metaphysical metaphor that derives from Plato's *Timaeus*. The creator or Artificer of the Universe deliberately represents himself in it; nature is virtually "a sensible God, the image of the intelligible." On Plato's use of this metaphor and its subsequent history, see Arthur O. Lovejoy, *The Great Chain of Being* (Cambridge: Harvard University Press, 1936), pp. 51ff.

[48]Edwards, quoted in Lowance, "'Images or Shadows'," p. 226.

[49]See Edwards, *Images or Shadows of Divine Things*, ed. Miller, pp. 69-70 (Image 70).

[50]Miller, introduction to *ibid.*, p. 26.

[51]This same correlation of perceiving and being was the heart of Edwards' more familiar treatment of the psychology of religious identity in *Religious Affections*, where the perception of God's beauty in and through the creation was made a test of redemption. The motivating question behind *Religious*

Affections was "what are the distinguishing qualifications of those that are in favor with God, and entitled to his eternal rewards? Or, which comes to the same thing, What is the nature of true religion?" (Edwards, *Religious Affections*, ed. Smith, p. 84). The question was answered by a careful discrimination between those religious experiences or forms of piety in which man's will or the devil might conceivably have had a hand--the unreliable tests--and those which could be attributed to nothing but the operation of grace, or God's self-communication. The analysis determined that the watershed between carnal and redeemed experience was the "new sense of things" that allowed mankind to perceive and enjoy God's beauty, the same sense that made him capable of "reading" the types in their spiritual sense:

> [I]f there be in the saint a kind of apprehension or perception which is in its nature perfectly diverse from all that natural nature; it must consist in their having a certain kind of ideas or sensations of mind, which are simply diverse from all that is or can be in the minds of natural men. And that is the same thing as to say, that it consists in the sensations of the new spiritual sense, which the souls of men have not. . . .(*Ibid.*, p. 271).

Thus, said Edwards, "True religion, in great part, consists in holy affections" (*ibid.*, p. 95). As a person perceives, so he is--and so he does, according to his new inclination or heart. The true Christian is, in essence, a right reader or right experiencer of God in and through the types.

[52]Edwards, "Dissertation Concerning the End for Which God Created the World," in Faust and Johnson, eds., *op. cit.*, p. 344.

[53]Bushnell, "Our Gospel a Gift to the Imagination," *Building Eras in Religion* (New York: Charles Scribner's Sons, 1910), p. 254.

[54]Bushnell, *Christ in Theology* (Hartford: Brown & Parsons, 1851), p. 66.

[55]See note 47 above.

[56]See M.H. Abrams, "Structure and Style in the Greater Romantic Lyric," in *From Sensibility to Romanticism*, ed. F.W. Hillis and H. Bloom (New York: Oxford University Press, 1965), pp. 535-36. Abrams discusses the Scriptual roots of this concept in *Natural Supernaturalism* (New York: W.W. Norton & Co., Inc., 1971), p. 88, n. 33.

[57]For a useful overview of the shifting uses of the term "analogy," see Victor Harris, "Allegory to Analogy in the Interpretation of Scripture," *Philological Quarterly*, XLV (January 1966), pp. 1-23.

[58]Quoted in Lovejoy, *op. cit.*, p. 86. The book as a whole provides a good survey of the roots and consequences of this school of thought.

[59]William Kirby, *On the Power, Wisdom and Goodness of God* (Philadelphia: Carey, Lea & Blanchard, 1836), pp. 466-68.

[60]See Abrams, "Structure and Style," in Hillis and Bloom, eds., *op. cit.*, pp. 533-39. It is tempting to dismiss such analogies as simple poetic conceits. Abrams insists, however, that behind the formal practice, at least at its inception, lay an active belief in the correspondences discovered. If nature seemed to have a moral meaning, it was because the world was assumed to be the work of an intelligent creator who left the mark of his own character on it.

[61]Edwards, *Images or Shadows*, p. 44.

[62]On the place of the Scottish philosophy in American philosophy and education in the early national period, see Herbert W. Schneider, *A History of American Philosophy* (New York: Columbia University Press, 1946), pp. 195-216. On its role in American critical thought, see William Charvat, *The Origins of American Critical Thought 1810-1835* (Philadelphia: University of Pennsylvania Press, 1936), pp. 27-58.

[63]Thomas Reid, *The Works of Thomas Reid* (New York: E. Duyakinak, Collins and Hannay, and R. and W.A. Bartow, 1822), vol. II, p. 411. Similarly, the critic Joseph Alison, who declared himself Reid's follower, wrote that "matter is not beautiful in itself, but derives its beauty from the expression of the mind." Quoted in Charvat, *op. cit.*, p. 50.

[64]Reid, *loc. cit.*

[65]Reid's position on this question is discussed in more detail in S.A. Grave, *The Scottish Philosophy of Common Sense* (Oxford: Oxford University Press, 1960), p. 159.

[66]Francis Wayland, "Discourse on the Philosophy of Analogy," in *American Philosophical Addresses, 1700-1900*, ed. Joseph Blau (New York: Columbia University Press, 1946), p. 353.

[67]*Ibid.*, pp. 353-363.

[68]Dugald Stewart, *The Works of Dugald Stewart* (Cambridge: Hilliard and Brown, 1829), vol. III, pp. 6-11, 108-62. It is worth noting that the Scottish view of the inherent structuring of moral experience is strikingly similar to Dilthey's view of the inherent organization of *Erlebnis*. Likewise, the Scottish theory of expressive communication has its counterpart in Dilthey's observation of the "curious psychological law"--that every physical event that expresses another's mental experience has the power to evoke a corresponding experience in the observer's mind. See H.A. Hodges, *Wilhelm Dilthey: An Introduction* (New York: Oxford University Press, 1944), p. 14.

[69]On the Scottish moral theory, see Grave, *op. cit.*, pp. 224-57. On its influence in America, see Meyer, *op. cit.*, pp. 33-59.

[70]Philosophers and theologians of the period frequently argued that to know what man is in the normative principles of his moral character is to know what God's moral character is like. They were quick to infer, in turn, that man's moral needs are a reliable revelation of things about God and the universe that we do not already know. If, for instance, mankind has a longing for immortality or the Trinity so "deep" as to be "native," then there is good reason to believe that these things are so, for God would not toy with his creatures by giving them longings he did not intend to make good on.
Arguments of this kind can be found throughout the range of American religious thought in this period. See for instance Charles Hodge, *The Way of Life* (Philadelphia: American Sunday School Union, 1841), pp. 20-21; and compare Emerson, *The Journal of Ralph Waldo Emerson*, ed. Edward W. Emerson and Waldo E. Forbes (New York: Houghton, 1909-1914), vol. I, pp. 210-11.
Bushnell went on to turn this principle into a slogan: "what we earnestly want, we know that we shall assuredly find." *Nature and the Supernatural* (1858; rpt. New York: AMS Press, 1973), p. 62.

[71]Emerson, *Journals*, vol. I, p. 186. On Emerson's debt to the Scottish philosophy, see Merrell R. Davis, "Emerson's 'Reason' and the Scottish Philosophers," *New England Quarterly*, XVII (1944), pp. 209-28.

[72]Stewart, *op. cit.*, vol. III, p. 161.

[73]This theory of the power of expression contributed both to the popular reverence for oratory and to the critical convention that literature can and ought to be didactic. See Charvat, *op. cit.*, p. 47.

[74]Barbara Cross makes much of Bushnell's "romantic sensibility" in *op. cit.*, pp. 21-30. See also Irving H. Bartlett, "The Romantic Theology of Horace Bushnell," Diss. Brown University 1952.

[75]See Mildred Kitto Billings, "The Theology of Horace Bushnell Considered in Relation to That of Samuel Taylor Coleridge," Diss. University of Chicago 1960; and Donald A. Crosby, *Horace Bushnell's Theory of Language* (The Hague: Mouton, 1975), pp. 96-107.

[76]Coleridge, quoted in Abrams, "Structure and Style," in *From Sensibility to Romanticism*, p. 556.

[77]Crosby, *op. cit.*, pp. 225-26. L.C. Foard tries to draw out the Kantian analogy in more detail in "The Copernican Revolution in Theology," Diss. Temple University 1970.

[78]See Schleiermacher, *On Religion* (New York: Harper & Row, 1958), p. 63.

[79]Cousin is mentioned in "Christian Comprehensiveness,"
The New Englander, VI (January 1848), p. 83; Neander first
appears in his "Argument for 'Discourses on Christian Nurture'"
(1847), in *Views of Christian Nurture* (1847; rpt. Delmar, N.Y.:
Scholars' Facsimiles & Reprints, 1975), p. 55, and is frequently
cited in later works; Schlegel figures in his "Discourse on
the Moral Tendencies and Results of Human History," (Hartford:
J.W. Judd, 1843), p. 21; Schleiermacher, Schlegel and Rauch all
appear in the "Preliminary Dissertation" to *God in Christ*
(Hartford: Brown & Parsons, 1849), on pp. 111, 34, and 37-38
respectively; Morell and Roethe are mentioned in *Christ in
Theology* (Hartford: Brown & Parsons, 1851), p. 84.

[80]The influence of Cousin is explored in detail by John
Edmund Howell, "A Study of the Theological Method of Horace
Bushnell and its Application to his Cardinal Doctrines," Diss.
Duke University 1963, pp. 59-70; the impact of Schleiermacher's
essay "On the Discrepancy Between the Sabellian and Athanasian
Method of Representing the Doctrine of the Trinity," trans.
Moses Stuart, *Biblical Repository and Quarterly Observer*, V
(April 1835), pp. 265-353, and VI (July 1835), pp. 1-116, is
noted by H. Shelton Smith, *Horace Bushnell* (New York: Oxford
University Press, 1965), pp. 6-8.

[81]Not only is there no record of such reading, but Bushnell
shared the scornful prejudice against German speculative philosophy that was commonplace in his day. See the quip recorded
in *LL*, p. 414.

[82]Bushnell first read Coleridge's *Aids to Reflection* either
while an undergraduate at Yale or while serving there as a tutor.
He reports that he encountered Coleridge while "in college,"
but adds that his conversion of 1831 followed "shortly after"
the reading. The later date is assumed by most commentators.
See *LL*, pp. 208-09.
        If we assume the later date, then it is likely that
Bushnell read the *Aids* in the new edition with a preliminary
essay by James Marsh (Burlington: 1829) which did so much to
spread Coleridge's influence in America.

[83]*LL*, p. 499.

[84]Williston Walker notes Coleridge's influence, but rightly
suggests that what Bushnell received was "inspired" rather than
"instilled" by his reading. See *Bushnell Centenary*, (Hartford:
Hartford Press, The Case, Lockwood & Brainard Co., 1902), p. 18.

[85]Coleridge, *Aids to Reflection*, 4th London edition, ed.
Henry Nelson Coleridge (1840; rpt. Port Washington, N.Y.:
Kennikat Press, 1971), p. 121.

[86]Bushnell, ["Natural Science and Moral Philosophy,"] MS
Yale Divinity School Library, pp. 1, 19 (my pagination).

[87]*LL*, p. 295.

CHAPTER II

EARLY WRITINGS

In this chapter, we will examine some of Bushnell's earliest writings to see how his own understanding of interpersonal communication took shape. We will begin with a pair of writings, one essay and one sermon, that Bushnell wrote while still struggling against the influence of his mentor, Nathaniel William Taylor (1786-1858) of Yale Divinity School. These works set the theme for two subsequent constructive essays, which we will analyse in turn. In "Revelation" (1839), Bushnell discussed the divine-human relation as mankind's communion with God through God's self-expression in nature and history. Here we will see how Bushnell reconstructed elements of the earlier American typological approach to similar issues. Then, in "Unconscious Influence" (1846), Bushnell examined interpersonal relations in greater detail, with an eye to showing how human community can serve as a medium for the communication of divine life. Bushnell's use and partial transformation of the Scottish model of communication introduced in Chapter I will receive special attention.

1. Bushnell Contra Taylor

Bushnell's interest in theology matured together with his commitment to the ministry, and reflected many of the same concerns. He entered divinity school with the impulses of his conversion still fresh. Through openness to God as he found him expressed in the promptings of his heart, Bushnell had discovered a new power and confidence. In theology, he sought explanations of that spiritual power and the means by which to communicate it. But if Bushnell took up theology with a clear sense of the questions he wanted it to answer, the terms in which his answers were eventually couched were unquestionably given after the fact by the theological education he received from Nathaniel William Taylor at Yale in the early 1830's.

Taylor's importance for Bushnell was complex. Bushnell was by no means a passive or credulous student. Taylor

35

recalled him grimly as one of the ones "t'other side" of every important question.[1] Further, Bushnell recoiled from the whole manner of doing theology that Taylor represented. Whereas Taylor reveled in strident controversy, Bushnell distrusted polemics. Whereas Taylor constructed his arguments on the assumption that language and logic could yield a precise representation of spiritual realities, Bushnell denied both the precision of language and the utility of logic to demonstrate or discover any truth not already immediately apparent to the intuition. Yet when it came to the ultimate aims and subject matter of theology, Bushnell assumed a common ground with Taylor to which he held throughout his career.

Briefly stated, Taylor's theological project was to mitigate the sharp split between mankind's natural abilities and his divine possibilities--nature and grace--a split which had grown accute in the Edwardsean school of Calvinism. Taylor did not deny sinful man's need for grace, as some Unitarians were doing at the time. He retained a radical or "right-angled" model of conversion as a spiritual transformation which no person can effect out of his own resources. But in place of the Calvinist emphasis on mankind's moral inability and total dependence on God to will and to do, Taylor wanted at least to give the natural man an active role to play in the drama of redemption. By stressing the co-operation of man and God in conversion, Taylor sought to make religion a "practical" affair, a possibility of existence continuous with human life in history.[2]

Taylor expressed his views on the relations of nature and grace most clearly in the position on the freedom of the will he adopted in opposition to Edwards.[3] In their discussions of the will, Edwards and Taylor faced a similar problem. Mankind is totally depraved according to Calvinism. Pragmatically, this meant that persons left to their own devices are invariably and inevitably sinful. But Calvinism also taught that human sin is voluntary, and therefore that persons can and must be held responsible for their acts. This resulted in an apparent paradox, put starkly by Calvin himself: "he who sins necessarily sins no less voluntarily."[4] The question arose, then, how sin could consistently be held to be both inevitable and free?

Edwards developed his answer in *The Freedom of the Will*
by means of a careful definition of "freedom." Freedom, said
Edwards, consists in a person's ability to do as he wills.
The will, however, "always is as the greatest apparent good
is."[5] What appears good, in turn, depends on the inclination
of one's heart, or what is the same thing, on one's capacities
of perception. The sinner, who lacks the "sense of divine
things" specially granted to the elect by grace, perceives
whatever good he can according to his faltering lights and wills
to pursue it freely. The saint wills according to his perceptions in exactly the same way, but because his perceptions are
regenerate, the goals he perceives to be good are those which
really are so in the divine scheme of things. The sinner sees
the world as an object of selfish desire; the saint sees it
truly as a type of the divine mind. The saint and the sinner
are therefore equally free and responsible, because both act
according to their perceptions and consequent wills. Nevertheless, the natural man's sin is inevitable because his inability
to perceive the typical significance of things--his lack of
holy affections--constitutes a "moral inability" to perceive
and do what is ultimately right. Edwards' solution to the
paradox of freedom in necessity was thus intimately related
to his aesthetic model of spiritual identity as an affair of
"holy affections" or a sense of the heart.

Taylor was unimpressed by Edwards' answer, primarily because he did not share Edwards' understanding of grace as the
communication of a new sense of divine things. In Taylor's
view of divine-human relations, the chief measure of spiritual
status was not the quality of one's perceptions, but the state
of one's conscience. The inward sense of guilt or righteousness was taken to be a sure index of one's standing before God.
The point Taylor wanted to maintain in his discussion of the
will's freedom, then, was human responsibility for moral
action. Without a clear consciousness of responsibility for
one's acts, he argued, one would not be likely to register
either guilt or complacency in the conscience. The clue to
human spiritual identity would therefore be lost.

Edwards had failed on exactly this point, thought Taylor.
Trying to make "freedom" compatible with necessity, Edwards

had ignored an essential feature of the common-sense understanding of responsible action: that for an act to be subject to praise or blame, the agent must have been able to do otherwise under the circumstances. Taylor held that two things are implied whenever we hold someone responsible for his acts: 1) that he knew the difference between right and wrong under the circumstances, and 2) that he could have done otherwise than he did. Taylor believed that this first condition was supplied in all cases by the presumed fact that God has built moral laws into "the very nature and structure of the mind."[6] Following the Scottish moral philosophers, that is, Taylor argued that certain basic moral principles are shared by all sane persons. Given that humanity is God's creation, and that the human moral constitution reflects the mind of its Author, then the voice of conscience must be a reliable guide to the moral constitution of the universe. No person can claim ignorance of the eternal moral law, for every person has a touchstone of the divine will in his own nature.[7] Second, said Taylor, because responsible action entails that the actor could have done other than he did--and given that responsible action is as important to God's moral schemes as it is to ours--so God must have created mankind free, with "power to the contrary," and left him so.[8] To deny that mankind is free in this sense, he argued, is tantamount to denying the entire divine-human relation. To lose actual responsibility--and with it the sense of responsibility--would be to lose the principle of one's moral identity, the clue to one's status before God. Persons without responsible wills would be rendered cosmically irrelevant. Therefore, Taylor allowed himself no doubts that mankind is free to choose sin or righteousness--that genuine spiritual options are open to mankind in his natural state. The sinner chooses to ignore the inward counsel of his conscience; the saint chooses to follow it and so occasions his own redemption.[9]

The heart of Taylor's theology, then, was his vision of the moral dignity of man--man's responsible will and God's scrupulous regard for it. Nevertheless, Taylor's strength was identical with his weakness in the eyes of Bushnell, his most precocious pupil. Bushnell was clearly impressed by Taylor's moral philosophy--his insistence on human freedom and his

assumption that the moral sense supplies mankind with an immanent voice of God in the conscience. Bushnell, however, was not
content to take the moral relation between man and God for the
whole of spirituality. In his own conversion of 1831, he had
discovered intrinsically valuable affections which he was inclined to call "divine" in a sense that Taylor's theology did
not seem to allow for. Thus, while Bushnell was inspired by
Taylor's attempt to bring redemption within the range of human
possibilities, he did not believe that Taylor had brought God
into the world in the right way. Taylor's attempt to mediate
between nature and grace remained curiously sterile to Bushnell's
mind, for it failed to acknowledge the possibility of an immediate communion between the divine and human natures.

Bushnell's ambivalence towards Taylor's theology appears
clearly in an essay written in May 1832, while Bushnell was
still a student at the divinity school.[10] The dominant theme
of Bushnell's untitled essay is the unfulfilled promise in
Taylor's vision of divine-human relations. On the one hand,
Bushnell heartily approved Taylor's idea that man and God
share a common moral nature. The inspiring quality of that
idea was enough to establish it as self-evident, he believed.
One who grasps it will cry with "the voice of a newly awakened
instinct," "my whole heart is in the character of God and all
my thoughts approve his goodness--he is my father."[11] On the
other hand, Bushnell saw Taylor's contention that the human
will is morally neutral--equally capable of good or evil under
all circumstances--as a betrayal of this primary insight into
man's likeness to God. That is, by representing sin as an or-
derly and explicable feature of the moral universe, Taylor
seemed almost to condone it.

> [E]very man knows that he is not what he was
> made to be. And yet much of our philosophy,
> I am sorry to believe, is in fact, though not
> professedly based on the spurious assumption
> that man is made for the evil he does. . . .
> A doctrine so dishonorable to God cannot be
> true.[12]

Likewise, Bushnell argued, by making mankind equally well disposed towards good or evil, Taylor's theory of the will effectively denied the native affinity for God that the doctrine of
the moral sense affirmed. It underestimated the "principle of

affinity ever impelling a re-union with the divine nature,"
and so left mankind "a wretched exile from a home he could
never have loved, and to which he can never have a desire of
returning."[13]

Several other specific differences between Bushnell and
Taylor could be discussed. If we stress their differences too
strongly, however, we are likely to lose sight of the degree
to which they remained in basic agreement. Taylor sought to
correlate the transcendent promise of redemption with capacities
inherent in the human condition. His means of doing so was to
show how human sinfulness could be overcome by an act of man's
own will. Bushnell was eloquent in his rejection of Taylor's
means, but he adopted the overarching project as his own. His
basic faith was that a point of correlation between human capacities and Christian ideals existed within the range of possibilities open to the natural man. Taylor's thoughts on this point
simply reinforced the lessons of his own conversion experiences,
where the impulses of his "heart" had proved to be congruent
with Christian belief. The aim of theology as Bushnell conceived
it, then, was to represent this correlation as a possibility
for man, and yet to do justice to the full range and complexity
of the human condition, from the heights of human potential to
the depths of sin and disorientation. The heart of theology
for Taylor and Bushnell alike was thus anthropological. But
Bushnell hoped to do Taylor one better. If theology was truly
to show the conjunction of the Christian possibility of existence with human needs, he believed, it must be more faithful
to human nature than Taylor's had been. Bushnell thus summed
up both his debt to Taylor and his reasons for striking out on
his own in a paragraph from his essay of 1832:

> If we must have a philosophy, let it be one,
> such as reveals itself in the spontaneous, we
> may almost say unconscious movements of the
> spirit. There is no other; and that is religion,
> Christianity itself. Speculate as we may, there
> is that in Christianity which is connatural to
> man. . . . The philosophy of Christianity is
> therefore the philosophy of man, or, as I have
> better said already, Christianity is itself the
> philosophy of man.[14]

Bushnell's first year as minister to the North Church of
Hartford, Connecticut, forced him to develop these student

thoughts more clearly. At the time of Bushnell's arrival, the church was in open conflict over precisely the issues on which Bushnell sought to distinguish himself from Taylor. Half the church supported Taylor's view that mankind has an inherent ability to lay hold of righteousness. The other half adhered to the Edwardsean position that because the human will is depraved, only grace can save sinful man from himself. Bushnell felt himself caught in the middle, like a plate "daintily inserted between an acid and an alkali."[15] For his own peace of mind, and in the interests of church harmony, he sought out a firm middle ground.

Bushnell attempted to define his position in a sermon titled "Duty Not Measured by Our Own Ability" (1833). Its basic argument is that man alone is neither strictly able nor strictly unable to do or be good, but that gracious help is available to man through "natural" channels. Bushnell relied on organic metaphors to explain himself. God's self-communicating Spirit is an environing condition for spiritual growth, he wrote; man depends on it as a seed depends on sunlight and water. But like sunlight, spiritual help is abiding and ubiquitous.[16] As he wrote elsewhere soon afterwards, "the doctrine of spiritual agency is grounded in the simple doctrine of God's omnipresence." God is "in-resident in his works;" spirit is an "air-medium, common, or present, both to the divine mind and to ours," a "fragrant wind."[17] That is, God's spirit is somehow present to us in creation, and its very presence is nurturing and inspiring. If only man is receptive to it, it fills him with a divine energy that expands his spiritual capacities and assimilates him to the divine nature.[18]

In practical terms, Bushnell's doctrine of the "abiding spirit" meant that when Scripture commands man to do the right, it asks what no fallen man can do himself, but not what it is impossible to do.

> It calls every man to earnest and hopeful
> endeavor by the consideration of an all-support-
> ing grace that can not fail;--Work out
> salvation with fear and trembling; for it is
> God that worketh in you.[19]

The doctrine of mankind's need for grace is

> only another way of generalizing the truth
> that God will co-work invigoratively, cor-
> rectively, and directively in all the good
> struggles of believing souls.[20]

Bushnell's church found this quite acceptable. The Ed-
wardseans recognized their characteristic doctrine of man's
total dependence on God; the Taylorites approved the stipulation
that man can and must struggle to fulfil the law. Bushnell thus
came through the challenge gratified to find his native inclination certified by success, and with the germ of his "comprehensive" theological method "experimentally proved."[21]

But Bushnell did not leave off theological reflection on
divine-human relations after his practical triumph. He knew
that these first halting steps beyond Taylor carried him into
a vast, unexplored territory--that they marked, in fact, a
sea-change in Calvinism.[22] By making grace an abiding force
in all lives--a "natural" condition of spiritual growth--he had
virtually eradicated the distinction of the elect from the
damned. He had effectively democratized Edwards' doctrine of
grace. No controversy arose at the time, but Bushnell went
on quietly to consolidate and extend his insights. Over the
next few years, this doctrine of the "abiding spirit" was carefully developed into a theory of divine self-communication in
"Revelation," and in "Unconscious Influence," into a social-
psychology of moral growth.

2. "Revelation"

"Revelation" was hastily prepared for delivery to the
Society of Inquiry at Andover, Massachusetts, in September
1839.[23] Bushnell never polished or published it, but we can
see in retrospect that it marked an important step in the
development of his thinking. It is the essay in which the outlines of his mature understanding of divine-human relations
first began to emerge. He had declared in his divinity school
essay against Taylor that "there is that in Christianity which
is connatural to man." Here he began to explore the mode of
that "connaturality" in detail.

Bushnell's general aim in "Revelation" was to define the
manner in which God is "in-resident in his works," and so, to
explain how created objects can become vehicles of spirit and

divine life. Specifically, he sought to understand the Bible
as a piece of language.[24] The Bible, he reasoned, is commonly
understood to be the primary locus of God's self-revelation to
mankind. And the Bible is a work in language. However the
Bible communicates God to man, then, "it reaches its end through
language" (p. 12). So, to understand the role of the Bible in
spiritual life, one must first understand the role of language
in the total life of the mind.

The chief function of language, Bushnell held, is to communicate the lives of other minds to us. Minds are "separate,
invisible, immaterial worlds" (P. 18). But through language,
minds are expressed and made public. Language is the medium
of our intersubjectivity. Bushnell's way of setting up the
issue thus led him to confront a problem that we have already
noted in our discussion of the Scottish philosophy's approach
to the interpretation of facial expressions and created works.[25]
How, Bushnell asked, is intersubjectivity possible? How are
we able to divine the thoughts and feelings behind another person's expressions, given that the mind or inner life expressed
never appears to our senses? Bushnell attempted to answer this
question by means of a theory of the origins of language. Because that theory reappears expanded and improved in several
later works, we will postpone treatment of it until Chapter IV
below. For now, it is enough to note Bushnell's conclusions.

"Language," he said, "is two stories high, being first a
language of sense or fact and next a language of thought or
truth" (p. 13). The first story of language is composed of
all terms that can be used to refer to empirical phenomena. The
second story comprises all terms for inward experiences of the
kind that never appear directly to the senses. "Rock," for
instance, is a term in the second. The two classes, in turn,
refer to their objects in different ways. Physical terms refer
ostensively; they are the verbal equivalent of pointing.
Their interpretation is therefore relatively unproblematic.
But terms in the second category cannot point to their objects.
They can only suggest them or evoke them by indirection
(pp. 9-10). Terms in the first category, we might say, are
notational; terms in the second category are expressive.

The key to the significance of language in life, Bushnell
believed, lay in how expressive terms manage to suggest their
referents. All terms in the second category are etymologically
derived from terms in the first, he assumed.[27] For instance,
"spirit" is derived from the word for breath, "comprehension"
from physical grasping, and so forth (pp. 12-13). The physical
image latent in the word is a vehicle for the invisible idea
it conveys. But how, he asked, can a notational image communicate an inward state? An image could only communicate an invisible thought effectively if it suggested the same thought to all
minds. And it could only do this if it were a natural sign
of that state, with an inherent power to evoke the appropriate
associations from all persons. Therefore, declared Bushnell,
since images do convey thoughts, it must be the case that they
are natural signs. Bushnell's reasoning here was *ad hoc*, but
the conclusion was apparently stirring enough to distract him
from its speciousness: "the whole outward world," he wrote,
"in its objects, colors, scenes, sounds, motions, wants and
the like is analogical to thought and truth and constitutes in
the whole a grand system of figure work, spiritually significant" (pp. 16-17).

The explanation for this inferred harmony of mind and
matter was equally obvious to Bushnell. God, nature's Author,
has formed the world for man's uses, both physical and
mental.

> Having his eye fixed on this necessity of man,
> [God] has constructed the outward world, i.e.
> our body and the realm of nature around us, so
> as to furnish a vast store house of types or
> images fitted to represent thoughts and be
> interpreted between man and man (p. 16).

Further, the same God who made the world for man's use made
man fit to use it. Man is

> a creature so quickened by the divine principle
> of intelligence that he feels the mysterious
> analogy between forms and truths and darts through
> one to the other scarcely conscious of the
> transition (pp. 8-9).

Thus, to account for intersubjective communication, Bushnell leaped to a remarkable set of conclusions about God's
relation to nature and mankind's relation to God. He drew on
the commonplace idea of the analogy of creation (discussed in

Chapter I above) to characterize the world as an analogy of
divine and human thought. He also called nature a store house
of "types," thus taking a stand with those of his New England
forefathers who saw nature as a type of the divine mind. Likewise, he held that the human mind is informed by a divine
principle of intelligence which manifests itself in our capacity to read the types and analogies of nature. And here we
can recognize something akin to Edwards' "sense of the heart"
transformed into a general theory of human understanding.

Bushnell's purpose in mounting this string of assumptions
was not to argue metaphysics and epistemology, however. It
was simply to indicate what the study of language could teach
about the nature of revelation. Having shown to his satisfaction that the fundamental characteristic of expressive language
is its ability to communicate inward thoughts and feeling through
concrete images, he went on to write similarly of revelation:
"The fundamental idea of revelation (I speak now of revelation
in the general) is that it brings truth into outward exhibition,
or into some one of the forms of the senses" (pp. 3-4). Revelation proper, then, is a special case of revelation in general.
The Bible is the expressive language of God. Thus,

> The great principle to be adopted is that all
> the presentations we meet of truth or spiritual
> doctrine in the Bible lie in figures and there
> must be studied. This is not peculiar to the
> Bible. All mental thought and moral truth lies
> in the same condition (p. 52).

His first premise, we will recall, was that whatever else the
Bible may be, "it reaches its end through language" (p. 12).
With these suggestions about the nature of language behind
him, then, he turned to consider what the Bible does as a work
in language.

The main point he wanted to make about the Bible was a
deduction from the principle that expressive language refers
to its objects by analogical or indirect means. The Bible is
an expression of the divine mind, he held; therefore, like all
expressive works, the Bible must communicate suggestively, by
indirection.

> [A] revelation never conveys truth from one mind
> to another; it only holds out some image which
> puts the beholder on generating for himself the

> thought intended, which he does out of his own
> sagacity quickened by the image presented
> (pp. 9-10).

This principle put Bushnell at odds with most Biblical theologians of his day. By and large, theologians in early nineteenth century America believed that the Bible provided material for an exact science of the divine mind. Biblical language, they held, described God and the operations of his spirit with absolute, algebraic precision.[28] Of course, it was acknowledged that the Bible also contains much that is figurative or metaphorical. But according to most current theories of rhetoric, figurative language was but garnish on the literal meat of the text. The entire business of theology was to isolate and pin down passages that could provide a straightforward map of the noumenal world.[29] Orthodox Calvinists and Unitarians alike shared this ideal of literal and logical precision. Unitarians found orthodox formulas wanting in logical or moral cogency and so discarded many of them.[30] Orthodox apologists struggled to prove Calvinism's greater faithfulness to the literal meaning of Scripture by means of their own canons of interpretation.[31] In both camps, figurative meanings were judged inconsequential, a distraction from the theological task.

Bushnell, on the other hand, believed that this ideal of literalness in the interpretation of Scripture was based on a tremendous category mistake. It assumed that talk about God could refer to him by notation, as if he were an empirical object. But God, by definition, transcends the world. He is no more available to our senses than are other minds. The language that represents him, then, must be expressive language, which is always figurative, never literal. Thus, Bushnell declared, it is no use trying to pin down literal language with reference to God.

> The distinction between literal and meta-
> phorical speech is a distinction of the rhetor-
> icians which philosophy does not tolerate,
> except so far as language is used to describe
> mere outward things. All the terms of thought
> and spirit are a figure work perfectly
> analogous to painting, and the reader or
> hearer only goes through a gallery of images
> or shapes which he studies with a painter's
> eye to get the sense (p. 53).

This understanding of the predominantly figurative character of Biblical language led Bushnell to another conclusion:
the impact of the Bible on mankind, he held, is primarily
aesthetic and educative in the manner of art. As he put it,
Scripture serves a "practical" function, not primarily a doctrinal one. As expressive language, Scripture conveys Mind to
mind by evoking the thoughts it carries in the minds to which
it is directed. It gives instruction in divine things, not by
setting them forth as facts, but by effectively developing a
person's capacity to reproduce them in his own experience, all
through the medium of language (p. 61). The text not only
shows God; it *gives* what it shows. To try to reduce the figurative "suggestiveness" of Scripture to scientific discourse,
then, is to deprive it of its practical effect. This is the
great "heresy" of orthodox and Unitarian alike. By concentrat-
ing on the letter of Scripture rather than the "spirit" expressed, they adopt an inappropriate attitude. They look for
a logical precision that is not there, and so miss the power of
instruction that is: "they thus put themselves out of the
range of the practical warmth of the gospel and destroy its
effect on the mind" (p. 71).

Scripture exercises this educative function, in turn,
wholly by means of the expressive power of its language.
Specifically, it provides a set of images which are the appropriate vehicles of Christian consciousness, just as the natural
world provides the forms by which we can express our natural
minds (pp. 45-46).

But in what sense are images educative, whether in nature
or Scripture? Bushnell provided an extended illustration. A
child, he wrote, first learns his own mind by drinking in the
forms of nature through his senses. The analogical significance
of the world does not immediately dawn on him, but when his
powers of abstraction and language awaken, his budding self-
knowledge will make use of, and be called out by, the images
he has on hand. Nature thus empowers the mind's development
(pp. 35-36). It is a providential arrangement for "the
schooling of the immortal creature for whom it was made"
(p. 34).

Likewise, Bushnell wrote, the Bible develops figures in
the Old Testament--sacrifice, atonement, priesthood, kingship,
and the like--which are the uniquely appropriate vehicles for
the ideas or spiritual truths of the New.[32] Without these
symbols to instruct and prepare their minds, people of Jesus'
generation could not have begun to understand him. With them,
they could both comprehend his mission and set it down in a
history which conveyed his power to future generations through
the medium of expression (p. 41). Thus, the Bible, conceived
as a store house of expressive symbols, is a necessary propaedeutic of Christian consciousness. Without expressive symbols, the spiritual efficacy of the gospel would be lost.[33]

Finally, Bushnell drew a conclusion about how Scripture
can be used to best effect in Christian life. The proper attitude of the Christian towards Scriptural symbolism, he held,
is receptive. "The forms and images of Scripture must not be
cast away but cultivated" (p. 72), for all the truth that it
has to offer is in them. For instance, when a Christian finds
that the atonement is described in Scripture by a whole raft
of diverse images--sacrifice, propitiation, expiation, satisfaction, and so forth--he should not try to reduce those suggestions to consistency. Rather, he should absorb the language,
fathom the spirit it contains, and so discover in himself the
complex response intended in it.

> Fall naturally into the impression they make on
> you as figures of speech--that impression is
> their truth (pp. 63-64).

Do not seize on any one formulation of a truth, he said; do
not paraphrase or define. Definitions lead to partisanship,
and partisanship in matters of religion only unsettles the
mind for right reading. So cultivate quietness, and the ability
to hear what God intends; transcend yourself by a reverence for
words as vehicles of the divine life.

> You must dwell secret and nourish your mind by
> your discoveries. You need ever to have a
> little reverence for words as being the mirrors
> of God and all knowledge (pp. 55-56).[34]

By such means, Scripture reaches its intended end as expression
--the communication of God to a connatural recipient:

look on here and follow after that we may
receive the practical effect and bring ourselves
into as deep an impression or as lively a
communion with God in these forms as is possible (p. 61).

To sum up: Bushnell in "Revelation" faced a problem similar to that we found addressed by the New England typologists--
how can redemption be mediated to man through his immediate
experience in nature and history? In what sense is grace an
"abiding" possibility for man in the world? Bushnell handled
the problem, in turn, with tools typical of the Scottish philosophy of mind. He introduced 1) a theory of expressive language
as a figurative representation of the speaker's mind, to be
interpreted by appropriate responses in similar minds; 2) the
germ of a theory of the inherent power of images to call forth
the experiences they intend; and finally, 3) a view of the
Scriptures as operating under the laws of expressive communication, reaching their end through images. Bushnell discussed
all these points at greater length in later works, so we will
spend no more time on his rather breathless treatment of them
here. The importance of "Revelation" is not its systematic
rigor (it has little), but the clarity with which it illustrates
how Bushnell, from the very beginning of his career, sought
clues for the solution of theological problems in the dynamics
of expressive communication

3. "Unconscious Influence"

In 1846, Bushnell preached and subsequently published a
sermon on "Unconscious Influence" which carried forward the
project he began in "Revelation." In the earlier work, Bushnell attempted to explain how God communicates himself redemp-
tively to mankind through creation and Scripture. His
explanatory model was human communication, conceived as the
expression of thought and spirit in concrete images. In
"Unconscious Influence," Bushnell significantly refined his
model, sharpening his concept of expression and extending his
analysis of interpersonal communication to include non-verbal
signs and influences. The work is thus primarily an essay in
social-psychology. But Bushnell's intention throughout was
to shed light on the nature and means of the divine-human

relation. He worked from the principle that "spiritual influences are never separated from the laws of thought in the individual and the laws of feeling and influence in society."[35] Therefore he assumed that the economy of redemption can be studied immanently, through analysis of the ways persons in society express themselves, respond, and grow.

Bushnell's starting point for reflection on the nature of interpersonal influence was his experience as a tutor at Yale. He had come to believe that persons are emulators, hungry for models. They form their identities around those to whom they are drawn. The Scottish philosophy, in turn, gave him a way to understand this phenomenon. Every person's language, behavior, and bearing, he held, is an expression that analogously represents his inward thought and feeling. To interpret self-expressions is to link up another's expressions with a similar thought or feeling in one's own mind. The interpreter quite literally mirrors or relives the mental contents expressed.[36] Expression as Bushnell conceived it thus has terrific power to reach into and mold the experience of others. Whatever a person expresses --or what he cannot help but show--reveals a pathway to selfhood that others may very likely follow. The power of example is subtle and pervasive:

> men are ever touching unconsciously the springs
> of action in each other. . . . We overrun the
> boundaries of our personality--we flow together.
> . . . And thus our life and conduct are ever
> propagating themselves by a law of social con-
> tagion, throughout the circles and times in
> which we live (p. 186).

Bushnell was keenly aware that this understanding of human interdependence put him at odds with his age. The common-sense view of human identity in Bushnell's America was radically individualistic; persons were thought to have their natures as they have their political rights--as inalienable possessions. The community was seen simply as a contractual arrangement for mutual benefit. In Europe, thinkers of a more or less romantic cast of mind were opposing this legacy of the Enlightenment with a more "organic" theory of society--e.g. Burke in his *Reflections on the Revolution in France* and Coleridge in his *Church and State*. Bushnell, too, eventually developed an organic theory of the state, though there is no direct evidence

that he was familiar with the European trends. Rather, he seems
to have developed his views from the guiding premise of "Unconscious Influence"--the theory of communication as a communion
of identity. If it is the case, as he wrote, that each individual is "a fractional element of a larger and more comprehensive
being, called society," it is because "in a certain department
of your nature, it is open, your sympathies and feelings are
open" (p. 194).[37] As an interpreter of expressions, every
person is open to the influence of those around him. By way
of illustration, Bushnell pointed to the common characteristics
of the members of a nation or a family and to the more ephemeral
contagion of feelings in crowds, wars, and economic panics
(p. 197). The reality of human life in society, in short, is
solidarity. We "flow together" in all the things that most
intimately shape our identities.

Assuming, then, that man is an expressing and interpreting
being, "thus qualified to communicate himself to others" (p.
191), Bushnell proceeded to analyze the means of expression and
interpretation. There are two basic types of self-expression,
he held. The first is deliberate speech and action, "that which
we exert purposely or in the endeavor to sway another, as by
teaching, by argument, by persuasion, by threatenings, by offers
and promises" (pp. 186-87).[38] It is voluntary, controllable,
and so, subject to conscious distortions. We "make an impression" by what we choose to do and say, sincerely or hypocriti-
cally (pp. 188, 192). The second form of expression, however,
is unconscious, involuntary, and so, perfectly representative
of the mind it expresses (p. 188). It consists in "that expression of the eye, the face, the look, the gait, the motion,
the tone or cadence, which is sometimes called the natural
language of the sentiments" (p. 192).[39] Such influences act
invisibly and inexorably. According to a natural law of influence, like begets like.

> [Influences] go streaming from us in all
> directions, though in channels that we do not
> see, poisoning or healing around the roots of
> society, and among the hidden wells of character.
> If good ourselves, they are good; if bad, they
> are bad (p. 188).[40]

We are always betraying and exerting ourselves in this way,
whether we are aware of it or not. And because it is so

constant and sure, unconscious influence is finally the more
powerful of the two modes of self-expression. The lightning
bolts of purposeful, intentional action may be highly impressive, but it is really the steady radiance of the personality
that makes the most difference in the world (pp. 189-90).
Thus, every person exerts a persistent, if small, moral force.
Even the most obscure man or woman inevitably makes a lasting
mark on society (pp. 201-02).[41] Every person, we might say,
is for Bushnell a miniature neo-Platonic God, whose selfhood
emanates and reproduces itself socially. At any rate, the
classic neo-Platonic metaphors of lamp and fountain dominate
Bushnell's account of the influential self: influence "flows
each moment, as light from the sun, and propagates itself in
all beholders" (p. 192).

Just as there are two modes of expression, there are two
"inlets of impression" through which expressions can become
powers over others. Explicit speech and action appeal to "the
ear and understanding." But unconscious influence is received
passively and subliminally through the "sympathetic powers,
the sensibilities and affections" (p. 192). Each person's native
feelings serve "for tinder to those sparks of emotion revealed
by looks, manners and general conduct;" like responds to and
reproduces like (p. 192).

Bushnell is not consistent, however, in distinguishing
these two inlets--understanding and sensibility--according to
the kinds of expressions they can receive. The sensibility is
not only the interpreter of non-verbal, emotive expression. It
can also interpret anything expressed in images or symbols.

> [T]hese sympathetic powers, though not immediately
> rational, are yet inlets, open on all sides, to
> the understanding and character. They have a
> certain wonderful capacity to receive impressions,
> and catch the meaning of signs, and propagate
> in us whatever falls into their passive molds,
> from others (p. 192).

The sensibility in this capacity is akin to what Bushnell
would later call the imagination, the faculty specifically suited
to interpret figures and analogies, to "catch the meaning of
signs."[42] Thus, as in the case of expressions, Bushnell regarded the unconscious mode of impression as the most comprehensive and consequential of the two. The influences that

make the most difference in life, he held, are unconscious influences, unintentionally broadcast and passively received.

To illustrate the role that unconscious influences and receptivities play in human society, Bushnell offered a few observations on the psychology of growth. Children begin life, he said, with an "instinct of imitation" (p. 195). The "souls" of children are "plastic" and "passive;" they are purely receptive natures. That is, in their first few years, they have no proper selfhood of their own. But they exhibit a genius for response to the non-verbal expressions of the selves around them. Their minds are thus called out--their habits and character formed--by signs. "The child looks and listens, and whatever tone of feeling or manner of conduct is displayed around him, sinks into his . . . soul and becomes a mold of his character ever after" (pp. 195-96). The infant is receptive because he is utterly passive. But the same hunger for models persists when the child develops a will of its own: "he begins voluntarily to copy every thing he sees. Voice, manner, gait, every thing which the eye sees, the mimic instinct delights to act over" (p. 196). And because the things copied are expressive of mind, the child learns not only the outward forms of behavior, but the feelings and qualities of character associated with them. His insides--his habits of thought and feeling--are formed along with his style, for mind and behavior are linked by the laws of expression.[43] Children thus receive "the deepest impulses of their life and immortality" from the forms and symbolic expressions they assimilate in growth (p. 196).

Later in life, "respect for others" takes the place of imitation, but serves the same function. By "respect," Bushnell meant the desire for approval, the urge to conform. We continue to imitate in order to win the good opinion of others, in fashion, aesthetic taste, morality, and religion. Thus, we fall into the habits of thought, feeling, action, and belief of our social circle. And adopting its habits, we adopt its insides. As we learn to express, so we are (pp. 196-97).

Bushnell, then, long before the researches of American social theorists like Josiah Royce, James Mark Baldwin, and George Herbert Mead, was alive to the role of imitation in

psycho-social growth.[44] Bushnell, however, was no academic
theorist, and never developed the insight in detail. For him,
the really momentous implication of this understanding of communication was one we would no longer even be inclined to draw.
Bushnell believed his theory implied that the growth process,
guided or shaped by the influence of others, has an inherent
ethical and religious orientation. His argument followed from
premises we have already reviewed. Intersubjective communication is only possible, Bushnell held, because persons have
similar thoughts, feelings, and impulses. To understand is to
share experiences, which entails a common capacity to experience.
He conceived this common human nature in connection with the
Scottish idea of the moral sense. All persons share at least
an innate ability to distinguish right from wrong. We are
linked by our "higher," ethical selves. The higher self, in
turn, is the image of God in man, an index of God's own moral
character. Understanding the normative moral expressions of
other persons, then, entails likeness to God. Similarly,
likeness to God is the presupposition of our ability to understand each other. Mutual understanding--indeed all symbolic
communication--is thus oriented towards the good. Through open
intersubjective communication, persons in community call out
or reinforce each others' common moral nature, in which their
likeness to God consists. The channels of interpersonal communication thus take on an inherently religious significance, which
Bushnell was anxious to explicate.

Bushnell's term for this normative possibility of existence,
in which the individual is at once most like other persons in
community and most like God, is "character." The word is
somewhat ambiguous in Bushnell's usage. On the one hand,
"character" is his shorthand for the inner root of human moral
nature, closely akin to "soul" or "self." It is mind, feeling,
habits of action and thought--anything than man or God conveys
through expression. In one view, then, every person has a
different character according to the state of his morals and
sensibilities. On the other hand, Bushnell also found it
proper to say that all persons have the same "character." The
word originally meant the stamp or graphic symbol which a
maker sets on his product, or an owner on his possessions.

Bushnell, with his characteristic flair for etymology, usually gave the term this twist. All persons, he wrote, are in the "character" of God; as his creatures, they bear his image. The character of a person is thus the norm of his being as well as the state he happens to be in.

Bushnell's treatment of the role of interpersonal influence in growth reflects the ambiguity of his concept of character. Influence is a medium of character in two senses. First, influence is a channel through which human sin and virtue are propagated indifferently. In this sense, all persons are influential. For good or evil, all persons "flow together" in society. Second, influence is a medium through which persons are awakened to their common wants and nature, their inherent impulses to a higher life. And in this sense, it is preeminently the Christian--the good person in sympathy with the mind of God--who lives and acts with influential power (p. 203). All persons shape our character, then, but normative or divine character can only be called out by one who himself expresses the image of God. And because that image resonates with our own inmost wants and affinities, normative character is the most powerful of all tools of influence. General influence generates local communities of like minds. Normative influence realizes the authentic, universal community of persons in their likeness to God.[45]

Bushnell thus believed that unconscious influence was a predominantly positive ethical force. He further believed it to be a positive religious force. Indeed, it promised to be "one of the most serious and fruitful chapters of Christian doctrine" (p. 186). In "Unconscious Influence," he began to indicate how that promise could be fulfilled. He noted, for instance, that this theory of communication could explain the redemptive power of Christ. Christ, said Bushnell, is both like and unlike other persons. He is like other persons in having a mind that reveals itself through expressions and exerts influence through what is revealed. He is unlike other persons in that his mind and character are identical with God's. The influence he exerts is thus perfectly normative or redemptive. Christ, as the image of God, propagates the image of God in man. He makes normative identity available through the natural channels of the sensibility.

> [A]n image, you know, is that which simply re-
> presents, not that which acts, or reasons, or
> persuades. . . . And here is the power of
> Christ--it is what of God's beauty, love, truth
> and justice shines through him (pp. 200-01).

Christ's self-communication has a special efficacy, then, because the image he bears is a perfect match for mankind's normative moral constitution. Being itself the pattern according
to which mankind was created, Christ's image prevails over the
more eccentric communicative powers of sin. He exerts "that
kind of influence which the spirit of truth may wield with the
more persuasive and subduing effect" (p. 200).

While Christ's influence is special in content, however,
it is not distinct in kind from the influence persons have on
each other. It was thus a short step for Bushnell from Christ-
ology to a theory of the Christian self. The Christian, he
held, can and should serve as a Christ to his neighbor, in the
very specific sense that he should bear and communicate the
image of God through his own character. Insofar as a person is
awakened to his normative being through the influence of Christ,
he too becomes a vehicle of divine life for others. By means
of revelation, he becomes revelation. It is to this end, Bushnell concluded, that God expressed himself in Christ in the
first place.

> It is the great idea of his gospel, and the
> work of his spirit, to make you lights in the
> world. His greatest joy is to give you character,
> to beautify your example, to exalt your principles,
> and make you each the depository of his own
> almighty grace (p. 203).

The Christian is thus to become what Christ was. Through the
natural means by which he communicates himself in society, he
is to become a vehicle of grace.

Bushnell accordingly drew a final, practical lesson from
this theory of interpersonal communication. In order to become
a vehicle of grace for others, the Christian must first set
his own inward life in order.

> You inhabit a house that is well nigh trans-
> parent; and what you are within, you are ever
> showing yourself to be without, by signs that
> have no ambiguous expression (p. 202).

In short, there is no place to hide. A parent, for instance, cannot hide his bad temper or weak principles from his children. Even if he never expresses them openly, the children will drink them in from the parent's look and general attitude. Therefore, to make his children good, the parent must make himself good. And to make then Christian, he must become Christian himself (pp. 202-03).

Bushnell's attempts to apply his theory of influence to theology here were sketchy and suggestive at best. Still, the outlines of a theology begin to emerge--a theology which is at once a fulfillment of the lesson he first learned as a tutor at Yale and a reaction against the theological education he received there. As he had already determined in "Revelation," God is not the remote moral judge that Taylor had made him out to be. Rather, God's spirit "abides" in nature, Scripture, and human history--the "language" of his self-expression. And through this abiding presence, God empowers persons for the higher self-knowledge in which their redemption consists. Christianity, therefore, like its chief vehicle, the Bible, "reaches its end through language." In "Unconscious Influence," Bushnell added reflections on how that redemptive end is reached on the human side. Man, he held, is a creature whose character and destiny are molded by the communicative power of expressions, verbal or non-verbal, human or divine. Persons will take on the image of evil almost as easily as that of good, but their self-knowledge is never complete until they find themselves fully expressed in the Christian norm. The human person, as a creature of language, is thus perfectly suited to the means of Christian redemption, and vice versa. Both being understood on the model of communication, religion and human growth become mutually interpreting categories.

NOTES

CHAPTER II

[1]Quoted in Cheney, *The Life and Letters of Horace Bushnell* (1880; rpt. New York: Arno Press, 1969), p. 62. This work will be cited hereafter as *LL*.

[2]Taylor's stance was that of a mediator--a friend of Calvinism who nevertheless sought to modify the orthodox understanding of divine-human relations in the direction of mankind's greater participation in the redemptive process. The best available accounts of the theological movement to which he belonged are Frank Hugh Foster, *A Genetic History of the New England Theology* (Chicago: University of Chicago Press, 1907); and Joseph Haroutunian, *Piety Versus Moralism* (New York: Henry Holt & Co., 1932). Each is strongly colored by its author's own theological preferences, and relies on questionable assumptions about Taylor's place in the tradition. For a cogent criticism of their assumptions about Taylor, see Sidney Mead, *Nathaniel William Taylor* (Chicago: University of Chicago Press, 1942).

[3]Taylor and the New Haven Theology he headed are generally classed as late representatives of the "New Divinity" party that took up the banner of Jonathan Edwards after his death. But in fact, Taylor freely and deliberately deviated from Edwards whenever he found Edwards' positions untenable. This was especially true with regard to the definition of freedom of the will. See Mead, *op. cit.*, p. 102.

[4]John Calvin, *Institutes of the Christian Religion*, trans. John Allen (Philadelphia: Presbyterian Board of Christian Education, 1928), vol. I, p. 285 (II, v, i).

[5]Jonathan Edwards, *Freedom of the Will*, ed. Paul Ramsey (New Haven: Yale University Press, 1957), p. 142. See also Roland Delattre, *Beauty and Sensibility* (New Haven: Yale University Press, 1968), pp. 86ff.

[6]Taylor, *Lectures on the Moral Government of God* (New York: Clark, Austin and Smith, 1859), vol. I, p. 200.

[7]For Taylor's moral philosophy and psychology, see W.S. Dutton, "Notes on Taylor on Mental Philosophy," MS Yale University Library. On the Scottish psychology itself, see S.A. Grave, *The Scottish Philosophy of Common Sense* (Oxford: Oxford University Press, 1960), pp. 207-19. On the role of Scottish philosophy in American religious thought generally, see Sydney Ahlstrom, "The Scottish Philosophy and American Theology," *Church History*, XXIV (1955), pp. 257-72.

[8]Taylor's slogan, "certainty with power to the contrary," is quoted and discussed by Mead, *op. cit.*, pp. 188-90.

[9]In his most famous and most controversial work--the
"Concio ad Clerum" of 1828--Taylor reconciled human depravity
with moral freedom by means of a distinction between "nature"
and the powers of the will. He allowed that persons inevitably
sin "by nature," which is to say that "they will sin and only
sin under all the appropriate circumstances of their being."
But Taylor was quick to add that mankind's universal disposition
to sin implies no cause compelling the will in that direction.
"Nature" is not the efficient cause of sin; it is only the
"occasion" of sin. Or, what is the same thing, the will itself
is always morally neutral. Good and evil are qualities ascribed
to one's nature according to the way one acts, not inherent
qualities of the will. The definitive property of the redeemed
has nothing to do with their perceptions, affections, or inclinations, then. It is simply that the saints choose righteous
action whereas sinners choose sin. Thus, redemption and sin alike
are behavioral rather than essential characteristics. They are
defined in terms of acts rather than inward states. "Sin is
in the sinning," not in some abstract status that constrains
the will in its sin. See Taylor, "Concio ad Clerum," in
Theology in America, ed. Sydney Ahlstrom (Indianapolis: Bobbs-
Merrill, 1967), pp. 213-49.

[10]["Natural Science and Moral Philosophy,"] MS Yale Divinity
School Library. The manuscript was originally untitled, but
this title has become standard.

[11]*Ibid.*, p. 33.

[12]*Ibid.*, p. 14.

[13]*Ibid.*, pp. 23,20.

[14]*Ibid.*, p. 30. It is arguable that Bushnell picked up
this emphasis on the possibility of divine-human communion not
from Taylor but from Samuel Taylor Coleridge, whose *Aids to
Reflection* Bushnell had been reading as early as 1831. See
Chapter I, n. 82 above. Coleridge teaches here, for instance,
that God and the human will are alike "supernatural," operating
independent of the principles of cause and effect that characterize physical nature (*Aids* [1840; rpt. Port Washington, N.Y.:
Kennikat Press, 1971], p. 236). Bushnell took over Coleridge's
distinction almost verbatim for his central definitions in
Nature and the Supernatural ([1858; rpt. New York: AMS Press,
1971], pp. 36-38). But is was not from Coleridge alone that
Bushnell could have learned to distinguish spirit and nature--
mind and matter--in this way. Nathaniel Taylor based his whole
theory of the responsible will on a similar distinction between
the mental and physical orders. The powers of the will, he
argued, are exempt from the laws of causation that pertain to
physical nature. If the will were causally determined, we
could not justly be expected to incur responsibility for our
acts. But we *are* responsible for our action, as consciousness
of sin and guilt proves. Therefore, the will must be a self-
active power (*Lectures*, I, p. 193). The cause and effect
relations that apply in nature simply cannot apply to a system
of free, responsible agents, and therefore do not apply to the
moral operations of the human mind. Bushnell was alive to this

aspect of Taylor's argument. His essay of 1832 refers to it
repeatedly, only to express regret that Taylor did not make
more of the distinction. Taylor professed to teach a philosophy
of mind, widely distinct in its principles from the philosophy
of matter, Bushnell wrote. But in fact, he went on, Taylor used
the lawlike regularity and concreteness of the physical universe
as a model for his interpretation of the spiritual. He tacitly
assumed that the moral order, in spite of sin, operated with
the same harmony and regularity as the physical. Bushnell, by
contrast, felt that to do justice to mankind, the idiosyncratic
qualities of the spiritual realm needed to be stressed. Philosophy should "allow to the spiritual in man, and more particularly to the will, a higher efficacy and more subtle power than
has hitherto been recognized." (Bushnell, ["Natural Science,"]
pp. 16, 26.) With a clearer view of the spirit in man, Bushnell
implied, theologians might break through to the conclusion
Coleridge had drawn from his own dualism, and which Bushnell
found so exciting: that of "the capacity and possible communion
of such spirit with the spiritual in principle," i.e. with God.
(Coleridge, *Aids* , p. 236.)

[15]Bushnell, "Twentieth Anniversary," (Hartford: Elihu
Geer, 1853), p. 8.

[16]Bushnell, "Duty Not Measured by Our Own Ability," in
Sermons for the New Life (New York: Charles Scribner, 1858),
p. 372. No earlier copy of the sermon exists.

[17]Bushnell, "The Spiritual Economy of Revivals of Religion"
(1838), in *Views of Christian Nurture* (1847; rpt. Delmar, N.Y.:
Scholars' Facsimiles & Reprints, 1975), pp. 126f, 129.

[18]Jonathan Edwards argued similarly. But where Edwards
made the gracious communication of a new sense to the elect
the condition of receptivity, Bushnell saw the "sense of the
heart" as man's birthright, the principle of his proper
humanity. In Edwards' view, the fall involved an utter loss
of higher spiritual insight, and so, of the capacity for righteous life. The "sense of the heart" was taken away and can be
restored to man only by grace. Bushnell, on the other hand, regarded the fall as the root of man's present moral disorientation, but he did not think that any capacity for righteousness
had been lost. Man's sin is a product of bewilderment and bad
conditioning, not the inevitable consequence of inability. For
a good discussion of this point, see H. Shelton Smith, *Changing
Conceptions of Original Sin* (New York: Scribner's, 1955).

[19]Bushnell, *New Life*, p. 373.

[20]*Ibid.*, p. 374.

[21]Bushnell, "Twentieth Anniversary," pp. 13, 14.

[22]See "Growth Not Conquest, The True Method of Christian
Progress," in *Views of Christian Nurture*, p. 157; originally
published as "The Kingdom of Heaven as a Grain of Mustard
Seed," *New Englander*, II (October 1844), pp. 600-19. My page
references are to *Views*.

[23]See *LL*, pp. 88-89.

[24]Bushnell, "Revelation" (1839), MS Yale Divinity School Library. I give my own pagination. Subsequent references to the work in this section will be given in the body of the text.

[25]See Chapter I above, pp. 29-35.

[26]I borrow this terminology from Philip Wheelwright, whose understanding of metaphor is similar in outline to Bushnell's understanding of the language of "thought and intelligence." See *The Burning Fountain* (Bloomington: Indiana University Press, 1968), pp. 3-17.

[27]Bushnell's authority here was most likely Josiah Willard Gibbs, Sr., a philologist with whom he studied at Yale. Gibbs' position is stated in his *Philological Studies* (New Haven: Durrie & Peck, 1857), pp. 14-15. Though published in 1857, the articles collected here reflect materials used by Gibbs in the classroom throughout his career.

[28]On this ideal of notational precision in theological language, see Crosby, *Horace Bushnell's Theory of Language* (The Hague: Mouton, 1975), pp. 80-96.

[29]This approach is exemplified by Taylor, *Lectures*, II, p. 152.

[30]See William Ellery Channing, "Unitarian Christianity," in *The Works of William E. Channing* (Boston: American Unitarian Association, 1897), pp. 367-84.

[31]See for instance Taylor's attempt to meet Andrews Norton's claim that the trinity is "merely" figurative by claiming that Biblical language is always literal, though in an extended sense of the term "literal." His refusal to step outside of the terms of the literal/figurative dichotomy is typical. See Taylor, *Essays, Lectures, Etc.*, (New York: Clark, Austin and Smith, 1859), pp. 92-101. For a discussion of the counter-point between Norton and Taylor, see Crosby, *op. cit.*, pp. 180-207.

[32]These figures are "types" of Christ, Bushnell wrote, in the same sense in which expressive terms are "types" of the thoughts they express. See "Revelation," pp. 39, 40-41.

[33]A seminal ambiguity should be noted at this point. Bushnell assumes that the power by which man divines the meaning of Scripture is the same as that which makes him capable of reading the analogy of creation. In both cases, God is present to man through his self-expression, "quickening" or calling out man's natural receptivities. This is the doctrine of the "abiding spirit;" God's presence provides empowerment to all who lay hold of it. But Bushnell was also convinced that man's natural capacities were injured in his fall. Man's likeness to God, and so his powers of perception, are dimmed. Scripture, in fact, is given to help overcome the failure of that very divine sympathy which makes its interpretation possible. This

paradox catches Bushnell in a version of the hermeneutical circle. On the one hand, "an experience is needed to interpret words" (LL, p. 208). We understand words as expressions of mind only if we recognize in them something we possess in our-selves. On the other hand, words--especially the words of Scripture--are given to call forth meaning-experiences that we are not already capable of. So what makes possible an advance in mankind's capacities for experience and interpretation? How do we become capable of perceiving more than we are already inwardly prepared to perceive? Bushnell would eventually answer this question by an appeal to "the wondrous art by which some men are able to propitiate and assist the generative under-standing of others, so as to draw them readily into higher realizations of truth" (God in Christ [1849; rpt. New York: AMS Press, 1972], p. 88). In "Revelation," however, he wavered between various approaches to the problem.

[34]Here, if anywhere, Bushnell shows the mark of Coleridge. Coleridge says in the preface to Aids to Reflection that one of his primary objectives is to direct his readers' attention to "the value of the Science of words," specifically to words as the bearers and inspiring force of thought and spirit: "lan-guage [is] not only the vehicle of thought but the wheels . . . such as Ezekiel beheld in the visions of God as he sate among the captives by the river of Chegar. Withersoever the Spirit was to go, the Wheels went, and thither was their Spirit to go: for the Spirit of the living creature was in the wheels also" (Aids, pp. 62-63). The words of Scripture, in sum, are the medium through which God's own spirit is made available to men. That is, by reflecting on the meaning of words as facets of our own experience, the secrets of a verbal revelation are opened to us. "For if words are not things, they are living powers, by which the things of most importance to mankind are actuated, combined and humanized" (Aids, p. 65).

[35]Bushnell, "Unconscious Influence," in Sermons for the New Life, p. 186. A comparison with a New York pamphlet edition of 1846 shows that the early and late published versions are iden-tical. I therefore refer to the more accessible edition of 1858. Subsequent references to this work in this chapter are included in the body of the text.

[36]Other theorists of interpretation, notably Dilthey and Collingwood, have reached similar conclusions about the nature of understanding, and yet have maintained a distinction between the experience we recapitulate in understanding and the exper-ience which is properly our own. Bushnell, unfortunately, made no such distinction. See Hodges, Wilhelm Dilthey: An Intro-duction (New York: Oxford University Press, 1944), p. 15; R.G. Collingwood, An Autobiography (London: Oxford University Press, 1939), pp. 112-14.

[37]For a similar statement, see Views, p. 187. In "Uncon-scious Influence," Bushnell appeared willing to give the individualistic social contract theory of the origins of the state some credence. Later, he dismissed the theory as "empty and worthless chaff," because it failed to acknowledge that human society is an organic unity. See "The Founders Great in

Their Unconsciousness" (1849), in *Work and Play* (New York: Charles Scribner's Sons, 1903).

[38]In Taylor's theology of moral government, transactions like these characterize God's moral influence on man. See Taylor, *Practical Sermons* (New York: Clark, Austin and Smith, 1859), pp. 102-03. Bushnell wanted to distinguish himself from Taylor's view of God's influence as deliberate persuasion or government, and so, in an earlier work, he repudiated the term "influence" entirely ("The Organic Unity of the Family," in *Views*, pp. 185-85.) In "Unconscious Influence" and later works, however, he reinstates "influence" in a broader sense, expanding it to include the "law of simple contagion" which he had earlier termed "organic."

[39]Compare Dugald Stewart on non-verbal "natural language," *Works* (Cambridge: Hilliard and Brown, 1829), vol. III, pp. 3-16.

[40]Compare Emerson: "We pass for what we are. Character teaches above our wills. Men imagine that they communicate their virtue or vice only by overt actions, and do not see that virtue and vice emit a breath every moment." *The Complete Works of Ralph Waldo Emerson*, Centenary Edition, (Boston: Houghton, Mifflin and Co., 1903), p. 58.

[41]This is a recurrent theme in Bushnell's work: viz. "The Age of Homespun," in *Work and Play*, pp. 375, 378-79; "Living to God in Small Things," in *Sermons for the New Life*, pp. 282-303. Ann Douglas makes the point that a similar theory of the power of passivity was used by women to rationalize their inefficacy in society. See Douglas, *The Feminization of American Culture* (New York: Alfred A. Knopf, 1977), pp. 44-48.

[42]See Bushnell, "Our Gospel a Gift to the Imagination," in *Building Eras in Religion* (New York: Charles Scribner's Sons, 1910), pp. 252, 265.

[43]The shaping relations between character and manner run in both directions. Not only do one's expressions represent character, but one's style shapes the inner life: "What [persons] express they will be likely to feel. . . ." *Views*, p. 221.

[44]For an excellent discussion of the interest in imitation in American social theory, see Ernest Becker, *The Structure of Evil* (New York: George Brazillier, 1968), pp. 120-25.

[45]When Bushnell speaks of analogical expressions as vehicles of "truth," he thinks of them as conveying "character" in its normative sense.

CHAPTER III

THE THEORY OF EDUCATION:
SOCIETY AND THE SUPERNATURAL

In his early essays on communication, Bushnell sketched out theories of how God communicates himself to the soul through the media of his self-revelation, and of how persons communicate their identities to their fellows in society by similar means, calling out possibilities of existence in others by the influence of their expressions. We have already stressed how these theories served as the framework for Bushnell's understanding of divine-human relations. The divine life enters the lives of persons, he said, in the same way that persons enter the common life of society. Personal identity is expressed or exteriorized through language and behavior and so becomes a factor in the experience of others. Likewise, God enters the web of human history and communicates himself to mankind through the forms of created nature and Scripture that manifest the divine nature. For God and man alike, all behavior--and every artifact of behavior--is a revelation of the creative life within. Further, said Bushnell, just as a person acquires "influence" through his self-expressions, communicating what is most characteristic of his life or personality through the forms that manifest it, so God's self-expressions act as a "self-replicating power" over mankind, inspiring a divine consciousness through the forms of the world. The common denominator of both these theories is an idea of the power of symbolic expressions of persons, human or divine, to influence the moral growth of others. Human society is a web of influences in which persons are educated by the images of selfhood expressed around them. Human communion with God, likewise, is a social relation in which persons come under the influence of God's character through their dealings with him as revealed in the world, and in which persons become assimilated to the inward life communicated by the image.

Bushnell developed this fundamental analogy between human social relations and divine-human relations in a series of works on Christian education: the "Discourses on Christian

Nurture" (1847), a collection of articles published as *Views of Christian Nurture* (1847), and an expanded and popularized version of these earlier works titled simply *Christian Nurture* (1861).[1] The basic premise of all these works was a simple but sweeping inference drawn from his ideas on interpersonal communication. If persons communicate their identities to others through the natural channels of social influence, and if a properly divine identity is available to persons through their converse with the mind of God expressed in nature and Scripture, then it follows that a redeemed individual--one whose identity has been decisively shaped by the divine self-expression--can communicate his derivative divine identity to others through his social interactions with them. Natural society, that is, can serve as a vehicle of grace, insofar as its members participate in the divine life. Individual Christains who have realized the divine image in their own character bring the possibility of redemption into the immanent life of the world, becoming vehicles of redemption through their natural power as persons to influence the moral growth of their neighbors.

In this chapter, we will examine Bushnell's writings on Christian education with an eye to the role played in them by his theory of communication. Before turning to the works themselves, we will briefly explore how Bushnell's views took rise from a critique of revivalism. In conclusion, we will note how the issues addressed in his writings on education were carried forward in a later work, *Nature and the Supernatural*.

1. Bushnell on Revivals of Religion

The aim of Bushnell's writings on Christian education was to give a fresh account of the Christian redemptive economy in the light of his insight into the potentially redemptive power of Christian personality communicated through social relations. He took up the task primarily to provide an alternative to the revival, the dominant force in New England church life in the early nineteenth century. Perhaps there is no easy way to characterize American revivalism in this period. It varied tremendously in style and substance from the exuberance of the frontier camp meetings at Cane Ridge, Kentucky, to the more

decorous tactics of settled clergymen in Connecticut.[2] It
shared no common theology and few common methods. Yet, as Perry
Miller has pointed out, the revival, for all its internal diversity, exerted a pervasive influence on American culture by
means of a few of its most characteristics themes. The movement's frequent internecine quarrels should not be allowed to
obscure its "terrific universality."[3]

Two of its most common premises were especially objectionable to Bushnell. First, the revival--explicitly or implicitly--
affirmed a radical dualism of sin and grace or world and
spirit. "The world" was viewed as a virtually unrelieved
desert of sinfulness, antithetical to all forms of righteousness. Revivals, by contrast, were seen as works of the spirit,
with a special power to triumph over sin by the force of God
that was in them. The revival's understanding of how persons
can attain redeemed status followed from this premise. The
worldly, sinful, and unconverted person was understood to be the
natural enemy of God. To be saved, he must be taken by storm,
literally shocked out of one state into another for which he
had little or no prior affinity. So, the kind of conversion at
which revivals aimed was conceived as a drastic break between
an old life and a new birth. Grace, if it comes at all, must
come to one suddenly, in an experience that is violent in pro-
portion to mankind's natural pugnacity, and wholly abstracted
from ordinary modes of consciousness. Lyman Beecher's account
of his own conversion typifies this ideal of sudden conversion.

> The sinking of the shaft was instantaneous.
> I understood the law and my heart as well as I
> do now or shall at the day of judgment. I
> believe the commandment came, sin revived, and
> I died, quick as a flash of lightning.[4]

Many of Bushnell's objections to this model of spiritual
transformation reflect a simple difference in attitude--what
William James has characterized as the "healthy-minded" religious person's lack of comprehension for the trials of the "sick
soul." [5] Bushnell had no patience with the doctrine of native
depravity on which the theory of sudden conversion was based.
He held, rather glibly, that the doctrine had been "forever
exploded" by a preceeding generation of theological liberals
and so would not deign to debate the issue himself.[6] More
to the point, Bushnell argued that the revival's insistence on

sudden conversion had consequences unfavorable to piety. Piety,
according to Bushnell, should be largely continuous with our
best worldly values. It should display "constancy, singleness
of aim, loveliness, purity, richness, blamelessness, and . . .
domesticity of character."[7] Revivalistic piety, however, seemed
to him jerky and uneven, loud and brash. It encouraged scenes
of extraordinary spiritual experience, but was content to regard
the everyday affairs of life as a spiritual wasteland. As a
consequence, said Bushnell, "the religious life, thus unskill-
fully ordered, is unhappy, wears a forced look, goes with a
perplexed and halting gait."[8] Bushnell thus set out to provide
a "happy" and "domestic" model of piety for persons untroubled
by erratic and intense spiritual needs.

Furhter, Bushnell objected to the revival's theory of
sudden conversion because it implied that conversion is a miraculous intervention of God in the affiars of a fallen world.
Revivalism seemed to divorce the process of redemption almost
entirely from the web of human affairs in which we live, move,
and form our identities. But this, Bushnell held, is psycho-
logically absurd. It makes religion

> a kind of transcendental matter, which belongs
> outside of life and has no part in the laws by
> which life is organized--a miraculous epidemic,
> a fire-ball shot from the moon, something holy
> because it is from God, but so extraordinary,
> so out of place that it cannot suffer any vital
> connection with the ties and causes and forms
> and habits, which constitute the forms of our
> history.[9]

Religion, according to his own experience, was a completion of
life in history--a possibility of existence communicated
through the same channels of influence that can shape our
growth toward other ends. Therefore, he claimed, to understand
religion as the revival does is both to mistake its true nature
and to mistake the means by which the interests of religion
can best be furthered. The revival's views of the "Divine
Husbandry," he wrote, are "unripe and partial, their notions
of Christian instrumentality confused, and their practice
desultory to the same degree."[10] He felt, in short, that
America needed a theory of the redemptive process better
suited to the interests of "healthy minded" piety.

A second common principle of revivalism to which Bushnell
took exception was its individualism. The relation between
God and the soul depicted in the revival's model of conversion
was entirely vertical. Salvation was a spiritual transaction
between God and the isolated soul. Consequently, little or
nothing was made of worldly institutions as means of spiritual
culture. The church, for instance, was viewed as a gathering
of converts after the fact--a "voluntary society, formed by a
voluntary compact" as Nathaniel Emmons put it.[11] The Christian
family was considered impotent to make converts out of its
children. Relations of blood and social proximity were irrelevant to the workings of grace.[12] Spiritual status could be
changed solely by the sudden, technically defined and certified
experience of conversion, which marked the individual's en-
counter with the spirit in the depths of the soul. The corollary of the revival's sharp separation of nature and grace,
then, was the spiritual isolation of the individual from society
--a view of human identity which harmonized nicely with the
individualism canonized in the social contract theory of the
nation.

For the most part, Bushnell's objections to this doctrine
were similar to those he leveled against the doctrine of sudden conversion. If we tear religion out of the social fabric,
he held, we lose a true understanding of religion along with
most of its benefits. Under the influence of revivalism, we
have "framed our theories of religion so as to justify the
incommunicable nature of persons as distinct units. While
thus engaged, we have well nigh lost, as was to be expected,
the idea of organic powers and relations."[13]

Bushnell gave special attention to what he took to be the
covert influence of spiritual individualism on child rearing.
According to the logic of individualism, he noted, there is
nothing a family can do to improve the spiritual state of its
children. No one can help the child but God. And God will
not help him until he is old enough to pass through the technical experience of conversion the revival prescribes. Thus,
said Bushnell, the inference was all too often drawn

> that [children] can do nothing right or accept-
> able to God till *after* their hearts are changed;
> or, what is the same, till after they have come
> to some advanced age.[14]

Children were therefore regarded as unregenerate sinners. And since it was assumed that the best way to insure the child's future conversion was to impress him with his innate hatefulness to God, children were too often brought up under a dark, depressing cloud, said Bushnell. "They are thus discouraged, and even *taught* to grow up in sin."[15]

Bennet Tyler, a noted theologian of the Connecticut revival, replied that Bushnell's interpretation of the revival's logic was spurious on this point. Christian parents do not teach their children to sin, said Tyler. Discourage them they certainly do, even to the point of despair. But despair, he held, is not so alien to Christian piety as Bushnell assumed. Mankind's plight is desparate, and desparate measures are called for.[16] Bushnell thought otherwise. Our spiritual state is certainly problematic, Bushnell held, but the cause is not so much our "evil heart" as our failure to use the spiritual resources that fill the world around us. Mankind's plight is his lack of receptivity to the divine self-communication. Therefore, Bushnell believed that any doctrine that might discourage a child or seal up his heart in despair could only frustrate his Christian growth. Discouraging doctrines dull the child to the divine influences that inform his life in history. A chief aim of Bushnell's writings on Christian education, then, was to teach Christian parents--both for their children's sake and their own--how to understand and use the immanent social expressions of the divine that revivalistic individualism led them to ignore.

2. Christian Nurture

What the revival lacked, then, Bushnell set out to supply: a theory of spiritual agency that would affirm continuity between Christian life and life in history, and a theory of Christian nurture in conformity with his understanding of the dynamics of religious growth. His criteria for a solution were set, in large measure, by the ambiguities of his own previous Christian experience and reflection. As we saw in his early essays against Taylor, Bushnell had a healthy respect for human sinfulness. Sin had shattered the perfect order of nature and left mankind alienated from God. Thus, mankind is

fallen and needs to be rescued by the aid of divine energies.[17]
While persons have an affinity for God, they lack the power to
save themselves. On the other hand, Bushnell also found much
to approve in Taylor's moral philosophy, insofar as it empha-
sized continuity between the moral core of the natural man and
the principles of Christian identity. "There is that in Christianity," he could say, "which is connatural to man."[18] Indeed,
Bushnell held that redemption would be morally meaningless unless it somehow made contact with human moral needs and affinities. Therefore, he sought some way to encompass both issues--
self-development and self-overcoming--within a single comprehensive account of the drama of sin and redemption.

His solution to the dilemma pivoted on the word "character."
As we have already noted, Bushnell often used "character" in a
normative sense, as a cognate for "redemption" or Christian
identity--the form which the divine nature assumes when it
enters a human life. "Character," so conceived, gave Bushnell
a common denominator between God and humanity--divine condescension and human self-realization. On the one hand, he held, the
aim of the Christian redemptive economy is to produce "character" in humanity, or what is the same thing, to communicate the
divine life.[19] To this end, God orders his entire creation.
He gives man a nature adapted to receive his own, institutes
natural means whereby character can be transmitted, and reveals
himself in a way calculated to be effective according to the
instituted means.[20] On the other hand, character is the built-
in *telos* of human development, in that man was made in the image
of God. No person is complete, no person fulfils his need for
a meaningful higher life, without character. The creature, that
is, longs to become what he was meant to be--an expression of
the divine life.[21]

Bushnell's concept of character also helped him to account
for mankind's present alienation from the norm of his being.
Normative character, he believed, is not a given in human life;
it is an achievement. The human soul contains only a "germ"
or "plastic law" of character which can receive either a good
or an evil development: "the soul itself is the principle
developed, and the good or evil, separate or mixed, is the
development."[22] This germ, as a germ of character, is

inherently oriented towards a normative development. Nevertheless, the native germ is sufficiently weak that its inherent orientation is easily overwhelmed. In general, the moral nature will take on the shape of the influences to which it is subjected. If the developing person is exposed to sinful influences, his potential for sin will be called out. As his habits form, his status will be fixed as a sinner. If one receives Godly influences, however, a Godly character will most likely result. Humanity in its present state is overwhelmingly inclined towards sin, Bushnell allowed, but only because the moral forces at large in the world conspire to give persons a bad education. Mankind has a chance for holiness, on the other hand, both because of his primal affinity for the good and because Godly influences have entered the world to counter-balance the influences that encourage and reinforce sin. In either case, moral growth must be understood as the result of interaction between a maleable subject and its environment.[23]

Bushnell's general position on Christian education, then, was that training should accentuate the Godly influences that will develop the normative moral character, while avoiding anything that will discourage receptivity to the divine. Accordingly, his leading premise in the works on Christian nurture was

> THAT THE CHILD IS TO GROW UP A CHRISTIAN. In
> other words, the aim, effort, and expectation
> should be not, as is commonly assumed, that the
> child is to grow up in sin, to be converted after
> he comes to a mature age; but that he is open on
> the world as one that is spiritually renewed,
> not remembering the time he went through a
> technical experience, but seeming rather to
> have loved what is good from his earliest years.[24]

From the beginning of life, that is, the child is to be exposed to and encouraged in love of the good, for through the good, his own goodness will be awakened. If he is understood to be "open on the world as one that is spiritually renewed," the chances are excellent that he will be renewed indeed.

Bushnell's program of education accordingly stressed two points over against the revival's doctrines of sudden conversion and spiritual individualism: gradualism and organicism. By gradualism, Bushnell simply meant that regeneration need not come through a spiritual crisis--a struggle with sin followed by a new birth in holiness. A regenerate character may be the product of an entire life of steady progress towards righteousness. The flowering of Christian character in adulthood, prepared by the nurture and training of the child, may dawn with no struggle or break with the past.[25] Once again, to use William James' characterizations, Bushnell spoke for the "once-born" religion of the "healthy minded" over against the spiritual requirements of the "sick soul."

Organicism is a topic that comes much closer to the heart of Bushnell's interests, so we will examine his treatment of it in detail. The use of organic metaphors in the discussion of social relations and personal growth was typical in early nineteenth century romanticism.[26] Where Bushnell picked up the concept is impossible to determine. What is clear, however, is that his ideas on the organic unity of society are closely tied to his ideas on how character is communicated. As he said in "Unconscious Influence," character of all kinds is contagious. And when character is normative, expressing the realized image of God, it becomes downright magnetic. It is "that which by principle and worth and beauty of feeling in one man, approves itself to another, and becomes a controlling and assimilative power over him."[27] Thus, the channels through which character is communicated--the natural pathways of interpersonal communication--function like the pathways through which sap is distributed to the leaves of a tree or blood to the bódy. Through social relations, a redeemed and redemptive life "flows into" the general stream of history. The organic metaphor was thus a direct translation of Bushnell's views on the moral significance of social communication. Character, he wrote, flows from one person into each member of society "just as naturally, and by a law as truly organic, as when the sap of a trunk flows into a limb."[28]

Bushnell found the organic metaphor useful in several other connections. For instance, organicism supported his view of moral growth as a result of interaction between native potentials and environmental conditions. An organic process, as understood by romantically inclined life-scientists in the early nineteenth century, involves the unfolding of an internal life principle, a *nisus formativa*, which draws on the environment

for resources in order to manifest itself outwardly.[29] By
applying this organic model to moral growth, Bushnell sought to
call attention to the role of environment in facilitating or
frustrating the development of man's native germ of Christian
character.[30] Further, the organic metaphor was useful to Bushnell as a popularizing device, since it would have been grasped
easily by anyone familiar with theories of the transmission of
racial characteristics by "blood."[31] Unfortunately, Bushnell
was sometimes carried away by this metaphor. He was frequently
on the verge of identifying social organicism with the unity
of the racial stock, and actually did so in a later work,
Christian Nurture.[32] In his early writing, however, the racial
metaphor served only to call attention to the psychological
principle that character is contagious. He had no stake in the
theory that the organic bonds of society are literally genetic
or racial. His aim was simply to drive home the point that no
person's identity is wholly his own creation.

> We possess only a mixed individuality all
> our life long. A pure, separate, individual
> man, living *wholly* within and from himself, is
> a mere fiction.[33]

The lesson Bushnell wanted to drive home in all this was
that these organic channels of interpersonal communication can
and should be turned to Christian uses. The character transmitted by expression may be either normative or aberrant, redeemed or sinful, depending on the character of the source.
Given the sinful state of the world, it is most often sin that
is transmitted.[34] However, since organic powers have such a
tremendous potential for beneficial uses, said Bushnell, it is
both unreasonable and disrespectful to God to assume that social
relations may not also become vehicles of grace. Since God,
in his providence, uses all things to produce normative character in man--to "form them to himself"--he must have intended
for social relations to play a role in the redemptive economy.

> The only supposition that honors God is that
> the organic unity of which I speak was ordained
> originally for the nurture of holy virtue. . . .[35]

Therefore, it is mankind's duty to recognize the divine intention and bring religious practice into conformity with it.
"Christianity or redemption must of necessity take possession
of the abused vehicle and sanctify it for its own uses."[36]

Bushnell developed this insight into a vision of the entire redemptive scheme. Redemptive influences entered the world through Christ, as sin entered it through Adam, operating "in and by the same laws of organic unity which sin has made the vehicle of depravity."[37] Through the personal power of Christ, passed on to his followers, the spirit has become "what the air is to the body--a Perpetual Element of inbreathing love; to dwell in families, to follow the individual and whisper holy thoughts, in solitary places and silent hours."[38] Wherever character is expressed, that is, it is communicated. And wherever character is communicated, the spirit is at work. Spiritual agency thus permeates Christian society. All that is wanting to make it effective in spreading redeemed life to all is a receptive attitude on man's part, and a clearer understanding on the part of Christians of the spiritual resources God has built into creation.

Bushnell accordingly issued a call to Christians to turn their attention back to the social context of their lives. They would find, he proclaimed, that God himself

> is dwelling as a power of good, a light, an
> aid, a regenerator and sanctifier, in the bosom
> of the world--a Spirit from God inhabiting the
> church as a church life, the Christian house, as
> a house life, the individual from infancy to the
> grave as the life of Reason and Love--Christ
> himself, present invisibly to all, breathing
> his own nature, and begetting his own image in
> their hearts.[39]

Specifically, Bushnell held, there are three forms of organic society--the nation, the church, and the family. Through some instinctive delicacy, perhaps, Bushnell did not discuss the redemptive capacity of the nation in detail.[40] But the church, conceived as the universal brotherhood of all who are spiritually united to Christ,[41] received an elaborate eulogy. The church has the distinction of an immediate relationship to Christ, the archetype of all normative character in human form. It should therefore possess the influential power of character to a superlative degree. As the body of Christ, "a perpetual Christ on the earth," it should be

> the light of the world as her savior was--a
> perpetual manifestation of the Spirit, or what
> is the same, of the Divine Nature. This too
> is the main source of her power over the

> world. . . . To be thus. . . a demonstration
> of the Spirit, to have the divine nature
> flowing out thus impalpably but really on the
> world, gives her an *assimilative power* in
> the nature of vitality.[42]

The proper power of the church is thus the power of character.
As a representative of Christ, the church manifests God, making
an appeal to man's higher sensibilities simply by the natural
magnetism of character.[43] Bushnell noted, however, that the
church has usually misunderstood its role. Rather than working
to make itself a more perfect expression of character, it has
repeatedly violated its nature under the impulse of ambition.
It has sought to make a conquest of the world through the use
of means external to character--philosophy, politics, warfare,
and superstition--and each flirtation with these forms of power
has weakened its inward principle. Therefore, by mistaking its
nature, the church has abdicated its mission as a vehicle of
character. To return to itself, the church must keep faith
with the quiet, impalpable, organic power which is its appointed
means of action.[44]

Bushnell's comments on family life ran parallel to his
views on the church. Like the church, the family has an awesome power to mold character. The relations between a parent
and a child are such that "the character of the one is actually
included in that of the other, as a seed is formed in the cap-
sule."[45] The child, that is, begins life as

> a mere passive lump in the arms, and he opens
> into conscious life under the soul of the
> parent streaming into his eyes and ears, through
> the manners and tone of the nursery.[46]

What the parent conveys to the child through his expressions,
the child passively absorbs. The impressions received in
childhood "are the seminal principles, in some sense, of the
activity that runs to language, and also of the whole future
character."[47] The parent thus has a power to develop the
child's character at a time when the child is most susceptible
to development. His example calls out capacities of experience
which will order the child's inner life ever after. And because the power is there, Bushnell assumed that the family also
has a divinely ordained responsibility to use its power to
serve Christian ends, to become a vehicle of grace. It must

know itself as a part of the ubiquitous divine scheme for the transmission of character and take up its appointed role.

> We can never come into the true style of living
> that God has appointed for us, until we regard
> each generation as hovering over the next, acting
> itself into the next, and casting thus a type
> of character into the next. . . .[48]

Bushnell's theory of nurture thus defined parental duties at the same time that it defined the susceptibilities of the child. The "true style" of Christian living that he recommends is founded on the premise that like begets like: "it is not what you intend for your children, so much as what you are, that is to have its effect."[49] The rule for parents, then, is eternal vigilance over their own character and piety.

> If a man were to be set before a mirror, with
> the feeling that the extant image of what he *is*,
> for the day, is there to be produced and left
> as a permanent and fixed image forever, to what
> carefulness, what delicate sincerity would he
> be moved.[50]

This is precisely the position of the parent, said Bushnell. Just as the earlier Puritans conceived themselves as standing before God in their every action, so Bushnell placed the Christian parent before his child as a constant reminder of his failings and need for growth. The stakes were high. The child's future, it was believed, is actually contained in the parent's character.[51] If that character is bad, the child will most likely follow suit. But if the parent's character is Christian, there is no reason to believe that the parent cannot be the child's medium of grace: "for the Christian scheme, the gospel, is really wrapped up in the life of every Christian parent and beams from him as a living epistle. . . ."[52] What we have here is something like a doctrine of the real presence of Christ in the Christian parent.

Bushnell's organicism thus amounted to the proposition that grace--redemption, the power of a divine life--can be communicated from person to person through the natural channels of communication. Not surprisingly, the position quickly made Bushnell's views on Christian nurture anathema to the orthodox theologians of New England, most of whom swore allegiance to Jonathan Edwards and many of whom were active in the revival.[53] Redemption was commonly understood in orthodox and revivalist

circles alike as a special, supernatural act of God, communicated
solely by the divine good pleasure. Bushnell, on the other
hand, seemed to tie grace to a string of natural causes, thus
making redemption a development of inherent human potentials.
While we can see today that Bushnell's basic position on the
nature of redemption--that grace consists in an ability to
apprehend the divine in the forms of nature and society--was
formally similar to Edwards' contention that grace consists in
a new "sense of the heart," early nineteenth century orthodoxy,
having failed to appreciate the more radical implications of
Edwards' position, had no ear for such resonances. From the
perspective of orthodoxy, Bushnell seemed simply to have transformed supernatural grace into natural growth. So, how, it was
asked, could Bushnell sustain his views on the nature of the
"Divine Husbandry" and continue to call himself a friend of
orthodoxy?

Bushnell believed he had an answer. To affirm his continuity with the tradition of New England theology, he called attention to the early Puritan doctrine of the "household covenant,"
according to which the children of converted parents were given
a conditional promise of grace. The Scriptural warrant for the
doctrine was God's promise to "be the God" of Abraham "and his
seed." It had been used to justify infant baptism, and later,
under the "half-way covenant," the qualified church membership
of the unconverted children of the saints.[54] The doctrine
did not deny that conversion was a supernatural act of God,
meeted out according to his good pleasure. But it did teach,
in an especially suggestive way, that God's acts were correlated
with the continuities of history. While the family was not
conceived as a proper vehicle of grace, nevertheless grace was
seen to follow family lines in a way that indicated a certain
harmony between the economy of redemption and the relations
of life in the world. Samuel Hopkins, a pupil of Jonathan
Edwards, put the case succinctly:

> if God has been pleased to make a constitution
> and appoint a way, in his covenant of grace with
> man, by which pious parents may convey and com-
> municate moral rectitude or holiness to their
> children, they, by using the appointed means,
> do it as really and effectively as they com-
> municate existence to them. In this sense,

therefore, they may convey and give holiness and salvation to their children.[55]

Bushnell believed himself to be the true heir of Samuel Hopkins in this regard. His theory of communication, he held, simply pointed out the natural laws by which the covenantal promise becomes effective--the organic, operative reality behind the doctrine. Hopkins founded his position on the covenant; Bushnell on the "philosophic conditions" of communication in general:

> I arrive at precisely the same results from a
> view of the relation itself, between parents and
> churches on the one side, and children on the
> other; that relation being considered as a
> vehicle of God, and thus a power. Dr. Hopkins
> takes the exterior view regarding the result as
> resting on a positive appointment of God. I
> have produced the interior view, that of
> inherent connection and causation.[56]

Bushnell thus held that his organic theory of society simply gave an immanent account of the same facts that orthodoxy treated transcendentally. The facts at hand are the possibility of redemption and mankind's need for help to achieve it. The question is, does that help come directly from God or is it mediated through the forms of our life in history? Is the Spirit supernatural or "abiding?" Bushnell held that the latter is true, and further, that the grace that abides in history is fully as supernatural as grace that strikes like lightning from above.

> If I say that [redemption] comes to pass in
> virtue of the parental character and treatment
> as an organic power; it is only in the certainty
> that this character and treatment are them-
> selves products of a supernatural grace.[57]

Grace, that is, is supernatural not because it is miraculously communicated; it may be communicated by purely natural means. Rather, it is supernatural because it is divine in its essence. Its source is God, and its issue is a God-like character. "The life of Christian piety is the life of God; its growth but a fuller participation of the divine nature in its power, goodness and beauty."[58] Character, we might say, is Bushnell's touchstone for the supernatural. Nothing that produces regenerate character, he held, can be judged merely natural, for whatever empowers character is supernatural by definition:

> the incarnation of the Son of God himself is
> not, as I believe, more truly supernatural
> than any agency must be, which regenerates a
> soul.[59]

The supernatural divine life, in sum, is that force in the
world that makes for character. Here, as always in Bushnell,
the theory of redemption and normative anthropology come to the
same point. Normative character is the touchstone of divinity;
divinity is the power and goal of normative growth.

Bushnell's defense of his position against the charge of
naturalism was unsatisfactory to most of his opponents because
it skimmed over what they regarded as the crucial issue: the
question whether grace can be communicated through the "constitution of nature" or whether it relies on a special "constitution of grace, as a strictly supernatural system."[60] From many
points of view, Bushnell's respondents argued that only the
latter alternative was acceptable. To illustrate this issue,
we will examine in some detail a critique of Bushnell's position
by Charles Hodge.[61]

Hodge, the guiding light and "beast of burden" of Presbyterian orthodoxy throughout the mid-century, found much to
approve in Bushnell's work. Like Bushnell, he opposed the revival in the name of the doctrine of the household covenant, and
like him, he affirmed that social relations play an important
role in Christian nurture. Hodge had little use for the term
"organic," but he was happy to acknowledge what Bushnell regarded as the crucial facts connoted by the term. There is,
said Hodge, an undeniable connection between parent and child
such that the Godly nurture of children will tend to make their
conversion in later life more probable. Families and communities cohere by virtue of a "subtle influence which pervades
the whole," "effective as the magnetic or electric fluid in
nature."[62] However, he said, there are three ways to account
for this phenomenon: 1) according to the Scriptural authority
of God's promise to Abraham; 2) by resolving the connection
to a law of nature, "accounting for [it] . . . in the same way,
or on the same principles which determine the transmission of
other forms of character from parents to children;" and 3) by
investing all redemptive power in the church and its sacraments. The first way, he said, was his own, the second was

Bushnell's. (The third, he noted in passing, was John Williamson Nevin's.[63])

Not all ways were equally acceptable to Hodge, however. Only the first preserves the genuinely supernatural character of conversion, he affirmed, and this was the root of his objection to Bushnell. God's covenant with Abraham, said Hodge, stipulated that

> early, assiduous, and faithful religious culture
> of the young, especially by believing parents,
> is the great means of their salvation.[64]

Human activity and God's spiritual agency are thus linked by the promise. But that linkage, he wrote, remains external. Redemption is not conveyed in religious training. Rather, a special influx of the spirit, an act of God apart from the laws of nature, is needed to renew the heart and confer Christian status. The Christian parent, assured by the covenant, may properly expect that his well-trained child is more likely than not to receive supernatural grace. Still, redemption is in no way causally linked to the educative process. It occurs by divine fiat alone, apart from all laws of nature. It is properly miraculous.

Bushnell's account of conversion, by contrast, seemed to link the miracle of grace to a train of natural causes. Therefore, Hodge found it less than Christian. Bushnell, as Hodge rightly noted, assumed that the operative power of the covenant was identical with the laws of expressive communication in natural society--that supernatural agency and natural processes were simply two ways of viewing the same facts. As Bushnell had written in 1847:

> there are two modes of viewing this whole
> subject, both equally correct. . . . If I
> take my position by the covenant of Abraham
> and hang my doctrine of nurture on that, . . .
> I realize indeed a form of unquestionable
> supernaturalism, in the mind of those who
> accept my doctrine. . . . Now just as the
> reality of the rainbow is in the world's laws
> prior to the covenant with Noah, so there is in
> the organic laws of the race, a reality or
> ground answering to the covenant with Abraham;
> only, in this latter case, the reality is a
> supernatural grace which inhabits the organic
> laws of nature and works its results in con-
> formity with them.[65]

Bushnell, that is, saw no contradiction in the assumption that
a supernatural agency may work within the laws of nature. Whatever expresses God serves as a vehicle of redemption; and whatever conveys redemption or character is supernatural by
definition.

Hodge replied that this is an "eccentric" definition of
supernaturalism, really no different from what most writers
mean by naturalism. For an event to be supernatural, on
Hodge's account, it must be miraculous, effected by some power
utterly distinct from those which operate in nature. Thus,
Bushnell's attempt to correlate the operations of nature and
the supernatural seemed self-contradictory to Hodge.

> The whole question is, whether the effect is due
> to a power that works in nature, or above nature.
> The German infidel who refers Christ's miracles
> of healing to animal magnetism, regards magnetism
> as a form of divine power, but he is none the
> less an unbeliever in the supernatural power of
> Christ, on that account.[66]

Bushnell's theology is not Christian at all, then. It is simply
cosmic theism, or pantheism.

Hodge's parallel between Bushnell and the hypothetical
infidel is not exact. Bushnell affirmed that grace is communicated by God's presence in social and natural phenomena. But
he did not say that the "power" of the natural, causal vehicle
of influence is identical with the power of God in it, no more
than the power of a word's meaning is identical with the force
of its vibrations on the ear. Causal relations are one thing;
God's intentions are another. The natural reality becomes a
vehicle of grace when God sees fit to put it to expressive use.
Thus, just as the rainbow becomes a sign of a promise, so organic social relations become effectively redemptive only because God has brought the image of character into the world to
be conveyed by them. The difference between natural and supernatural events lies not in the means by which the event comes
about, but in what the event is capable of expressing.

Hodge's quarrel with Bushnell, in sum, focused on the
question

> whether regeneration is a natural sequence or
> not; whether its proximate antecedent, its true
> cause, is nature or grace; some organic law, or
> the mighty power of God.

According to Hodge

> these two views are as far apart as the poles.
> They cannot be brought together by saying, God
> is in nature, as well as in grace, for the two
> modes of his operation is all the difference.[67]

Bushnell, on the other hand, simply did not acknowledge the
kind of difference between nature and grace indicated by Hodge.
But Bushnell, in turn, drew a distinction that Hodge did not
acknowledge--the difference between the fact viewed as a piece
of nature and the fact as an expression of a divine intention,
conveying the supernatural mind at its source. Hodge understood
only causal efficacy; Bushnell was more interested in the power
of symbolic expressions to shape character, and built
his theology around the conviction of the reality of this power.

Another criticism leveled against Bushnell's organicism
deserves our attention here. Some of Bushnell's critics flatly
rejected his theory of a quasi-organic influence between parent
and child through which identity is communicated. Bennet Tyler
in particular scorned it as "an assumption without a particle
of proof."[68] The charge is a fair hit. Bushnell indeed offered
no hard evidence for his theory. He simply illustrated it with
presumed facts of social-psychology--e.g. the "family resemblances" that characterize cultural groups--which he invited
his audience to acknowledge. Bushnell recommended a way of
seeing social phenomena; he did not try to explain them. Tyler
simply refused to accept Bushnell's invitation; so the conversation might have ended before it began.

Tyler went on, however, to argue quite cogently that the
theory of an organic connection of character is inconsistent
with experience. Its obvious implication is that all the children of Christian parents should be regenerate, for if grace
is "hereditary" in the same way that sin is, its effects should
be inescapable, as those of sin are. However, Christian parents
are often disappointed in their children. So, Tyler asked,
how can Bushnell account for the fact that some individuals
exposed to constant revelations of Christian character will
fail the succumb to its magnetism?

To meet the problem, Bushnell made a distinction between
the influences that shape character and the acts of will by
which the self appropriates those influences. Passive

sensibilities are one thing, he argued; the choices by which
we put our perceptions of value into action are another. And
it is the latter that finally define human character or moral
status. Thus, he distinguished between a "natural" attraction
for character and a Christian love.

> [W]hen we speak thus of a love to what is right
> and good, we must of course discriminate between
> the mere excitement of a natural sensibility to
> pleasure in the contemplation of what is good
> (of which all minds are more or less capable)
> and a practical subordination of the soul to its
> power, a practical embrace of its law.

Previous to this act of the will or "practical embrace" of the
good, he insisted, there "can be no proper goodness in the
soul."[69] Bushnell thus made Christian character depend on an
act of the individual will as well as on the communication of
grace. It followed that the unregenerate children of Godly
parents could be held responsible for their own state. The
fault lay not in the laws of organic connection, but in their
own failure to appropriate the influences communicated to them.

Moral voluntarism, thus introduced, contradicts a main
theme of the theory of communication. In "Unconscious Influence," for instance, Bushnell had been at pains to show how
the influence of Christian character "flows into" a person.
The powers of self-expression are passively received, molding
the mind quite apart from the conscious will. Here, however,
Bushnell brought an active component into the redemptive process.
For redemption to become actual, the free, voluntary involve-
ment of the whole person is demanded. Passive reception and
active appropriation must co-operate. Bushnell never fully
reconciled the two, but he solved his problem, in a way, by
juxtaposing them, affirming that human character is shaped by
a willed appropriation of forces that are passively received.

> [C]haracter may be, to a great extent, only
> the free development of exercises previously
> wrought in us, when other wills had us within
> their sphere.[70]

Or as he put it more fully, redeemed character

> is rather a state of being than an act or series
> of acts; and if we look at the causes which
> induce or prepare such a state, the will of the
> person himself may have a part among those causes
> more or less important, and it works no absurdity
> to suppose that one may be even prepared to such

> a state, by causes prior to his own will; so that,
> when he sets off to act for himself, his struggles
> and duty may be rather to sustain and perfect
> the state begun, than to produce a new one.[71]

In sum, Bushnell argued that Christian character has a willed
component but that in essence it is a quality of experience or
mind which only an extrinsic, educative power can call out.
No one develops Christian character--or any other kind of
character--apart from acts of the will. But unless the Spirit
of God were at large in the world, informing nature and human
society, salvation would not even be a possibility of existence
for mankind. Grace, communicated through nature and history,
co-operates with mankind's striving for self-realization.

3. *Nature and the Supernatural*

Two crucial issues thus emerge from Bushnell's attempt to
interpret the Christian redemptive economy in terms of his
theory of interpersonal communication: the question of the
relation of natural and supernatural means in the communication
of character, and that of the relation of active and passive
elements in its reception. Bushnell addressed both of these
issues in a later work, *Nature and the Supernatural as Together
Constituting the One System of God*. The book is long and discursive, but we will briefly review its central tenets on these
topics to show how Bushnell continued to defend the possibility
of "a really supernatural training" within the terms of his
theory of communication.[72]

Bushnell's chief concern here, as his title indicates, is
to define and distinguish the roles of natural and supernatural
forces in the ways of the world. As in the works on Christian
nurture, he stressed their interdependence. Natural processes
are the media through which supernatural intentions are
carried out. His approach to the problem in the later work
shows a significant change of emphasis, however. In the earlier
writings on Christian nurture, he defined his own position over
against the supernaturalism of the revival and the doctrine of
the household covenant. In *Nature and the Supernatural*, he
addressed a naturalism far more thoroughgoing than his own,
and attempted to sway it in a more supernaturalistic direction.

Indeed, this is the one book in Bushnell's *ouvre* that can be
termed a work of Christian apologetics.

He began by noting the spread of a new, naturalistic common
sense in American religious thought, represented variously by
phrenology, mesmerism, Unitarianism, Fourierist associationism,
transcendentalism, "popular literature," and the higher
Biblical criticism.[73] Taken as a whole, he allowed, the movement was not an unmitigated evil. On the contrary, it called
attention to many things that Bushnell himself embraced gladly.
Bushnell seems to have had Theodore Parker in mind when he
characterized the whole movement as follows:

> It finds a religious sentiment in all men, which
> in one view, is a truth. It finds a revelation
> of God in all things, which is also a truth. It
> discovers a universal inspiration of God in human
> souls; which, if it be taken to mean that they are
> inherently related to God, and that God, in the
> normal state, would be an illuminating, all-moving
> presence in them, is likewise a truth.[74]

The common error of all brands of naturalism, however--that
which made them naturalistic--was that they took these native
capacities for a complete definition of the human spiritual
condition. They denied the possibility of a sin from which mankind cannot save himself, and so, the need for self-overcoming.
Consequently, they could not believe in the necessity or possibility of a supernatural agency operating on persons from
outside their own wills. Naturalism, in other words, tried to
reduce all life to a single system, the system of natural law,
and to derive all religious values from its inherent operation.

Bushnell's primary objection to naturalism, so conceived,
repeated his objection to the theology of his teacher, Nathaniel
William Taylor. Naturalism denied two "facts of consciousness:"
the human conviction of sin, or sense that mankind is not all he
ought to be, and the consequent felt need for supernatural
redemption, or for a power capable of raising persons to heights
they cannot attain by the action of the sinful self.[75] Bushnell
claimed that these sentiments are universal, implanted by the
creator himself. So, he held, they must have some correlate
in the constitution of the world, for

> what we earnestly want, we know that we shall
> assuredly find. The prophecy is in us, and
> whether we call ourselves prophets or not, we
> shall certainly go on to publish it.[76]

Bushnell therefore went on to develop a view of the world in conformity with these presumed moral intuitions.

His moral cosmology was oriented around two premises: first, that there is sin and that there is a supernatural redemption from sin, but second, that redemptive agency does not violate the lawful order of nature.[77] Nature and the supernatural are distinct in kind, but together they co-operate as "the one system of God." As in the writings on Christian nurture, Bushnell insisted that the supernatural economy of redemption works in harmony with the natural laws of human development, effectively communicating the spirit through them as mind is communicated through expressive forms. He offered definitions of "nature" and "supernatural," in turn, designed to correlate man's plight with his possibilities without collapsing them into one.

Bushnell's definitions of nature and the supernatural repeated those suggested by Samuel Taylor Coleridge in the *Aids to Reflection*. He defined nature as a self-contained physical system, governed entirely by mechanical laws of causation, a "chain of causes and effects." The supernatural, on the other hand, is whatever is "either not in the chain of natural cause and effect, or which acts on the chain of cause and effect, in nature, from without the chain."[78] At first glance, this appears compatible with Charles Hodge's idea that a supernatural act is one that breaks miraculously into the chain of natural causes from without. When we look more closely, however, we find that what Bushnell meant by a supernatural act is not what Hodge meant by miracle. No supernatural agency, according to Bushnell, can violate the laws of nature. The supernatural only turns natural laws to ends that would not be reached by the operation of nature on its own. For instance, when a person builds a house, he subordinates the laws of nature to his will, and produces effects that nature alone does not. An act of will is thus a fully supernatural act according to Bushnell's definition.[79]

> [I]f the processes, combinations, and results
> of our system of nature are interrupted, or
> varied by the action whether of God or angels
> or men, so as to bring to pass what would not
> come to pass in it by its own internal action,

under the laws of mere cause and effect, the variations are, in like manner supernatural.[80]

Bushnell thus defined the supernatural realm as a system of selves, acting on nature to express and communicate themselves through their free, self-reproductive acts. The supernatural is related to nature just as a mind is related to the forms by which it expresses itself. In Bushnell's own terminology, the supernatural is the realm of "powers," "having all, in the matter of their will, a power transcending cause and effect in nature. . . ." The natural, by contrast, is the realm of "things," the material objects acted upon.[81] The two realms operate according to separate laws, just as mind and body are separately organized. Yet there is a natural correspondence between them, just as the natural types of language, taken from the physical world, prove to be appropriate to the expression and communication of mind.[82] Nature, like language, is a vehicle for minds. It is "only the platform on which [God] establishes his kingdom as a kingdom of minds, or persons. . . ." Again, it is "only stage, field, medium, vehicle, for the universe; that is, for God and his powers;" a medium for the "serving and training of men."[83] Finally, he wrote that God's end in it all is the education of persons into likeness with himself, as the exemplar or archetype of all created minds.

This vision of the natural world as a vast stage for the supernatural training of persons turned Bushnell's attention to the question of the receptivity of the trainees. He explored the means of this training in detail with an eye to the role of human free will in the process. We cannot follow all his peregrinations here, but in sum, his scheme is as follows. Humankind, he wrote, was created for immediate participation in the life of God, for a-cosmic union and beatitude. But of necessity, human souls were created imperfect. Adam lacked the stronger qualities of character, because character is something that can only be schooled into man by experience in history. Thus, Adam was made for union with the divine, but he had no staying power. He became distracted by the first challenge to his virtue that came along. And in his fall, he set a pattern of sinful behavior that has become mankind's habit ever since. Man's will has become self-will; his consciousness "alienated" from God. But the historical world into

which man had fallen is not a pointless wasteland. History is
designed to make good on the very qualities the original,
"innocent" man lacked. We find ourselves "embodied in matter"
in order to exist in society, and we find ourselves in society
in order to be schooled into the values and laws attendent upon
our solidarity--to learn love, duty, and the consequences of
evil. In short, society trains man in the habits of a righteous
character, and character relates man to God. God frames the
world for our "practical profit; to bring us up into His own
excellence, and establish us eternally in the participation
of his character."[84]

To this end, God has instituted a two-fold economy of
training for the race: law and gospel. Under the law, the
mind is drilled in the externals of character; its sin is
"worn down" under the futile effort to put itself right by the
mere power of the will.[85] But the law only fulfils itself by
making persons more willing to receive the second stage of
their training, under which Christ or any Christian person
representing the divine character communicates the inward principle of character directly to the human heart, or rather, calls
out the principles that slumber there. Law prepares man's
receptivity for grace by training his will to appropriate it.
Grace, in turn, calls out the capacity for redeemed life sub-
merged in sin. Life moves towards liberty through a drill in
the law,[86] toward passive receptivity to the divine life through
concerted moral effort, toward spontaneous joy and "play"
through work.[87] The whole process is supernatural, orchestrated
by God's governing intentions, but the end is one in which the
will, properly prepared, must co-operate.

This formula for the relation of human activity and divine
initiative in the redemptive economy actually brings Bushnell
no closer to consistency than he had been in the works on
Christian nurture. The extent to which human activity is guided
by influences passively received remains unclear. Still, Bushnell's treatment of the question in *Nature and the Supernatural*
was more elaborate and comprehensive. It presented what Bushnell regarded as an empirical psychology of growth, and correlated it suggestively with the traditional Christian conun-
drum of the relations between law and gospel. This correlation

was to prove decisive in Bushnell's handling of the atonement, which we will examine in Chapter V.

The heart of Bushnell's vision, in sum, remained here what it had been in the writings on Christian nurture. He sought to show that the world, understood as a medium of divine and human self-communication, is a fit vehicle for conveying and nurturing mankind's potential for a redeemed or normative existence. He had personally discovered that it is possible for a person to learn to "be" fully and integrally by means of receptivity to the forms of natural life. In these later writings, his continued attempt to interpret and refine his understanding of that discovery led him to insist that such redemptive lessons can be attributed, in part, to the grace of God. *Nature and the Supernatural* made much show of argument against naturalistic science, because naturalism denied that there was a supernatural grace to be received. But his arguments, which are quite weak, are in a sense a distraction from the book's primary strategy. Bushnell was not so much arguing a position as he was recommending an attitude towards experience which he had found effective in transforming his own life--a way of seeing the world as divine revelation and human development as participation in God. The problem of correlating supernatural agency with natural development addressed here would occupy him throughout his career. His most creative thought, however, appears not in his attempts to argue his position apologetically, but in the works in which he develops his vision confessionally. Bushnell found his voice best in his attempts to give Christian thought a new development from within. To those writings we now turn.

NOTES

CHAPTER III

[1]"Discourses on Christian Nurture" was published originally
by the Massachusetts Sabbath School Society in 1847. It was
reprinted with other articles in *Views of Christian Nurture and
of Subjects Adjacent Thereto* (1847; rpt. Delmar, N.Y.: Scholars'
Facsimiles & Reprints, Inc., 1975), which will be the source
for our references. *Christian Nurture* (New York: Scribners,
1861), has been reissued several times by Yale University Press
in a "New Edition" by Luther A. Weigle.
    This chapter will deal mainly with the early materials
collected in *Views*. The 1861 *Christian Nurture* includes some
new material--primarily practical advice on child rearing--but
represents no real advance on Bushnell's earlier thought.

[2]On the revival as Bushnell knew it in Connecticut, see
Charles Roy Keller, *The Second Great Awakening in Connecticut*
(New Haven: Yale University Press, 1942).

[3]Perry Miller, *The Life of the Mind in America* (New York:
Harcourt, Brace & World, Inc., 1965), p. 7.
    Bushnell never mounted a concerted attack on revivalism
in general. It drew his attention only insofar as its practices
and premises contradicted the motifs of his own Christian
experience. Therefore, it is fair to say that Bushnell's
sketch of the revival in these writings is parochial and, in
some ways, misleading. He focused his fire on revivalism as
he found it in Connecticut. Therefore, he tended to speak as
if the whole movement had an Edwardsean orientation. Nevertheless, the features of revivalism which Bushnell picked out for
criticism are those which are well nigh characteristic of the
movement as a whole: its view of conversion as dependent on a
sudden and miraculous influx of the spirit, and its consequent
understanding of spiritual life as a vacillation between periods
of decline and renewal.

[4]Lyman Beecher, *The Autobiography of Lyman Beecher*, ed.
Barbara Cross (Cambridge: Harvard University Press, 1961),
vol. I, p. 28.

[5]See William James, *The Varieties of Religious Experience*
(New York: Collier Books, 1961), pp. 78-80, 143-59. James
gives no precise definition for either "healthy minded" piety
or the religion of the "sick soul." Nevertheless, the impression one gains from his copious illustrative material is that
the religion of the healthy minded is predominantly optimistic
in tone, while that of the sick soul is pessimistic, preoccupied with moral failure and self-doubt. For the healthy minded,
a close, saving relation to God seems an easy thing to attain
in the present order of the world; the healthy minded person's
religion is therefore "once-born." The sick soul, on the
other hand, finds salvation infinitely problematical because
of his sense of man's radical evil and God's otherness; for
him, salvation requires a second, supernatural birth, and so
James characterizes his religion as "twice born."

[6]Bushnell, *Views*, p. 89.

[7]*Ibid.*, p. 8.

[8]*Ibid.*, p. 125.

[9]*Ibid.*, p. 69.

[10]*Ibid.*, p. 123.

[11]Nathaniel Emmons, quoted in Barbara Cross, *Horace Bushnell* (Chicago: University of Chicago Press, 1958), p. 62.

[12]While the revival also spawned numerous social reform organizations dedicated to reversing the tide of "barbarism" in the West and infidelity in the East, it could not consistently see these efforts as contributing directly to its redemptive aims. For a recent analysis of the Protestant voluntary organizations, see Gregory H. Singleton, "Protestant Voluntary Organizations and the Shaping of Victorian America," *American Quarterly*, XXVII (December, 1975), pp. 549-60.

[13]Bushnell, *Views*, p. 184.

[14]*Ibid.*, p. 166.

[15]*Ibid.*

[16]Bennet Tyler, *Letters to the Rev. Horace Bushnell* (Hartford: Brown & Parons, 1848), p. 6.

[17]Bushnell, *Views*, p. 102.

[18]Bushnell, ["Natural Science and Moral Philosophy,"] MS Yale Divinity School Library, p. 30.

[19]Bushnell, *Views*, p. 128.

[20]*Ibid.*, pp. 132-33.

[21]Bushnell had very little to say about precisely what qualities make up character, human or divine. Like St. Paul discussing Christian virtue, he was quick with lists of cognate terms, but finally left a great deal to the imagination. For instance, Bushnell wrote that character involves principles like "truth, justice, rectitude, benevolence" and feelings of "courtesy, gentleness, condescention, pity, gratitude, forgiveness, charity," and the greatest of all, "domesticity." (*Views*, pp. 170, 8.) More often than not, Bushnell omitted even these blunt characterizations and said simply that to have character is to be like Christ; for as Christ was the divine in human form, so is the norm of character.

[22]*Views*, p. 102. He did not understand the "germ" of identity in an Edwardsean sense as an all-inclusive inclination of the heart which determines the subject's will and destiny from within. Rather, this germ is merely a possibility of future development.

23*Ibid.*, pp. 107-08.

24*Ibid.*, p. 6.

25*Ibid.*, pp. 12-13.

26See M.H. Abrams, *The Mirror and the Lamp* (New York: Oxford University Press, 1953), pp. 184-225.

27Bushnell, *Views*, p. 169.

28*Ibid.*, p. 19.

29See Bushnell, "Life, or the Lives," in *Work and Play* (New York: Charles Scribner's Sons, 1903), pp. 273, 304.

30Bushnell, *Views*, p. 147.

31*Ibid.*, p. 108. See also "The True Wealth or Weal of Nations," in *Work and Play*, pp. 63-64.

32See Chapter 8 of *Christian Nurture*, on "The Out-Populating Principle of the Christian Stock." (New Haven: Yale University Press, 1967), pp. 163-89.

33Bushnell, *Views*, p. 22.

34This truth, he felt, was acknowledged in the Calvinist doctrine of Adam's "federal headship" of the race, which held that the sin of the founder of humanity is communicated to all his descendents. All men sin because a sinful influence entered the world through Adam. As we will see again below in connection with the doctrine of the household covenant, Bushnell saw himself as providing the "interior" view, the "philosophic conditions," of the orthodox doctrine. *Ibid.*, p. 28.

35*Ibid.*, p. 187.

36*Ibid.*, p. 199.

37*Ibid.*, p. 200.

38*Ibid.*, p. 214.

39*Ibid.*, p. 223.

40Bushnell believed that America had a special role to play in the history of redemption, but he did not hang any of his theological opinions on this conviction. See, for instance, "Christian Comprehensiveness," *The New Englander*, VI (January 1848), p. 97.

41*Views*, p. 236.

42*Ibid.*, p. 174.

[43]Bushnell's conception of the church displays significant similarities to, and even more significant differences from, the ecclesiology of one of his critics, the German Reformed theologian from Mercersburg, John Williamson Nevin. Both Nevin and Bushnell understood Christian identity as a supernaturally empowered possibility of existence that entered the world "really and historically" in Christ, and which is transmitted through the organic unities of society. The supernatural becomes natural because, in Christ, the divine life took on human form.

Nevin and Bushnell differed, however, over the question, what are the means of the organic transmission of Christian character? Bushnell found all channels of expressive communication effective in conveying the divine mind. Nevin, on the basis of a somewhat different theory of organic relations, held that the Church and its sacraments alone were capable of conveying redeemed life. The organic transmission of Christ's life depends, Nevin held, on physical communion with the body of Christ. And only the Church, through the Eucharist, can provide this. Redemption thus "accords with the organic constitution of life," but requires a distinct, supernatural "constitution of grace"--a vehicle of the divine body--to be communicated. Bushnell's theory of nurture thus appeared to Nevin to be a churchly philosophy without the church, a kind of incipient naturalism.

Bushnell replied that Nevin's own theory of the church could be accounted for wholly within the terms of his own theory of communication. The power of the church for Bushnell was just one instance of the powers of natural human communication. See John Williamson Nevin, "Educational Religion," *The Weekly Messenger of the German Reformed Church*, XII, New Series, June 23, June 30, July 7, & July 14, 1847. Bushnell's reply is in *Views*, pp. 95-108.

[44] The church, in short, must accept the same limits that Bushnell had imposed on himself. It must give up worldly ambitions in the name of exemplary influence. See *Views*, p. 160. This critique of Christian activism is developed in the entire article published in *Views* as "Growth, Not Conquest."

[45]*Ibid.*, p. 18.

[46]*Ibid.*, p. 19.

[47]*Ibid.*, pp. 105-06.

[48]*Ibid.*, p. 108.

[49]*Ibid.*, p. 206.

[50]*Ibid.*, p. 107.

[51]Bushnell lived in an age when the child was a focal point of Christian and domestic concern. New England in the early national period was in the throes of a vast social transformation. Family patterns were shifting. Young men were quitting rural society in increasing numbers to make their way in the cities or in the West, where fortunes were made, temptations

abounded, and morals declined. Prodded by a sense of the tran-
sitoriness of family life and fearful for their children's
moral safety, parents longed to make the most of the control
they had over their children's early years. In response to
this need, the literature of the age united to prove that the
fate of the tree was truly in the twig. Associationist psychology supplied a theory of the power of early impressions in the
formation of character. Numerous child rearing manuals, especially aimed at mothers, popularized and applied the theory to
stereotyped situations, to teach bewildered parents their roles
and assure them of their lingering influence. Gift book fic-
tion consummated parental wish-fulfilment, in turn, through
countless stories of wayward adolescents snatched from the
jaws of destruction by a memory of their mother's prayers and
tears. See Cross, *Horace Bushnell*, pp. 58-60, 67; also
Douglas, *Feminization* (New York: Alfred A. Knopf, 1977),
pp. 74-75.

[52]*Views*, p. 14.

[53]For a brief review of the controversy aroused by Bushnell's
"Discourses on Christian Nurture," see H. Shelton Smith, ed.,
Horace Bushnell (New York: Oxford University Press, 1965),
pp. 375-78.

[54]For a lucid discussion of these traditions, see Perry
Miller, *The New England Mind: From Colony to Province* (Cambridge: Harvard University Press, 1953), pp. 82-104.

[55]Samuel Hopkins, quoted in Bushnell, *Views*, p. 71.

[56]*Ibid.*, p. 72.

[57]*Ibid.*, p. 104.

[58]*Ibid.*, p. 173.

[59]*Ibid.*, p. 97.

[60]J.W. Nevin, "Educational Religion," July 7.

[61]Charles Hodge, "Bushnell on Christian Nurture," *Biblical
Repertory and Princeton Review*, XIX (1847), pp. 502-39. This
article was reprinted as a pamphlet that same year by Leavitt,
Trow & Co., in which form it gained a wide distribution. Page
references in what follows are to the pamphlet edition.

[62]*Ibid.*, pp. 3-4.

[63]*Ibid.*, p. 19.

[64]*Ibid.*, p. 8.

[65]Bushnell, *Views*, p. 99.

[66]Hodge, "Bushnell on Christian Nurture," p. 23.

[67]*Ibid.*, p. 25.

[68]Bennet Tyler, *Letters*, pp. 16-20.

[69]*Ibid.*, p. 16. For another treatment of this distinction, see the sermon "Religious Nature and Religious Character," in *Sermons on Living Subjects* (New York: Charles Scribner's Sons, 1890), pp. 129-47.

[70]*Views*, p. 20.

[71]*Ibid.*, p. 21.

[72]Bushnell, *Nature and the Supernatural* (1858; rpt. New York: AMS Press, 1973), p. 17.

[73]*Ibid.*, pp. 22-28.

[74]*Ibid.*, p. 17. Similarly favorable comments on Parker are made by Bushnell in a letter to James Freeman Clarke, October 18, 1854, MS the Houghton Library of Harvard University.

[75]Bushnell, *Nature*, pp. 149-63, 17.

[76]*Ibid.*, p. 62.

[77]*Ibid.*, p. 31.

[78]*Ibid.*, pp. 36-37. Coleridge made the distinction similarly in the *Aids to Reflection* (1840; rpt. Port Washington, N.Y.: Kennikat Press, 1971), pp. 108n, 110, 236.

[79]Bushnell, *Nature*, pp. 42-63. Bushnell probably found inspiration for this view in Nathaniel Taylor, who taught that the will is self-determining, independent of all natural laws of causation. See Chapter II, n. 14 above.

[80]*Ibid.*, p. 38.

[81]*Ibid.*, pp. 84-85.

[82]*Ibid.*, p. 189. This passage shows the inaccuracy of Cross's comment that Bushnell's theory of language does not figure in *Nature and the Supernatural*. See Cross, *Horace Bushnell*, p. 118.

[83]Bushnell, *Nature*, pp. 58, 90.

[84]*Ibid.*, pp. 99-101.

[85]*Ibid.*, p. 119.

[86]*Ibid.*, p. 100.

[87]See Bushnell, "Work and Play," in *Work and Play*, pp. 9-42.

CHAPTER IV

THE THEORY OF LANGUAGE:

THE THEOLOGIAN AS EDUCATOR

Bushnell's works on religious language and symbolism are
his most vibrant and characteristic products. Bushnell himself
referred to his "Preliminary Dissertation on the Nature of
Language as Related to Thought and Spirit" as an epitome of his
"thinking habit."[1] Subsequent commentators have called the
theory of language the "key to Horace Bushnell."[2] We concur
with this judgement, and simply add that the theory of language
epitomizes more than Bushnell's theological strategy. It encom-
passes and gives voice to all the conflicting concerns, personal
as well as intellectual, that shaped Bushnell's career. To
show its place in his developing intellectual project, then,
we will first review its immediate background in his life and
thought before going on to an analysis of the works that con-
tain it.

1. Backgrounds

In the aftermath of the minor pamphlet war aroused by his
writings on Christian nurture,[3] Bushnell had two major preoccupations. The first centered on questions raised in the Christian
nurture controversy itself; the second concerned the differences
between orthodox and Unitarian theologians in New England. We
will discuss each in turn.

a. Divine and Human Loves

Bushnell's chief interest in the works on Christian nurture
was the communication of Christian identity. Communication for
Bushnell was the process by which one mind or spirit conveys
its subjective expreience to another. A person's mind is expressed in his manner, his acts, his speech, and his products.
If the natural human capacity to "read" those expressions is
operating, an "impression" exactly correspondent to the quality
of mind expressed is made on the mind of the recipient. The
transmitter's influence thus tends to shape the receiver's

mind into the image of his own character. Persons "beget" themselves in others through the communicative power of the forms
in which they express themselves.

Communication, so conceived, seemed to Bushnell to be the
key to understanding both the means of human growth in history
and the means by which Christ effects mankind's redemption.
The principal aim of God in Christ, Bushnell assumed, was the
communication of normative, divine character. The power of a
parent over the character of a child provided him in turn with
a suggestive model for the power of Christ over fallen man.
Christ, like the parent, communicates life and character to
other persons through example, expression, and influence, shaping the inward spirit of others by the force of his own inwardness as manifested in his life. In Christ's case, this inward
character is identical with the divine life; it is a divine,
redemptive life that he communicates. The "supernatural"
process by which persons are redeemed is thus perfectly con-
formed to the "natural" means by which persons are educated.
The substance of salvation--a consciousness in union with the
divine life--can be communicated through the same channels
that shape natural human identity.[4]

The reviewers of the writings on Christian nurture were
disturbed by Bushnell's close correlation of nature and the
supernatural. Each critic in his own way confronted Bushnell
with a serious question: how is Christian redemption, communicated *through* history, to be distinguished from a possibility
within history? What makes the possibility of existence offered in Christ different from the options open to the natural
man? Another related point raised by most of Bushnell's critics
concerned the theory of communication itself. Bushnell's
theory implied that a fundamentally Christian character will
be communicated willy nilly to all members of a Christian
household, just as parental character is supposed to be "organi-
cally" transmitted to children. The same should hold true, to
a lesser extent, for all members of a Christian society, insofar as persons "flow together" in all their interactions. However, said Bushnell's critics, this flatly contradicts the observed facts. Not all children of truly pious parents become
Christian; some members of predominantly Christian cultures

are not even remotely good. Redemption may not be a wholly
random occurrence, but it certainly does not seem to follow
inexorable "organic laws." Orthodox Calvinism had a way to
account for the sporadic distribution of Christian souls: redemption depended ultimately on God's sovereign will.[5] Bushnell however wedded redemption to historical relations, and so
he had trouble accounting for variations in piety with a human
group.

Bushnell's critics, in sum, were asking him to sharpen his
distinctions. His treatment of grace in terms of the theory of
communication seemed to collapse the difference between natural
and supernatural energies and to belie the facts of Christian
experience. Bushnell was challenged, then, to find some way
to account for the observed facts and do justice to the special
qualities of grace within the terms of his theory.

Bushnell's work on these problems lay fallow for a year
after the publication of *Views of Christian Nurture*. Then, in
February of 1848, Bushnell experienced an insight into the means
and ends of Christian redemption that he frequently referred
to afterwards as a turning point in his life.[6] It is difficult
to determine just what he took the content of that insight to
be, or to discover the precise train of thought and circum-
stance that led up to it. It is our contention, however, that
the questions that arose from the Christian nurture controversy
were the trigger of Bushnell's crisis. What he discovered in
1848 was primarily a way to answer his critics without sacri-
ficing his own most characteristic concerns.

The records of Bushnell's experience describe it only in
glowing generalities. His wife recalled a long period of tension followed by a sudden release. (She speaks of herself here
in the third person.)

> On an early morning of February, his wife awoke
> to hear that the light they had waited for, more
> than they that watch for the morning, had risen
> indeed. She asked, "What have you seen?" He
> replied, "the gospel." It came to him at last,
> after all his thought and study, not as some-
> thing reasoned out, but as an inspiration--
> a revelation from the mind of God himself.[7]

Bushnell himself recorded the experience as a "personal discovery
of Christ, and of God as represented in him."[8] The account is
meager, but it suggests at least that Bushnell's new

apprehension of Christ remained with the terms of his theory of
communication: Christ came to him as a "representation" or
expression of God.

There is more to be said about what Bushnell was going
through at the time than can be inferred from this scanty record, however. We hear, for instance, that he had been reading
Quietistic literature prior to the experience. His wife refers
to his interest in Upham's translation of the *Life of Madam
Guyon*, *The Interior Life*, and the writings of Fenelon.[9] A manuscript sermon dated January 1848 (therefore written just prior
to his experience), suggests the reason for his interest. The
sermon, titled "Pure Love," attempted to distinguish the pursuit of holiness from the pursuit of happiness, sanctity from
external virtue. "Perfect obedience," said Bushnell, is frequently raised as the ideal of the religious life. Obedience,
however, is a poor term for what is special in Christian piety.
Obedience is an affair of the will, he wrote, but religious
character is an inward state of the mind and heart, characterized
by the self-less love the Christian feels for God. What is
unique in Christian life, then, is self-less love. Growth in
the Christian life in turn is the cultivation of a divine love
to the exclusion of selfish natural desires. Natural loves
must in fact be "crucified" for the sake of divine love. Bushnell's reflections at this time thus led him to cast self-love
and love of God as irreconcilable enemies.[10]

Here the question posed by Bushnell's critics--how is
redemption to be distinguished from the possibilities of life
in history?--was transposed into a new key. The theological
issue became a devotional issue: do natural loves for the things
of this world have any place in a properly religious character?
In this sermon, Bushnell seems to doubt it. Natural desires
and the love of God seem to be at odds, in such a way that the
religious goal requires the crucifixion of all worldly loves.
To preserve the unique value of Christian consciousness, then,
Bushnell suggested his willingness to scrap the complex harmony between history and transcendence developed in his theory
of communication.

In the end, however, Bushnell did not abandon his earlier
position on the relevance of social relations to Christian

growth. Instead, he went on, with tremendous energy, to develop
his theories, to condense them into a fascinating theory of symbolism and its interpretation, and to apply them throughout the
remainder of his life to the cardinal issues of Christian doctrine. His experience in early 1848 seems to be one of the
major reasons why he took the course he did.

Our best evidence for what his experience meant to him in
this regard is a sermon written immediately after the insight
dawned titled "Christ the Form of the Soul."[11] In this sermon,
Bushnell reaffirmed the understanding of Christ and his work
that had grown up in connection with his theory of communication.
The sermon's text is Galatians 4:19: "Until Christ be formed
in you." In this phrase, said Bushnell, Paul sums of "the
grand object and even the whole object of the gospel plan."[12]
"Form," Bushnell assumed, is an analogy for the characteristic
style of the spirit or inward life: "What form is to the body,
character is to the spirit."[13] To have Christ formed in one is
thus to become like him in character. Bushnell pinned down
this terminological nexus with a paraphrase of the "kenosis"
hymn in Philippians 2:6-11: "Being in the *form of God* the eternal word assumed humanity that he may bring into humanity the
form of a *divine character*."[14] He then drew a further conclusion: to become like Christ in character is to share in the
divine life of which he is the "express image," for the identity of man is as the character that represents it. Bushnell
thus took Paul to mean that redemption is participation in the
divine nature (in the sense that one takes on its "form"), and
that this participation is made possible by the power of forms
to communicate the life they represent. This principle, he
claimed, is clearly stated in II Cor. 3:18, which he paraphrased as follows:

> But we all with open face beholding as in a
> glass i.e. in Christ the glory of the Lord are
> changed into the same image from glory to
> glory.[15]

In this law of expression, he wrote, we are given "the whole
scope of the gospel as a renovating power."[16]

All of these ideas had appeared previously in Bushnell's
work. They represent, in fact, the same line of thought that
ran him into difficulties with the critics of his stand on

Christian nurture. For here again the question could be raised, if Christ communicates character simply by virtue of the express image of God he bears, why doesn't the expression he makes have the same power over all persons? Bushnell met this difficulty here, however, by drawing a new implication from his theory of communication. Communication, he noted, is a two-part process. A complete exchange requires both a matter expressed in a vehicle and a receiver with adequate power to interpret and realize the meaning expressed. Therefore, if not all persons respond to the divine power expressed in Christ, the fault must lie in their receptive capacities. Some persons are mysteriously "blind" or "deaf" to the gospel communication; their "hearts are hardened" and will not be transformed. Taking his lead from both Calvinistic and Quietistic devotional thought, Bushnell attributed such failures to the interference of worldly and selfish concerns. The soul becomes "filled" with self, so that there is no room to "receive" the operative image of Christ. Christian redemption can thus be distinguished from natural influence by the special attitude that is necessary to receive it.

One name for this special attitude of receptivity, said Bushnell, is "faith." Faith is not assent to a proposition, but openness to a transforming influence. It is the act of receptive love by which a fallen person "embraces" the communicative power of God in Christ.

> Our love to Him gives him welcome in our soul
> and entertains him there. This we may call
> repentance, faith, conversion, regeneration or by
> whatever name. The sublime reality is that the
> divine has made a juncture with our nature, and
> Christ has begun to be formed within us.[17]

Faith, then, marks the overcoming of spiritual deafness and, by implication, the overcoming of the fallen self. In a person who has faith, the communicative power of the image can work itself out "from glory to glory," while a person without faith remains alienated from the life he has no capacity to respond to. What Bushnell has done, in short, is to turn the law of gospel communication which he found in II Cor. 3:18 into a *conditional* principle.

> *If* you are to behold in Christ as in a glass
> the glory of the Lord and be changed into that
> image, you must look with *open* face.[18]

The condition of human salvation is thus defined in terms of the theory of communication. The Christian is one who can receive Christ as the express image of God, and so complete the divine act of self-communication. The non-Christian, by contrast, is one who does not get the point, who remains deaf and dumb in the face of God's perpetual attempt to get through.[19] For purposes of determining religious status, then, as one perceives, so one is.

In "Christ the Form of the Soul," then, Bushnell consolidated and refined the understanding of the Christian redemptive economy developed in his theory of communication. As Bushnell later wrote, his experience just prior to writing the sermon was one in which "elements which I had before held separately and without perceiving the mode of their agreement" snapped together into an integrated vision.[20] So, in this sermon, Bushnell's conviction that a divine life can be communicated through receptivity to this world was integrated with his concern to preserve the distinctly "supernatural" dignity of Christain character. The entire diagnosis and cure of the human condition, he discovered, could be represented in terms of divine self-communication and mankind's attempt to interpret it. The Christian, he held, in a formula reminiscent of Edwards and the typologists, is one empowered by the spirit to become a right reader of God's self-expression in the creation. The Christian by definition sees God in all things and lives in the joy of that consciousness. The condition that is at once the presupposition of his ability to perceive and the substance of his joy, in turn, is his participation in the divine nature. Christian character both begins and ends in expressive communion with God.

The elegance of this vision accounts in large measure for the inspiring impulse it gave to Bushnell's career. Having discovered the power of his theory of communication to encompass both the mystery of iniquity and the highest peaks of spiritual attainment, he went on to explore its implications for a theory of religious language and symbolism.

b. Orthodox Memories and Unitarian Hopes

Bushnell's renewed energies were drawn to questions of the
nature of religious symbolism by contemporary doctrinal disputes
between orthodox and Unitarian theologians in New England. On
the one hand, orthodoxy stood firm against doctrinal change in
the conviction that sound doctrine, firmly grasped, was an
indispensable helpmate in the Christian life. It found tradition a source of spiritual power. On the other hand, what was
a helpmate to the orthodox was a stumbling block to the Unitarians. They found orthodoxy's most prized doctrines uniformly
appalling: Calvinism's concept of God's wrath and unsearchable
justice was morally objectionable; the trinity as usually conceived was logically absurd. In the Unitarian view, piety
consisted in moral earnestness fired by a sense of kinship
with God. But who, they asked, would be encouraged by kinship
with a wrathful God who taught absurdities? The Unitarian response to these difficulties was elegantly direct; all the
imagery that made Christianity logically inconsistent or morally
complex should be abandoned. They would win consistency at the
expense of traditional symbolism.[21] This difference in outlook
between the orthodox and Unitarian parties has been captured
nicely by R.W.B. Lewis, who characterizes orthodoxy as the party
of memory and Unitarianism as the party of hope. The orthodox
sought to preserve the past; the Unitarians proposed to scrap
it in the interests of a brighter spiritual future.[22]

Bushnell's allegiances in this dispute were divided. He
shared many of the Unitarian "difficulties" with orthodox doctrine. He also shared their moral model of piety, as his tendency to identify redeemed status with character indicates. His
sympathies were such, in fact, that in 1847 he could declare to
James Freeman Clarke, a prominent Unitarian:

> I have little doubt that if I had lived in the
> day when [Unitarianism] came into the field, I
> should have been found among its zealous adher-
> ents.[23]

However, Bushnell believed that the Unitarian break with tradition was a deadly error. The lesson of his own experience
had been that the past is a medium through which present possibilities of spiritual existence are transmitted. Therefore,
he feared that by jettisoning some of the symbols and forms

that had educated generations of New England Calvinists, the
Unitarians would find they had lost the practical key to Christian experience. Without traditional symbols to mold belief,
he wrote elsewhere, "the tone or tonic energy of the gospel"
would be lost.[24] If Unitarianism still had power to inspire
and elevate life, it was thanks to the education its founders
had received in the "resonant and somewhat brassy energies of
Calvinism."[25] But this energy will fade as time carries the
Unitarians away from their source. Without the doctrinal tensions that Calvinism embraces, Unitarianism has no educative
power: "it fails to impart to those who grow up under it from
childhood, that deep, vibratory sense of religion, which is
needful to its volume and power."[26] In sum, Bushnell wrote,
Unitarianism will die of its virtues; it is "very simple, perfectly comprehensible, never difficult, a last fruit of reason,
a completed model of--inefficiency."[27]

Bushnell thus cherished a hope that these two parties
might someday be reconciled. A concise expression of his
ecumenical interest can be found in the letter to Clarke already cited. Here he stated his conviction that

> if an orthodox man and a Unitarian could be
> melted into one it might possibly make a Christ-
> ian. And why not go further and say what is truer
> still, that if all the sects could be melted
> into one, they would each add something wanted
> by all the others. For what are we all, but so
> many *partialities* toiling after the infinity of
> truth.[28]

Orthodoxy and Unitarianism "want" each other, he said, because
each contains only half a truth; neither alone supplies suste-
nance for a full spiritual life. Orthodoxy needs the Unitarian
stress on religion's immediate relevance to human moral and
rational interests; Unitarianism, in turn, needs orthodox sym-
bolism--the stretched passion generated by a sense of God's
otherness--to sustain the "vitality" and "tonic energy" of its
spiritual impulse.[29] In sum, the present needs of spiritual
life must be integrated with the ways the past has taught us to
deal with them. Only thus, said Bushnell, can a person become
a whole Christian or a complete human being.

The implications of this principle for theology were clear
to Bushnell. Orthodox symbols should be retained, but they
must be given a "new development."[30] Unitarianism rejected the

trinity, the divinity of Christ, and the orthodox theory of the
atonement because it found them irrelevant and even harmful to
the interests of spiritual life, which it identified with the
love of God and the cultivation of character. Bushnell, by
contrast, believed that orthodox symbols properly understood
would be found to be the best means to the Unitarians' own ends.
A new development or fresh presentation of the doctrines was
needed, then, to make clear their practical power and moral
significance.

> If, now, we wish to be clear of scripture, made
> into logical jargon on the one hand, and unmade
> or emptied of divinity and grandure on the other,
> I know no better method than to accept these great
> truths . . . as realities or verities addressed
> to faith: or what is not far different, to
> feeling and imaginative reason.[31]

When Bushnell wrote to Clarke in 1847, he was convinced
that such a new development of doctrine was possible, and that
once accomplished, it would reconcile all the warring factions
in New England. Bushnell's "first conviction" in that year was

> that all serious, earnest men have something in
> their view which makes it truth to them; there-
> fore that all serious, earnest men, however
> repugnant in their words, have yet some radical
> agreement, and if the place can be found, will
> somewhere reveal their brotherhood.[32]

The "place" of agreement between orthodox and Unitarian was the
divine life or consciousness in which all Christians participate.
All that they needed to realize their practical unity was a
truer idea of the variable relations between expressive language
and truth--a tool by which to penetrate behind the "repugnant"
surfaces of words to the one truth expressed.

After his experience in 1848, Bushnell was confident that
he had discovered the key to this new age of faith in his theory
of communication. He set to work that year and throughout the
remainder of his career to apply his theory to a complex of
concerns at once theological, cultural, and personal.

2. The Theory of Language

Bushnell's mature reflections on language and symbolism are
contained in three works: the "Preliminary Dissertation on
Language" contained in the volume *God in Christ* (1849); the
opening chapter of *Christ in Theology* (1851) titled "Language

and Doctrine;" and a much later essay, "Our Gospel a Gift to
the Imagination" (1869).[33] These writings differ in purpose,
emphasis, and organization, but are substantially similar in
content and in their range of implications. Our analysis of
Bushnell's theory will draw on all three.

a. Language as the Medium of Divine-Human Relations

Bushnell's chief interest in his works on language and
symbolism was to demonstrate the relevance of traditional Christian symbols to moral growth and character development--the en-
richment and intensification of the spiritual life. He approached
the task by way of an analysis of the meaning of words and symbols in general, and of their role in the formation and transformation of the self.

> What I design is, principally, to speak of language
> as regards its significancy, or the power and cap-
> acity of its words, taken as vehicles of thought
> and of spiritual truth.[34]

The key words in this passage are "power" and "vehicles." The
first underscores something we have already observed: that for
Bushnell, words are not inert labels which we stick on the
facts of experience; they have a power to change selves in and
through the process of communication. As Coleridge put
a similar point, "if words are not things, they are living
powers, by which the things of most importance to mankind are
actuated, combined, and humanized."[35] Bushnell's use of
"vehicles" in turn indicates that words exert such power because of the expressive, "sign-ificant" relation they bear to
thought and truth. The power of words, "taken as vehicles of
thought," is their capacity to call out similar thoughts in
the mind of the recipient. The communicative process does not
leave the participants unchanged. In fact, Bushnell was anxious
to show that the meaning of a certain kind of words--Christian
symbols among them--is identical with the state of the soul
evoked in the process of coming to understand them. Words, by
their very nature as expressions, are shaping powers over life;
they nurture qualities of mind similar to those they express in
all who understand them. Bushnell, in sum, aimed to show that
the relevance of religious symbols lies in their effective power
to generate inward experiences and shape character, and that this

power is exerted according to simple, universal laws of expression and interpretation.[36]

Bushnell's first step upon declaring his intention to hunt out the power of words was to begin speculating on the origins of language.

> To understand the precise power of words, or the true theory of their power, without some reference to their origin, will be difficult or impossible; for it is, in fact, the mode of their origin that reveals their power.[37]

The genesis of words "reveals" their power, said Bushnell, but it does not explain it. That explanation depends on psychological and cosmological principles--the presumed "laws of expression," according to which any human or divine expression perfectly represents the mind at its source and is interpreted by experiences identical with those expressed. Bushnell thus had little at stake in the origin story as such: "what we say of [the power of words] may be true, in general, if what we say of their origin should not hold in every particular."[38] Bushnell spent some time in his "Preliminary Disseration" criticizing alternative theories of origin, but he never felt pressed to answer later critics of his own theory.[39] And in later treatments of language, he skipped over the story of origin entirely to state the principles unadorned. We may conclude, then, that Bushnell's interest in the origin of words was subordinate to his interest in what he called their "significance"--their educative power as expressions of mind.

Nevertheless, there is an imaginative cogency to the story that makes it worth retelling. In outline, the story is the same that Bushnell told in "Revelation." Bushnell proposed a thought experiment. Imagine, he said, that two people are thrown together who have never even heard language used before. They are human beings, and so they will have an innate capacity for language--"a certain free power of self-representation or expression"[40]--but as yet, that capacity is unrealized. How will they get along? Bushnell assumed that they would have no trouble developing a language to name empirical phenomena and physical objects. They can simply point to any physical object they care to name, since physical objects are equally available to the senses of each. One will point to a rock, say "rock," and so get the other in the habit of associating the sound with the thing. Thus, a noun-language is developed. Verbs, adjectives, conjunctions, prepositions, and grammatical relations, in turn, will all be developed out of nouns and observable spatial relations.[41] Simple ostensive reference, then, is supposed to explain the genesis of a tolerably adequate language for describing objects and operations in the physical world.[42]

To Bushnell's mind, however, this is really the least interesting kind of human speech. What fascinated him was the "language of intelligence," the language by which persons express their inward thoughts or emotions, their minds. This, he assumed, is a wholly different kind of language from that which refers to physical objects. One reason why it is different is that it could not have been learned or originated in the same way as the language of sense. If one of the parties in our thought experiment wants to give a name to a thought or emotion, he cannot literally show the other person what he has in mind. His thoughts, his hopes, and his fears are invisible. How, then, can he communicate subjective experiences to his companion? Bushnell's whole story was designed to bring us to this puzzle, for the clue to the spiritual significance of language, he claimed, lies in its solution.

The solution is simple, but the principle it presupposes is vast. Our namer will refer to his thought by using the name of some physical object or operation--some word he already knows. Bushnell supported his conjecture with etymological evidence suggested to him primarily by Josiah Willard Gibbs, Sr., his former professor at Yale. All words that presently refer to thought and spirit, he claimed, have a physical base: e.g. "spirit" comes from the word for breath, "prefer" means set before, "rectitude" means straightness, and so on for all words of thought and feeling, however deeply buried their roots.[43] All language of thought and feeling is therefore "metaphorical," in the sense that it uses some physical form as the objective correlative of a subjective experience.

The question remains, however, how will our namer's companion understand the metaphor? How is intersubjective communication possible? Bushnell answered that since intersubjective communication is an accomplished fact, and since thoughts and

emotions are expressed by means of words of physical reference,
there must exist a natural analogy between certain thoughts and
certain things,[44] by virtue of which we intuitively associate
thoughts with their appropriate images, both in our own use of
words and in our interpretation of the expressions of others.

> It is only as there is a Logos in the outward
> world, answering to the logos or internal reason
> of the parties, that they can come into a mutual
> understanding in regard to any thought or spirit-
> ual matter whatever. To use a more familiar ex-
> pression, there is a vast analogy in things which
> prepares them, as forms, to be signs or figures
> of thoughts, and thus, bases or types of words.[45]

Bushnell's repeated use of "logos" in this passage is
striking. He used the word, first of all, to make the point
that the physical universe is so well suited to the uses of
thought that it is like a language itself; it exhibits an organization that is like the organization of our minds.[46] Further,
the neo-Platonic connotations of the logos concept imply an
explanation for the facts it identifies: if the universe is
like a language, it is because God is its "Author." In this
contention, Bushnell presupposed an understanding of the analogy
of creation similar to that we examined in Scottish philosophy
and aesthetics. The physical world is an expression of the
divine mind, and an expression in a very specific sense:

> if the creation of the world be issued from
> God, it must represent the mind by which it is
> conceived, and must, in all its particular forms
> or objects, reveal those archetypes of thought
> in God which shaped them in their birth.[47]

As Wayland had put it, the creation bears "in all its lineaments
the traces of the character of its Author."[48]

The universe is like a language, then, because like language,
it is an expression of mind. And being the expression of the
same mind that created us, the world is suited to become the
expressive vehicle of our minds. "[T]he external grammar of
creation answers to the internal grammar of the soul, and becomes its vehicle,"[49] for there is

> an eternal and necessary connection between the
> *forms* God has wrought into things--thus into
> language,--and the contents, on the one hand,
> of his own mind, and the principles, on the
> other, of all created mind.[50]

If there is a mysterious, preestablished harmony between what

is "inmost in our souls" and the forms of creation, it is because creation itself expresses the inwardness of a kindred
soul. "[T]he outer world is seen to be a vast menstruum of
thought or intelligence."[51]

Bushnell's theory of language thus bore first fruits in a
vision of divine-human relations. The universe is an expression
of God, and man is a creature sufficiently similar to God to
understand God's self-expression. Mankind, indeed, has the
potential for an immediate insight into--even a communion with--
the mind of God in all things.

b. Language and the Human Condition

Bushnell did not end his research into the power of words
with this insight into divine-human relations, however. His
primary interest in the theory concerned the power of words
and symbols to foster human growth through the dynamics of
interpretation. This interest, in turn, led Bushnell back for
a closer look at the nature of words.

Bushnell's story of origin led to the conclusion that
there are two distinct departments of language.

> First, there is a literal department, in which
> sounds are provided as names for physical objects
> and appearances. Secondly, there is a department
> of analogy or figure, where physical objects and
> appearances are named as images of thought or
> spirit . . . .[52]

Following our practice in Chapter II, we will refer to Bushnell's
first category as notational language, and to the second as
expressive language. We have already seen how Bushnell distinguished these departments according to their presumed origins.
More significantly, however, he distinguished them according to
the different kinds of things they indicate and the different
ways in which they refer. Notational language refers to empirical data ostensively; expressive language refers to inward,
mentalistic phenomena by suggestion or indirection--i.e. by
means of analogies, metaphors, figures, or types.[53] Bushnell's
interest is primarily in the latter category, the language of
mind.

Bushnell's terminology for expressive figures was rather
loose. Symbol, metaphor, analogy, and type were all one to
him; he used them interchangeably, and offered precise

definitions of none. But at least part of what he meant it
clear. A term in the language of intelligence has two distinct
aspects: vehicle or form, and content or "truth." The form
which carries the meaning is taken from the physical world;
the content pertains to the realm of mind or spirit which it
expresses. Thus, the essential fact about a symbol, by whatever name, is that it is a device for manifesting and transmit-
ting the inward life of a mind. All verbal "expression" is
symbolic; conversely, the meaning of any symbol is the inward
mental quality it communicates.

This model of expressive language had important implications
for Bushnell's understanding of how the language of intelligence
communicates and is to be interpreted. First of all, because
the content of an analogical expression is an inward state of
the soul, to understand such an expression is to re-experience
the mental state expressed. The meaning, or "truth," of symbols is not an object external to mind, but a spiritual state.

> What [symbols] carry into our soul's feeling is
> their only truth, and that is a simple, internal
> state of the soul itself.[54]

The problem of all symbolic communication, then, is the transmission of an experience from one mind to another through the
medium of form. Symbolic language does not complete its communicative role by conveying neutral bits of information. The
"truth" in which it deals is never propositional. Rather, the
meaning of a symbol is the effect it has over the receiver's
mind as he comes to understand it.

> [Symbols] do not literally convey, or pass over
> a thought out of one mind into another. They
> are only hints, or images, held up before the
> mind of another, to put *him* on generating or
> reproducing the same thought . . . .[55]

Symbolic communication is thus essentially instrumental, or as
Bushnell loved to put it, "practical." The symbol is a tool
for producing truth in a soul.

The question how such symbols are to be interpreted brings
us to the radical interest of the subject. To explain how symbols help to generate inward states, Bushnell drew a distinction
between the ways in which his two departments of language need
to be interpreted. Understanding physical language, he said,
requires no talent different in kind from what an animal

possesses. Animals can learn their own names and the names
of a few important objects in their experience. "But no animal
ever understood a metaphor."[56]   To interpret analogical language
requires a higher faculty, one that sets mankind apart from
lower beings. Bushnell called this faculty "intelligence" at
times, and at other times "imagination," "heart," "sympathy,"
"faith," and "love."[57]   In any case, it can be defined as

> a power to see, in all images, the faces
> of truth, and take their sense, or read
> (*intus lego*) their meaning, when thrown up
> before the imagination.[58]

The definition is *ad hoc*. Bushnell simply attributed a power
he had observed in persons to a faculty which he assumed them
to possess (like Moliere's doctor who ascribed the soporific
powers of opium to its "dormative properties"). However, the
imagination or intelligence, so defined, is pivotal in Bushnell's vision of the communicative process. The imagination
is the interpretive correlate of the expressive capacity, in
which the meaning of expression is converted back into experience. It is that which "receives impression from expression."[59]
Therefore, this faculty is the immanent reason for the power of
words in personal experience. Because man has an imagination,
he can reproduce the contents of symbols. And because he has
access to their contents, words can become vehicles of "spirit
and life"--vehicles of a power which transforms the soul.[60]

    Symbols cannot transform a person, however, in the sense
of making him something he had no prior capacity to become.
Understanding requires a common ground and some co-operation
between the parties. One person understands another "only as
he has the same personal contents, or generative power out of
which to bring the thought required."[61]   Symbols call out
capacities of thought and feeling; they do not create them.
It follows that a person's capacity to interpret symbols is
correlated with his inward receptivity, his responsiveness.
As in "Christ the Form of the Soul," Bushnell insisted on the
conditional character of interpretation. We can receive
another's self-communication only if we are properly receptive,
or only if the ground of understanding pre-exists in us.[62]
Because persons, on the whole, are capable of understanding
each other, and because they are frequently responsive to the

Word of God, Bushnell was confident that the preconditions of both secular and sacred communication exist, at least potentially, in all persons. Simply as users and interpreters of language, human beings manifest their likeness to God and to each other.

But the curious fact remains that not all persons are equally aware of their capacities, or have developed them to the same degree. The problem, Bushnell was convinced, was not due to any failure of the rational understanding. The interpretation of symbols cannot proceed according to explicit laws or principles, for the relation between form and content in any given symbol is ultimately mysterious.

> On the one hand, is form; on the other, is the formless. The former represents and is somehow fellow to the other; how, we cannot discover.[63]

Interpretation, rather, is an intuitive capacity, made possible by human kinship with the divine mind who first prepared the world to be a vehicle of thought. Interpretive facility thus depends less on technical skill than on the intimacy of one's relation to God.

> [T]here will be different measures of understanding, according to the capacity or incapacity, the ingenuousness or moral obliquity of the receiving party--even if the communicating party offers only truth, in the best and freshest forms of expression the language provides.[64]

The reference to "moral obliquity" here gives the clue to Bushnell's meaning: the capacity of interpretation correlates with the spiritual status of the interpreter. The pure in heart shall see God and man in their expressions; the impure have lost the inward capacity to "generate" them. If the capacity to read truth in form is the mark and measure of our likeness to God, the failure of that capacity is the mystery of sin.

Bushnell thus used his theory of interpretation to reformulate the Christian diagnosis of the human condition. Mankind's fallenness consists of his inability to respond fully to God's self-communication, or in the moral obliquity that deafens him. Salvation, in turn, is the restoration of human sensibility to the divine meaning or presence in things, a renewal of the capacity to receive the divine life expressed in the world, and so, to participate in that life as a perceiver

or interpreter of it. The problem of spiritual life, then, is
how to make a realization of the power of expressive symbols,
how to become receptive.

c. Theology as Pedagogy

Bushnell believed that theology, properly conceived, could
play a role in restoring human receptivity to God's self-communication. His works on language all climaxed in a discussion
of this point. He began, in each case, with a critique of
theology's prevalent self-understanding and ended with a prescription for reform. His guiding principle was that theology
should not strive to be an exact descriptive science, for
exactitude with regard to the divine mind was ruled out by the
very nature of expressive language. Rather, theology should
cultivate the resources for effective communication it has in
its heritage of symbols, conceived as vehicles of redemption.
The norms for theology are to be determined according to the
laws of expressive communication.

Bushnell characterized the history of Christian theology
as a comedy of errors in the interpretation of language--the
language of Scripture, the language of creed, and the language
of previous theologies. The ultimate root of error is human
sinfulness, man's stubborn refusal to take words in the sense
in which they are offered.[65] More specifically, Bushnell
pointed to two ways in which theologians generally fail to
comprehend language, the medium they share with God's self-
revelation in Scripture.

First, said Bushnell, theology has misunderstood the true
relation between literal and figurative language. In making
this charge, he had in mind theologians like Nathaniel Taylor
who assumed that the language of Scripture and theology can be
taken to provide an exact and reliable map of the noumenal
world.[66] Scripture is often figurative, Taylor allowed, but
its language can be purged of metaphorical imprecision and translated into direct, literal statements of truth. Theology, in
principle, can provide the same precision and certainty as
algebra. Bushnell, by contrast, held that Scripture is an expression of the divine mind and as such is figurative by its
very nature. All language of thought and spirit (with a few

exceptions[67]) is figurative or expressive. Thus,

we have no properly literal language, save in
reference to matters of the outward physical
state. When we come into the world of mind or
spirit, words get their significance, I have
insisted, under conditions of analogy, and
never stand as a direct and absolute notation
for thought.[68]

For example, the word "sin" in theology is an expressive term,

signifying an inward spiritual condition that never appears to

sense. Therefore, it must be interpreted intuitively as an

analogy. Its meaning must be "generated" out of the inter-

preter's own repertory of experiences. But this entails that

every interpreter will understand it somewhat differently,

depending on his personal stock of "temptations, wants and

repentances." Disputes over the precise meaning of "sin" are

therefore interminable, simply because its meaning is of the

kind that can never be determined with precision.[69] The theo-

logian who ignores the distinction of literal and figurative

language thus commits a disastrous category mistake. "This, I

conceive, is the almost universal sin that infests the reason-

ings of mankind concerning moral and spiritual subjects."[70]

Second, Bushnell held that theology errs in its belief that

valid consequences can be drawn from the language of Scripture

by the use of strict logical method. Bushnell here had in mind

something like the theological style recommended by John

Cotton:

Every shred of Gold hammered, or drawn out of
a wedge of Gold, is as well Gold, as the whole
lumpe and wedge. Whatsoever is drawn out of the
Scripture by just consequence and deduction, is
as well the word of God as that which is an
express Commandment or example in Scripture.[71]

Bushnell's criticism of deductive logic in theology again fol-

lowed from his views on the expressive imprecision of Scriptural

language. Symbols do not lend themselves to logical treatment

because of their basic double nature. "They impute form to

what is really out of form;" they express something that has

"no shape or sensible quality" in a sensible image. Thus, in

a sense, "they always affirm something which is false."[72]

Every reasoner must therefore be on guard against confusing

the essential implications of a symbol with its accidental

connotations. But logic alone is undiscriminating in this

regard. "Thinking," said Bushnell, "is nothing but the handling
of thoughts by their forms."[73] Therefore, since truth--the inner meaning of the word--is only accidentally related to its
form, logical reasoning frequently leaves truth behind.

To illustrate the pitfalls of logical theologizing, Bushnell cited the disputes over "moral ability," that raged in
his own day. The question at hand was whether the human will
has an inherent ability to turn to God, or whether an antecedent grace is necessary for conversion. The problem is as old
as Christendom, but Bushnell believed it to be fundamentally
misconceived. Moral ability, he noted, is commonly discussed
under the imagery of "antecedent" conditions and "consequent"
acts--before and after.[74] The "form element" in the words
implies that human moral life consists in a unilinear train of
causes and effects. But such is simply not the case, Bushnell
insisted. The will is part of a different order of being,
where laws of cause and effect do not hold. Therefore, images
of before and after cannot be applied consistently to psychological operations. The passage in which he made this point
deserves quoting at length:

> What endless debates have we had in theology
> concerning questions of priority--whether faith
> is before repentance, or repentance before faith;
> whether one or the other is before love, or love
> before them both; whether justification is before
> sanctification, and the like. We seem to sup-
> pose that a soul can be taken to pieces, or have
> its exercises parted and put under laws of time,
> so that we can see them go, in regular clock-
> work order. Whereas, being *alive* in God when
> it is truly united to Him, its right exercises,
> being functions of life, are of course mutual
> conditions one of another. Passing out of
> mechanism, or the empire of dead atoms, into the
> plastic realm of life, all questions of before
> and after we leave behind us. We do not ask
> whether the heart causes the heaving of the lungs,
> or whether the lungs have priority, and keep up
> the beating of the heart; or whether the diges-
> tive faculty is first in time, or the assimila-
> tive, or the nervous. We look at the whole body
> as a vital nature, and finding every function
> alive, every fibre active, we perceive that all
> the parts, even the minutest, exist and act as
> mutual conditions one of another. And so it is
> in spiritual life. Every grace supposes every
> other as its condition, and time is wholly out
> of the question.[75]

The point here is that attempts to lay out the elements of
spiritual life in terms of a casual sequence necessarily end in
perplexity because the terms themselves are inappropriate.
The knottiness of the problem simply reflects the confusion of
the thinkers who find it problematical. When language is rightly used, the apparent complexities of the issue dissolve into
the "infinity" of a lived truth. Bushnell, we expect, would
have heartily approved Wittgenstein's therapeutic aphorism,
that the only real solution to a problem in thought consists
in the dissolution of the problem. Everything depends on a
just sense of the limits and possibilities of words.[76]

For the same reasons that theologians tend to be naive
about the imprecision of figurative language, they are also
insensitive to its resources, said Bushnell. Bushnell saw
New England theologians struggling to eliminate metaphor and
multiplicity from Christian language. They did so in the name
of "sound doctrine," thinking that the only brand of truth
worth having was that which is fixed in meaning and logically
self-consistent. Bushnell's theory of language, however, suggested that just as there are two kinds of language, so there
are two kinds of truth: a truth of reference, which can be
contained in relatively precise verbal formulas, and a truth
of expression, which cannot.[77] A truth of expression is ultimately a state of the soul, a quality of life, whose "truth"
is its self-evidencing value as a mode of experience. It is a
"truth" that closely resembles "beauty" on the subjectivist
account--i.e. it is not a property of an object or statement
but a quality of our response to a form. As such, the truth
of expression is "immediate" or intuitively present to the soul.
We know such truths just as we know of our own existence or
have our self-consciousness.[78] Notational language, in sum,
communicates an abstract truth directly; expressive language
communicates an immediate, living truth by indirection. Notational language conveys information; expressive language aims
to set another person on "generating or reproducing the same
thought."[79] Bushnell's criticism of the logical method in
theology, then, is that by overstressing notational precision,
it ignores the linguistic resources by which religious symbols
can become an effective power for growth.

Bushnell's favorite case of theology's mistaken attitude toward language was its approach to paradox and contradiction in Scripture. The Bible, he said, is the most contradictory book in the world.[80] For instance, it calls Jesus both man and God; it represents his mission as a ritual sacrifice, the payment of a debt, a propitiation of God's wrath, and an expression of God's love, to name only a few of the symbols of the atonement. This rich profusion of symbols makes both orthodox Calvinist and Unitarian nervous, said Bushnell, because they don't know how to comprehend it all as notational truth. The orthodox generally try to reduce the confusion to system by seizing on one form to the exclusion of the others--e.g. representing the atonement exclusively under the figure of penal satisfaction, literally understood. Different factions choose different figures, and so, theological controversies arise. The Unitarians, on the other hand, respond to the confusion with a program "to decoct the whole mass of symbol, and draw off the extract into pitchers of [their] own."[81] What neither party sees, however, is that no single expression or scheme can translate the Bible's multiplicity. The subject matter of the Bible is ultimately the mind of God--"God coming into expression."[82] The language that bears its truth is therefore expressive language--language whose meaning is its operative power to beget that mind in us. The Bible, in other words, is a "practical" book, designed to make an impression and employing the linguistic strategies best suited to produce the desired effect. If it employs contradiction and paradox it is because they are well-calculated to make the right impression.

The practical value of paradox is as follows. Single statements affirm something false in their forms, and are likely to be misleading. But opposed statements, carefully balanced, can correct each other's defects and work together to produce the desired effect, producing a kind of vector quantity of oblique forces.

> [A]s form battles form, and one form neutralizes
> another, all the insufficiencies of words are
> filled out, the contrarieties liquidated, and the
> mind settles into a full and just apprehension
> of the pure spiritual truth. Accordingly we
> never come so near to a truly well rounded view
> of any truth, as when it is offered paradoxically;

> that is, under contradictions; that is, under
> two or more dictions, which taken as dictions,
> are contrary to one another.[83]

Several finite representations may therefore be necessary to
give us the idea of a single spiritual reality. Thus, for
instance, Bushnell approached the trinity as an "instrumental"
verity, a set of expressions which unite to drive our mind "in
a resultant motion towards the infinite."[84]

For similar reasons, Bushnell adopted a relativistic attitude towards doctrines and creeds.[85] Doctrines are the expressions of inward truth, he held. They are valuable only if
they help to communicate the consciousness they express. A
doctrine which is effectively true under one set of circumstances
may thus lose its power, and hence its "truth," under other
circumstances. For example, the forms that the original writers
of Scripture used to express their experienced truths may no
longer mean the same to us, since we are "different men, living
as parts of a different system of things and thinkings and deny-
ings and affirmings."[86] Similarly, expressive forms tend to
fade into apparent literalness with constant use over time.
Metaphors die, and when one dies the element of falsehood in
its form comes to dominate the truth of its spirit. Therefore,
Bushnell concluded, to keep the Christian truth fresh and effective, it must constantly be reinterpreted and re-expressed.
"It may even be necessary to change the forms to hold us in
the same truths."[87]

His attitude toward existing creeds was correspondingly
accomodating. The creeds of the various sects, he said, all
represent Christian truth from somewhat different angles. The
forms by which they do their expressive work are different.
As operative pieces of language, however, all Christian creeds
are fundamentally alike; the resultant of the repellent forces
within them points in the same direction. Thus,

> when they are subjected to the deepest chemistry
> of thought, that which descends to the point of
> relationship between the form of truth and its
> interior formless nature, they become, thereupon,
> so elastic and run so freely into each other,
> that one seldom need have any difficulty accepting
> as many as are offered him.[88]

Bushnell's contemporaries saw his commodious attitude toward theological truth as sheer irresponsibility. Bushnell, by

contrast, understood himself to be facing up to the real conditions under which truth is offered in language. The result,
he was sure, would be both better theology and a more intense
spiritual life. Logical theology, by railing against paradox
and expressive elasticity, cripples the truth-capacity of language. It deprives religion of its proper cogency, which is
identical with its power over life. Bushnell crystallized this
point by drawing an analogy between religion and poetry.
"Religion," he said, "has a natural and profound alliance with
poetry."[89] Both religion and poetry, that is, are expressive
media. Poetry expresses a human author; religion expresses
God, e.g. in the Bible, "the grand poem of salvation."[90]
Thus, if it would be absurd to try to "compress the whole tragic force of Lear into some one sentence of Edgar's gibberish"
or to represent in a single formula the impression we receive
of Goethe from his poetry, so it is even more absurd to think
that the meaning of the Bible can be paraphrased by a scientific theology.[91] The meaning of the Bible, like the meaning of
a poem, consists in the comprehensive manifold of impressions
it makes on the attentive reader. Take away the manifold, and
you take away the power, the "tragic force," in which its
truth consists.[92]

Bushnell's own program for theology followed from these
observations. The goal of theology should not be to make language more precise, but to cultivate receptivity to existing
Scriptural and theological forms, conceived as expressive vehicles of Christian character.

> The principal difficulty we have with language
> now is, that it will not put into the theoretic
> understanding what the imagination only will
> receive, and will not open to the head what the
> heart only can interpret.[93]

He was convinced that religion left in the terms of expression
is richer and more healthful than any scientific theology
could ever be, even if such a theology were possible.[94] The
following passage suggests his reason:

> Indeed, if it were possible to get religious
> truth into shapes and formulas having an absolute
> meaning, like the terms of algebra, as clear to
> the wicked as to the pure, and requiring no con-
> ditions of character in the receivers, it would
> very nearly subvert, it seems to me, all that

is most significant and sublime in the discipline
of life.[95]

The important phrases here are "conditions of character" and
"discipline of life." We will examine each in turn.

The conditions of character required for understanding,
as we have seen before, follow from the very structure of expressive communication as a transfer of inward states.

> In this matter of understanding, two things are
> requisite; first, a matter which is understand-
> able; and second, a power that is capable of
> understanding . . . .[96]

Because the content to be understood in an expression is an
inward state, the power of understanding is a power of "sympathy"--a power to reproduce the expressed experience out of
one's own resources. This means that the interpreter must
1) be sufficiently like the speaker to have some clue to the
character of his experience, and 2) make the exertion of patience,
candor, and love that is always required to enter into the
feelings of another.[97] That is, there must be both a ground
of sympathy and a willingness to act on it. The ground of
sympathy is the common character of all persons as creatures
in the image of God; the willingness is in fact exercised
whenever expressive communication occurs. Bushnell was confident that both of these conditions can be met and that the result is a more or less perfect intersubjectivity between the
communicating parties.

Bushnell noted, however, that in many cases these "conditions of character" are not met in practice. We often need to
make an extraordinary effort to enter into another's experience.
To illustrate this point, Bushnell referred to the experience
of reading a "difficult" writer, one who uses words in unusual
ways or makes leaps of thought that strike one as mysterious.[98]
Difficult writing was a hotly debated topic in the literary
criticism of Bushnell's day. German philosophy, Carlyle's
essays, and romantic literature in général seemed incomprehen-
sible to the more conservative American critics, who considered
the difficulty of the works a vice. The rationale they offered
for their judgement involved a theory of interpretation very
similar to Bushnell's. Understanding is made possible by sympathy, they held. The common elements in human moral character--

the universal intuitions and moral experiences of mankind--
provide the bridge by which we can enter into another's feelings,
interests, and thoughts. But in the new romantic literature
and philosophy, said the critics, "subjectivity" had run ram-
pant. Literature had begun to express the private fantasies
and associations of individuals rather than the common elements
in human nature. For these critics, in other words, the universal in human nature was closely associated with popular standards of usage and taste.[99] Bushnell, by contrast, did not
identify the universal with the popular. The universal in
humanity is the image of God. And given humanity's fallen
estate, this norm of taste and character is extraordinary rather
than ordinary. Bushnell was therefore willing to give difficult
writing the benefit of the doubt. An author may exceed our
grasp, he held, because he is closer to the norm than we are.
What confounds us may be his spiritual superiority, manifested
in the strangeness of his words. The problem of understanding
then is a problem of spiritual culture. The interpreter must
somehow "draw himself into the same position" as the author.[100]

Bushnell conceived the "discipline of life" associated
with the understanding of expressive language on the model of
how one comes to understand a difficult writer. The difficult
writer stands "above" us and beckons us to join him. Our problem is to extend our sympathy so as to realize the possibility
of experience he offers. The means of this discipline or
culture are two-fold. To an extent, we can make an advance by
our own efforts, purifying and clarifying our vision through
study and reflection. But even more, the author himself must
assist us through the educative art of the work--"the wondrous
art by which some men are able to propitiate and assist the
generative understanding of others, so as to draw them readily
into higher realizations of the truth."[101] The spiritual culture of the understanding thus combines active and passive
moments. The interpreter must be receptive to the leadings of
the spirit expressed in the work, and he must also work to prepare his receptivity by study and analysis.

Everything that Bushnell said about understanding the
difficult writer applies quintessentially to understanding the
self-expressions of God. God is the difficult author *par*

excellence. His inward life exceeds ours in quality as far as any possibly could. He sets the norm of all character and identity. Therefore, the "conditions of character" required to understand his expressions--in nature or history, in Scripture, and in Christ--are no less than the perfections of the divine life itself. In short, man must participate in the divine life in order to have "sympathy" with God. There should be nothing surprising in this requirement, said Bushnell, for it is perfectly in accord with the common laws of expression.

> If it requires a degree of sympathy, generously extended and for a length of time, to allow us to come into the whole sphere of another, and feel out, in a manner, the real import of his words, before we can be sure that we understand him, it ought not to be a hard necessity that a like sympathy with God is requisite to make any true doctrine of God, whether in the words of man or of Scripture, intelligible and clear to the mind.[102]

This may not be a "hard necessity," but it does make the problem of the "discipline of life" rather sticky. For it follows from the principle that "this condition of sympathy requires a large infusion of the Divine Spirit, which is itself a divine experience and an immediate knowledge."[103] To understand God, one must already participate in his nature. And what can any amount of self-discipline on the part of fallen man do to meet this condition?

Bushnell's answer involved the same blending of active and passive moments we found in his approach to the difficult writer. On the one hand, the interpreter must actively cultivate whatever seed of sympathy with the divine nature that he already has by virtue of his humanity. Fallen man is alienated from God, Bushnell held, but he has not lost all resemblence to the divine nature. For instance, all persons are capable of love, which Bushnell calls a "true interpreter" of the divine: "He that loveth knoweth God, for God is love."[104] By cultivating this inherent power of insight, then, human persons can grow into greater intimacy with God, realizing that "immediate, experimental knowledge of God, by virtue of which, and partly in degree of which, Christian theology is possible."[105] On the other hand, Bushnell insisted that ultimately the only way to enter the life of God is to take a purely receptive attitude toward his expressions:

> giving ourselves to truth as set before us in
> living expressions, under God's own forms, yielding
> them a pure heart in which to glass themselves,
> would fill us evermore with senses of God and
> his truth otherwise unattainable.[106]

Interpretation thus requires one "to offer a living ingenuous heart to what God expresses to us," "an imagination that is open and a living and believing heart."[107] This he elsewhere calls the way of faith.[108]

If theology is to aid in the "discipline of life," then, it must contribute to the realization of those conditions of character that make a living knowledge of God possible. Theology, as a discipline of the mind and heart, must become one with the practice of the presence of God. Bushnell sensed that the goal was possible:

> we can know God as being with us and in us,
> filling our argumentations, opening to us the
> senses and powers of words, imparting himself
> to our secret experience as the light of all
> seeing . . . .[109]

However, he was obliged to point out that theology's resources for the task are limited. Theology can never become "Divinity." "Divinity" in Bushnell's usage is the immediate participation of the divine nature in the soul of man, the very stuff of Christian piety.

> It is that influx and intergrowth of the divine
> nature that is consciously experienced, when
> every inlet of the soul is opened by love, and
> faith, and prayer, and holy living, and patient
> waiting upon God. It is interpretation made by
> experience,--a knowledge had of God through the
> medium of consciousness, and resembling the
> knowledge we get of ourselves in the same manner;
> or . . . it is not a doctrine or system of
> doctrine, but a Living State, the Life of God
> in the soul of man.[110]

"Theology," by contrast, is the discursive, reasoned presentation of religious consciousness. A theology based on genuine Divinity may be called Christian theology; a theology based on merely natural consciousness is sheer speculation.[111] But in neither case does theology constitute a definitive body of knowledge of God. The only real knowledge of God is Divinity itself. Theology, insofar as it suffers under the limits of language, always contains something "undivine."

Bushnell's enthusiasm for theology was thus rather severely qualified. His most frequent comments on theology, in fact, were almost uniformly scornful. For example, he loved to reiterate that precision in theology is pretense. Theological systems are "soap-bubble worlds, rising by their own levity."[112] Systems appear substantial only because

> the dogmatizer solidifies the smoke he is in,
> by the concentrating force of his dullness;
> becoming the most precise of teachers, because
> he is so mystified by his own vagueness, that
> he hews it into solid blocks of knowledge.[113]

Dogmatic theology has one redeeming feature, albeit an ironic one: it is its own gravedigger. That is, the futility of the effort of theological construction gradually awakens us to the real character of theological language, and the proper means of receiving its truth.

> [I]n so many dialectic buildings and destruc-
> tions, our mind is sharpened, by what we suffer,
> to a closer, keener inspection of the forms of
> truth, and gradually convinces itself, by its
> own miscarriages, that real truth is to be found
> only by insight, and never by the extempore
> clatter of logical judgements.[114]

This may seem like faint praise, but it does show that Bushnell had reservations about rejecting theological systems out of hand. In several passages, he insisted on the practical value of theological system-building, or on the value of the powers of mind that motivate it. "System is the instinct of intelligence," he wrote, implying that it should not be suppressed; "to crucify the instinct of system is, in one view, to crucify the intelligence."[115] Likewise, Bushnell repeatedly praised theology as an exercise in discernment, valuable quite apart from its dubious concrete results.[116] But Bushnell also allowed that there is some value in the systems themselves. Rightly employed, they can be useful as guides to the spiritual life, "pocket systems of the infinite." They accomodate our ignorance, not so much in order to lift us into truth as to put a restaining weight on our fancy. As he put it in one of his finest images, theological systems

> are to the disciple what the iris is to the
> eye, drawing its opaque and variously-colored
> curtains round the aperture of sight, that only
> just so much of the light may enter as will make
> the tiny picture within distinct and clear.[117]

Theology, then, can have instrumental value as an aid to immediate spiritual insight; it serves as a schoolmaster for
"Divinity," not so much by what it does as by what it fails to
do. Even more positively stated, "the instinct of system, and
a certain actual determination towards it are, in one view,
necessary conditions of insight and true interpretation."[118]
The partial blindness attendant on mankind's fall is thus,
paradoxically, a means to mankind's restoration, serving to
clarify the image whose power is the power of redemption.

What Bushnell was trying to work out through these complex
qualifications is a comprehensive attitude toward the theological past. His own researches had led him to believe that an
educative theology--an authentic discipline of the knowledge
of God--would have to be something quite different from what
had formerly passed under the name. The logical measures of
men's minds cannot handle the things of God. But Bushnell's
reservations about theological logomachy did not carry him all
the way to a rejection of intellectual methods in favor of form-
less sentiment, as commentators frequently suggest.[119] Bushnell's was not the temperament to say, with Melville, "To the
dogs with the head!"[120] Bushnell wanted to do theology. But
he wanted to do it in such a way as to minimize the head/heart
tensions that he, along with his culture, so often perceived.
The theory of communication, in its developed form as a theory
of language, showed him a way to proceed. By stating theological problems as problems of understanding and interpretation,
he could at once solve them in a new way and demonstrate their
immediate relevance to experience, according to "the close relationship of God's revelation with the inlet function to which
they are given."[121]

To sum up, Bushnell believed that theology will begin to
play an educative role in the life of the spirit when it achieves
a just sense of the limits and expressive potentials of language.
The discovery will change theological practice in certain respects. The true theologian, using Divinity as a touchstone,
will test all doctrines to see if they retain a genuine power
to stimulate the growth of character. Some doctrines will be
abandoned as "scholastic rubbish;" other will prove to have
lasting relevance "as a re-acting basis for the mind, in

climbing into a divine experience."[122] Theology carried on in
this fashion will have no proper "method" at all besides the
method of receptivity or insight. Aware of its instrumental
role, it will not pretend to precision or definitiveness. It
will thus be more open to changing forms of expression, and
more willing to use expressive language itself in a direct,
unanalyzed way. Theology, it might be said, will become more
like preaching in its use of symbols for their effect rather
than their scientific value. But at base, it will still be the
same kind of enterprise as the old theology. The theologian
is inevitably a headworker who more or less indirectly serves
the interests of the heart. Bushnell's theologian, like the
poet in Wallace Stevens' adage, "represents the mind in the
act of defending us against itself."[123] The more consciously
this is done, the better. But even the most benighted past
theologians played this role to some degree in what they did
to preserve and clarify the force of expressive images. Thus,
the same principle by which Bushnell prescribed a new way of
doing theology allowed him to give qualified approval to the
tradition.

Bushnell employed his theory of language, then, to reconcile a tension common to his own biography and the cultural
situation reflected in the controversy between orthodoxy and
Unitarianism: the tension between inherited tradition and
the immediate interests of human character development.
Bushnell was alive to the claims of the past on the human
personality; he affirmed that persons are products of the past,
and that they cannot sever contact with their social and historical conditions without loss. On the other hand, the inner
life of each individual advances its own claims to be expressed,
and expressed anew. Solidarity and originality are values with
equal merit. Many thinkers in Bushnell's age wrestled with a
similar ambivalence. Bushnell's solution to it was one of the
most sophisticated. He dealt with the tensions between past
and present, memory and hope, in the context of language as a
medium of character development. The past of language shapes
human personality in the present, calling out its capacities
in accordance with the resources of the tradition. Persons, in
turn, use language to express their innermost experience.

Tradition and self-realization are thus co-efficient values.
Language transmits, and is in turn transformed: "The future
must be of the past, and the past must create a future."[124]
The "bigot" who insists that the future be identical with the
past and the "radical" who would discard the past are equally
mistaken. As Bushnell wrote to James Freeman Clarke, it would
take both a bigot and a radical--both an orthodox man and a
Unitarian--to make a whole person or a whole Christian.

The solution to the complex problems of human experience
lies not in any simple formula, then, but in the complex interactions of opposed claims on man's allegiance. Past and present, history and transcendence, must all be allowed to exert
their force. For it is with persons as it is with language.
The truth will not be formed by destroying contradictory energies, but by following them to their end,

> offering our mind to their impressions and
> allowing it to gravitate inwardly toward the
> truth in which they coalesce.[125]

NOTES

CHAPTER IV

[1]Bushnell, *God in Christ* (Hartford: Brown & Parsons, 1849), p. 11.

[2]Cheney, *Life and Letters of Horace Bushnell* (1880; rpt. New York: Arno Press, 1969), p. 203. This work will be cited hereafter as *LL*. See also p. xvii above, n. 1.

[3]See Chapter III, n. 53 above.

[4]See Bushnell, *Views of Christian Nurture* (1847; rpt. Delmar, N.Y.: Scholars' Facsimiles & Reprints, 1975), p. 97.

[5]See Bennet Tyler, *Letters to the Rev. Horace Bushnell* (Hartford: Brown & Parsons, 1848), pp. 17-20.

[6]*LL*, pp. 191-93, 445.

[7]*Ibid.*, p. 192.

[8]*Ibid.*, p. 193.

[9]*Ibid.*, p. 191.

[10]Bushnell, "Pure Love," MS Yale Divinity School Library.

[11]Bushnell, "Christ the Form of the Soul," MS Yale Divinity School Library. An abridgement of the sermon is included in a posthumous collection of Bushnell's papers, *The Spirit in Man* (New York: Charles Scribner's Sons, 1910), pp. 39-51. Our references are to the MS.

[12]*Ibid.*, p. 7.

[13]*Ibid.*, p. 1.

[14]*Ibid.*, pp. 7-8. My italics.

[15]*Ibid.*, p. 9.

[16]*Ibid.*, p. 18.

[17]*Ibid.*, pp. 10-11.

[18]*Ibid.*, p. 33.

[19]*Ibid.*, pp. 61-62.

[20]Bushnell, *God in Christ*, p. 101.

[21]Channing's "Unitarian Christianity" is the quintessential expression of the movement's position in that age. See Channing, *Works* (Boston: American Unitarian Association, 1897), pp. 367-84.

[22]Lewis, *The American Adam* (Chicago: University of Chicago Press, 1955), pp. 7, 28-32. Lewis has shown that these attitudes typify a dialogue that was being conducted on virtually every level of American culture in the early nineteenth century. It is not surprising, then, to find that Bushnell mirrors this ambivalence in his own character, in the tension between allegiance to the past and self-reliant ambition we noted in Chapter I.

[23]Bushnell, Letter to James Freeman Clarke, Hartford, August 30, 1847. MS the Houghton Library of Harvard University.

[24]*God in Christ*, p. 99.

[25]*Ibid.*, p. 100.

[26]*Ibid.*

[27]*Ibid.*, p. 110.

[28]Bushnell, Letter to Clarke, Hartford, August 30, 1847.

[29]*Ibid.* See also *God in Christ*, p. 99.

[30]*Ibid.*

[31]Bushnell, *God in Christ*, p. 14.

[32]Bushnell, "Christian Comprehensiveness," *The New Englander*, VI (January 1848), p. 87.

[33]"Our Gospel a Gift to the Imagination" appeared first in *Hours at Home*, X (December 1869), pp. 159-72. It was reprinted in *Building Eras in Religion* (New York: Charles Scribner's Sons, 1910). All subsequent references to this essay will be to *Building Eras*.

[34]Bushnell, *God in Christ*, p. 12.

[35]See Coleridge, *Aids to Reflection*, 4th London edition, (1840; rpt. Port Washington, N.Y.: Kennikat Press, 1971), p. 65.

[36]For a modern version of the position that a symbol's meaning emerges from the reader's "engagement" or interaction with it, see L.C. Knights, "Idea and Symbol: Some Hints from Coleridge," in *Further Explorations* (London: Chatto, 1965), pp. 155-68.

[37]Bushnell, *God in Christ*, p. 13.

[38]*Ibid.*

[39]For a fine survey of technical objections raised against Bushnell's theory of language, see Crosby, *Horace Bushnell's Theory of Language* (The Hague: Mouton, 1975), pp. 229-82.

[40]Bushnell, *God in Christ*, p. 17.

[41]*Ibid.*, pp. 26-29. Bushnell's authorities for the idea that nouns are the basic form of language are Horne Tooke and Josiah Willard Gibbs, Sr. On Gibbs, see Chapter II, n. 27 above.

[42]Willard Quine makes the point that even when experiences are shared, synonymy is not assured. We mention this only as one of the more interesting of the myriad objections that can be raised against Bushnell's theory. See Quine, "Meaning and Translation," in *Problems in the Philosophy of Language*, ed. Thomas Olshewsky, (New York: Holt, Reinhart & Winston, Inc., 1969), pp. 517-37.

[43]*God in Christ*, pp. 24-25, 51-53. Many of Bushnell's examples of etymology also appear in Gibbs, *Philological Studies* (New Haven: Durie & Peck, 1857), pp. 14-16.

[44]Bushnell, *Christ in Theology* (Hartford: Brown & Parsons, 1851), p. 33.

[45]Bushnell, *God in Christ*, pp. 21-22.

[46]*Ibid.*, p. 30.

[47]*Christ in Theology*, p. 36.

[48]Wayland, "Discourse on the Philosophy of Analogy," in *American Philosophical Addresses, 1700-1900*, ed. Joseph Blau, (New York: Columbia University Press, 1946), p. 353.

[49]*God in Christ*, p. 28.

[50]*Christ in Theology*, p. 31.

[51]*God in Christ*, p. 30. For Bushnell, this principle spelled liberation from what he regarded as a bankrupt tradition of natural theology. Whereas natural theology in Bushnell's age sought to infer God's existence from "evidences of Christianity" in the intelligent design of the world, Bushnell found an expressive power in the unanalyzed facts of nature which, to his mind, constituted its own evidence. Persons are "always in the presence of divine thoughts and meanings;" God

> stands EXPRESSED every where, so that, turn whichsoever way we please, we behold the out-looking of His intelligence. No series of Bridgewater treatises, piled even to the moon, could give a proof of God so immediate, complete, and conclusive.

See *ibid.*, pp. 31, 36.

[52]*Ibid.*, p. 39.

[53]*Christ in Theology*, p. 16. A close modern parallel to Bushnell's distinction is Philip Wheelwright's distinction of "steno-language" and "expressive language." See Wheelwright,

The Burning Fountain (Bloomington: Indiana University Press, 1968), pp. 3-17.

[54]*Christ in Theology*, p. 17.

[55]*God in Christ*, p. 46.

[56]Bushnell, *Building Eras*, p. 252.

[57]Frequently, several of these terms are clustered together. Linkages are established by usage, making the terms rough equivalents of each other. For example, see *Building Eras*, p. 252; *Christ in Theology*, p. 39.

[58]*Building Eras*, p. 252; see also *God in Christ*, p. 24.

[59]For the relations between impression and expression, see Bushnell, "The Gospel of the Face," in *Sermons on Living Subjects* (New York: Charles Scribner's Sons, 1907), p. 366.

[60]*God in Christ*, p. 78.

[61]*Ibid.*, p. 46.

[62]One of Nevin's most telling criticisms of Bushnell's "Discourses" was that Bushnell failed to distinguish between the "ground" of a fact and its "occasion" in discussing the possibility of human virtue. Bushnell slid too easily, he held, between the observation that a receptivity to the divine self-communication has been prepared or "occasioned" in Christians by their education and the assumption that the capacity for reception is grounded in their participation in the divine nature. "Educational Religion," *The Weekly Messenger of the German Reformed Church*, XII, New Series, July 7, 1847.

[63]*God in Christ*, p. 46.

[64]*Ibid.*, p. 46.

[65]*Building Eras*, p. 267.

[66]See Nathaniel Taylor's treatment of "law" in *Lectures on the Moral Government of God* (New York: Clark, Austin and Smith, 1859), vol. II, p. 152.

[67]Bushnell believed that a few terms in the intellectual department have precise meaning: the "necessary ideas" of "space, cause, truth, right, arithmetical numbers, and geometrical figures." *God in Christ*, p. 46. These were noted, not because Bushnell believed that precision was an attainable ideal in intellectual language, but simply as exceptions that prove the rule of its generally figurative character.

[68]*Christ in Theology*, p. 40.

[69]*God in Christ*, p. 47.

[70]*Christ in Theology*, p. 16.

[71]Quoted in Williston Walker, "Dr. Bushnell as a Religious Leader," *Bushnell Centenary* (Hartford: Hartford Press, The Case, Lockwood & Brainard Company, 1902), p. 22.

[72]*God in Christ*, pp. 48-49.

[73]*Ibid.*, p. 52.

[74]*Ibid.*, p. 63.

[75]*Ibid.*, p. 64. Bushnell did not mean that the organic metaphor is any more literal than the mechanical; he meant only that we have a wide range of optional analogies to choose from, and that the organic analogy is a more appropriate vehicle for the case at hand.

[76]Bushnell's version of this point is that because demonstrative proof is impossible where expressive language is involved, doubt can never be stopped; it can only be "dissolved." See "The Dissolving of Doubts," in *Sermons on Living Subjects* (New York: Charles Scribner's Sons, 1890), pp. 170-71.

[77]Bushnell was also aware that even referential language has only a qualified precision, because its terms refer to generals, not individuals. He got this point from Alexander Bryan Johnson's *A Treatise on Language* (1828 & 1836), ed. David Rynin, (Berkeley: University of California Press, 1959).

[78]Bushnell did not believe that knowledge of truth is ever "intuitive" in the sense that it is available to minds independent of any act of communication. When he said that "we may directly intuit truth, without symbols or representations of language," he meant only that the content of a communicated truth, once it is conveyed into the mind, is possessed in consciousness independent of the symbols that convey it. See *Christ in Theology*, p. 15. See also "The Immediate Knowledge of God," *Sermons on Living Subjects*, pp. 114-28: "we should know God himself as a presence operative in us; even as we know the summer heat by its pervasive action in our bodies."

[79]*God in Christ*, p. 46.

[80]*Ibid.*, p. 69.

[81]*Ibid.*

[82]*Ibid.*, p. 74.

[83]*Ibid.*, p. 55.

[84]*Ibid.*, p. 144.

[85]It was his position on creeds more than anything else that made *God in Christ* notorious among the orthodox. See *ibid.*, pp. 81-82. The same position is upheld in *Christ in Theology*, pp. 53-55.

[86]*God in Christ*, p. 80.

[87]*Ibid.*

[88]*Ibid.*, pp. 81-82.

[89]*Ibid.*, p. 74.

[90]*Ibid.*

[91]*Christ in Theology*, p. 33; *God in Christ*, p. 69.

[92]Bushnell's stress on the "wholeness" of a work here epitomizes his characteristic drive to comprehend contraries within
the unity of his lived experience. A "real man," he said, can
only be described by all the possible representations of his
experience: "the only way to make up a real man is to put
the whole dictionary into him." Likewise, the only way to make
a whole Christian is to put the whole Bible into him, filling
his mind with all the contrary values of spiritual life--bondage
and freedom, history and transcendence--and "allowing it to
gravitate inwardly towards that whole of truth in which they
coalesce." *God in Christ*, pp. 73, 71.

[93]*Christ in Theology*, p. 30.

[94]Cross, *Horace Bushnell* (Chicago: University of Chicago
Press, 1958), pp. 101-02. Cross entirely misunderstands Bushnell on this point. She mistakes his belief that the advancement of science will precipitate greater depth and power in
figurative language for a hope that figurative language will
someday be replaced by literal speech. For Bushnell's own
explicit attempts to avoid this misinterpretation, see "Revelation;" *God in Christ*, pp. 78-79, 308-09; *Building Eras*, pp.
271-72; *Christ in Theology*, pp. 29-32; *Nature and the Supernatural* (1858; rpt. New York: AMS Press, 1973), pp. 523-28.
See also Crosby, *op. cit.*, pp. 174-75n.

[95]*Christ in Theology*, p. 66.

[96]*God in Christ*, p. 86.

[97]*Christ in Theology*, p. 65.

[98]Bushnell seems to have had in mind his own experience in
reading Coleridge. Compare *God in Christ*, p. 87, with *LL*,
p. 208.

[99]See William Charvat, *The Origins of American Critical
Thought*, pp. 7-26.

[100]*God in Christ*, p. 89; *LL*, p. 208.

[101]*God in Christ*, p. 88.

[102]*Christ in Theology*, p. 65.

[103]*Ibid.*, pp. 65-66.

[104]*Ibid.*, p. 40.

[105]*God in Christ*, p. 93.

[106]*Christ in Theology*, p. 32.

[107]*Ibid.*

[108]*God in Christ*, p. 111.

[109]*Christ in Theology*, p. 66.

[110]*Ibid.*, p. 83.

[111]*Ibid.*, pp. 83-84. On pp. 84-87 of this work, he states his basic approval of Richard Roethe's attempt to ground theology in Christian consciousness. He knew of Roethe only from the 19 pages of translation that were appended to John Morell's *Philosophy of Religion* (New York: D. Appleton & Co., 1849), pp. 340-59.

[112]*Christ in Theology*, p. 73.

[113]*Ibid.*, p. 71.

[114]*Ibid.*, p. 22.

[115]*Ibid.*, p. 64.

[116]*God in Christ*, p. 82; *Christ in Theology*, pp. 80, 86.

[117]*Christ in Theology*, p. 80.

[118]*Ibid.*, p. 81.

[119]See for instance Cross, *op. cit.*, p. 11; Clebsch, *American Religious Thought* (Chicago: University of Chicago Press, 1973), pp. 115-16, 120.

[120]Quoted in Leo Marx, *The Machine in the Garden* (London: Oxford University Press, 1964), p. 278.

[121]Bushnell, *Building Eras*, p. 263.

[122]*Christ in Theology*, p. 87.

[123]Wallace Stevens, "Adagia," in *Opus Posthumous* (New York: Alfred A. Knopf, 1957), p. 174.

[124]Bushnell, "Christian Comprehensiveness," *The New Englander*, VI (January 1848), p. 87.

[125]*God in Christ*, p. 71.

CHAPTER V

THE ATONEMENT:

SYMBOLISM AND GROWTH

After his spiritual crisis of 1848, Bushnell set out to
explore the theological implications of his theory of interpersonal communication. His goal, as we have seen, was at
once conservative and progressive. He felt a strong attachment to traditional Christian language and yet sought to make
ancient doctrines freshly intelligible by showing their congruence with the natural "laws of expression" through which
persons communicate thought and influence in society. Several
doctrines seemed to translate easily into the terms of his
theory. The doctrine of the trinity could be interpreted by
the general law that several contradictory forms of expression
may be necessary to drive an interpreter's mind to a single
expressed truth. The incarnation became comprehensible in the
light of the presumed fact that concrete images always serve
as the vehicles of invisible, spiritual meanings.[1] Above all
others, however, the doctrine of the atonement seemed to Bushnell to be the connecting link between the theological past
and his own vision of divine-human relations. The subject matter of the atonement, Bushnell believed, was no less than the
ways and means of the "Divine Husbandry," the continuing work
of God to draw us into communion with himself. The clue to
the process was given, in turn, by the principle that whatever
Christ does for the redemption of mankind, he does as an expressive symbol. Christ awakens our dead receptivities through the
expressive power of his character and biography, and so con-
forms us to the divine spirit that is the necessary precondition
of our ability to understand him. The doctrine of the atonement
thus gave Bushnell a broad compass in which to develop his
theory of communication as a diagnosis and prescription for the
human spiritual condition.

In a sense, the story of the final 28 years of Bushnell's
career is the story of his gradually enlarging reflections on
the atonement. His first major project after his spiritual

crisis of 1848 was an address on the atonement delivered at
Harvard. The book in which the address was published, *God in
Christ*, gained Bushnell an immediate reputation as a theological
innovator and, it was suggested, a heretic. In general, New
England theologians judged that the old wine had not survived
transfer into Bushnell's new bottles.[2] To answer charges of
heresy, Bushnell wrote another book in 1851, *Christ in Theology*,
again including a long section on the atonement. The second
book was not the least bit conciliatory; it retreated from
none of his former positions. Nevertheless, his local minister-
ial association found it acceptable, and there the matter should
have ended. But Connecticut's more conservative preachers were
not yet appeased. Harassment continued for several years.
Ministers throughout Connecticut refused Bushnell the common
courtesy of exchanging pulpits; their attitude towards him in
public was cold and distrustful.[3]

Bushnell, who had no original intention of isolating himself, felt this enforced isolation keenly. And along with the
sense of isolation went a deepening self-doubt. He knew that
he had taken risks in *God in Christ*. His correlation of the
Christian redemptive economy with the presumed laws of expressive communication was, after all, a personal insight, nurtured
in private rather than in the ring of public debate. Therefore,
the frequently leveled charge of "subjective delusion" had
some power to unsettle him. Where, after all, could he find
fellow spirits? His acquaintance with European liberal theology
was too meager for him to feel anything but a hint of community
there. He felt kinship with no local theological party, salon,
or sub-culture. And while the friends who stuck by him were
warm, they were, with a few exceptions, uncomprehending.[4] So,
with no external props for his confidence, nothing in his inward life seemed to retain the power of truth it once had. He
felt haunted by "an angel of dryness; . . . one that lets me
eat and work, and bids me go on, but laughs all the while at
the foolish figure I make."[5] If his former harmonious engagement with Christianity had been the charm that allowed him "to
sufficiently be," this new, uncharacteristic self-consciousness
left him unable to "be, or more than half be, anybody."[6] As a
result, "I have become wholly dissatisfied with myself."

Finally, as a kind of objective correlate to this crisis of identity, his health failed. A collapse in 1852 initiated a long series of rest cures and travels, interspersed with bouts with a vaguely tubercular lung disease.[7] Acquaintances in later life remembered him as robust and active, but in fact, he never fully recovered his health.

Buhsnell eventually recovered his psychic equilibrium, however, by means of simple patience towards his persistent doubts and debilities. This quality of his mind can be illustrated by an address on "The Dissolving of Doubt" in which the patient turned therapist, offering advice to the young on how to handle their own spiritual crises. He argued that because the truths of religion and life are of the expressive sort, they are never logically necessary. All of the most important truths, in fact, are inherently dubitable. Doubts can never be stopped. But they can be "dissolved" by a process of spiritual culture that brings one into immediate consciousness of the realities behind the indemonstrable truth.[8] This process of growth is slow, he allowed, but he was confident that for all sincere persons, it would be sure. He had found in the past, and continued to find throughout his life, that out of these periods of wise irresolution "new light" would dawn. Sometimes the dawns were false. The "devil of invention, ingenuity, discovery" could masquerade as an angel of light.[9] But even the chance of self-delusion could be met with a human tolerance for uncertainty, or with what is probably best described as a sense of humor.

> Perhaps our new seeing in such matters is, at times, but our mood; and yet perhaps our mood may be our gift of seeing.[10]

When new light did dawn for Bushnell, it came in the form of fresh insights into the doctrine of the atonement. His lifelong preoccupation with the nature of human community, stirred perhaps by his personal isolation and certainly by his sense of the tragedy and redemptive promise of the American Civil War,[11] gave the impulse for his major work on the subject, *The Vicarious Sacrifice Grounded in Principles Interpreted by Human Analogies*, published in 1866. As the book's title suggests, his aim here was to demonstrate the congruence between the redemptive work of Christ and more familiar forms of human interaction. He did not believe that the atonement could be "reduced" to natural

facts and processes. But as a general rule, he was convinced
that unless a doctrine made a close approach to human nature--
appealing to man's immanent interests and sentiments--its transcendent significance could never become accessible. His chosen
task as a theologian was to discover and clarify appropriate
analogies for Scriptural truths, thus to bring the truth "so
much closer to the common life of men, and settle its hold just
so much more firmly on their convictions."[12] In his works on
Christian nurture, Bushnell had presented a practical key to
the traditional doctrines of native depravity and the "covenant
of Abraham" in the laws of communication and expression. In
The Vicarious Sacrifice, then, he set out to do something
similar. He believed he had discovered a connecting link between divine redemption and human growth in "vicarious love."
Like "character," vicarious love served in Bushnell's system as
a highest common factor of moral natures, and thus as a ground
of their possible communion.

   The Vicarious Sacrifice was followed in 1874 by the final
major work of Bushnell's career, *Forgiveness and Law*, which
pursued this line of thought a step further. It developed an
analogy between the psychology of human forgiveness and the
role of Christ's suffering in the atonement, intended as a translation of the orthodox concept of propitiation. His appropriation of yet another orthodox concept here represents no fundamental change in the style or direction of his thought.
Forgiveness and Law simply pushed Bushnell's "new development"
of orthodoxy forward on a new front.[13]

   Bushnell's major works on the atonement, then, include the
relevant chapters of *God in Christ* and *Christ in Theology*, *The
Vicarious Sacrifice*,[14] and *Forgiveness and Law*. As we have
suggested, the doctrine they teach is cumulative, each work
complementing and extending the thought of the others.[15] We
will therefore treat Bushnell's works on the atonement simul-
taneously in this chapter. Our discussion of the themes of the
writings will follow the order in which Bushnell took them up
to a certain extent. But where a topic or theme receives attention in several of the works, as is often the case, we will draw
freely on all the available materials.

1. Objective Atonement and Subjective At-one-ment

As Bushnell saw it, the doctrine of the atonement defines not only the meaning of Christ's life and death, but the nature and means of all human spiritual growth. The value of the doctrine therefore, on his own principles, should lie in its power to clarify the norms of character and to inspire persons to attain them. By this standard, Bushnell weighed the theories of the atonement then current in New England and found them wanting. The orthodox theories were irrelevant; the Unitarian theory was insipid. A doctrine suited to enhance human spiritual experience should be neither. But Bushnell's attitude toward existing formulas was not totally negative. Both orthodox and Unitarian theories, he believed, had a germ of genuine intelligibility relative to human life. The Scriptural language of the orthodox formulas had an undeniable power to capture and move human sentiment. The Unitarians made their contribution, in turn, by portraying the atoning transaction in a straightforward and comprehensible way, as something done for man in accordance with God's unambiguous intentions. Bushnell's aim relative to the tradition, then, was to develop a view of the atonement free from previous errors but retaining the features that gave former doctrines their cogency.

Orthodox theories of the atonement current in Bushnell's day fell into two main classes: substitution or satisfaction theories and Grotian or governmental theories. Both types held that the atonement serves primarily to resolve a tension between justice and mercy in the mind of God. Their first premise was that sinful man richly deserves cosmic condemnation. But God is a loving God, who would forgive mankind if he could do so without violating the strict terms of his own justice. According to the satisfaction theory, God solves this problem by sending Christ to pay the debt of suffering due to his justice, thus leaving himself free to be merciful to mankind. Christ pays for our sins "vicariously" through his death, and so "purchases title" for our redemption. According to the Grotian theory, on the other hand, God sends Christ not to make a payment for human sin, but rather to show mankind that although God has determined to be merciful, he is still concerned that the law be upheld. In Christ's life and suffering death, God makes a powerful public declaration of his love of right and his abhorrence of sin. Thus, God "satisfies" his justice wholly by expressing his continued regard for the law, lest humanity should think it is being let off too easily.[16]

Unitarian thought about the atonement began from quite different premises, and reached quite different conclusions. God, it was held, is a purely good and benevolent being, a loving and lovely Father to mankind.[17] Indeed, God is eternally disposed to forgive man. There are no barriers or conflicts in God's nature to be overcome. Therefore, Christ's work is understood to be entirely for mankind's moral benefit, not a device for resolving a mysterious intra-divine ambivalence. Christ comes to draw mankind into oneness of character with God; his moral teaching and his exemplary behavior serve, as William Ellery Channing wrote, "as the means of purifying the mind, of changing it into the likeness of his celestial excellence."[18] The Unitarians held, in short, that the atonement is a matter of moral pedagogy. Atonement is at-one-ment with God, achieved through the cultivation of the character. Christ's suffering and death help make his moral teachings impressive, but they are otherwise irrelevant to his work. Therefore, it was held, the traditional language of atonement theory--the language of sacrifice, propitiation, and penal suffering--is wholly inappropriate and should no longer be used.

Bushnell's objections to these existing theories define the territory on which he planned to build his own doctrine of the atonement. On the one hand, he rejected orthodox theories because they represented the atonement as something remote from the dynamics of human moral growth. Christ, said Bushnell, does not come to earth to balance God's ledgers; rather, "the end of his mission is declared to be a moral effect, wrought in the mind of the race."[19] Thus, Bushnell was at one with the Unitarians in his belief that the end of the atonement must be "to bring men into union with God, to reconcile them unto God."[20] Its object must be to produce character.[21] On the other hand, Bushnell objected strongly to the Unitarian conclusion that the traditional language of Scripture and doctrine should be scrapped. The orthodox doctrines may be misleading, he allowed, but they have proved their tremendous

power to mold Christian character and to inspire believers and
martyrs throughout the centuries. Thus, there must be some
"power of divine life" in the orthodox representation of the
case which any genuine doctrine should try to "reclaim and restore."[22] Bushnell therefore set out to frame his doctrine so
as to balance or comprehend the interests of subjective relevance and objective efficacy.

> All that is real and essential to the power of
> this orthodox doctrine of atonement, however
> held, I hope to set forth as the DIVINE FORM
> of Christianity, assigning it a place where it
> may still reveal its efficacy . . . .[23]

When Bushnell wrote his first essay on the atonement in
1848, he believed he had discovered a way to combine these interests. A double view of the atonement could be maintained,
he held, in which the traditional representations of the atonement could be understood as means to a subjective at-one-ment,
just as figurative vehicles served as the means of intersubjective understanding in expressive communication. The atonement,
that is, could be understood as an expressive transaction between God and man, operating on the same principles as human
communication and likewise reaching its end in the shaping of
human character.

Bushnell found warrant for this approach in Scripture; or
rather, he found it in the very diversity of Scriptural pro-
nouncements on the atonement. On the one hand, he held,
Scripture gives a subjective account of the atonement, one
designed to have an inward, transforming effect on the reader.
It tells the simple, tragic story of Jesus' life and death by
means of narrative art--i.e. in a way that has a powerful effect
on the reader's feeling and sensibility. Moving on the feelings,
it awakens the divine thoughts and sentiments that Christ him-
self--and God in Christ--expresses. Thus, as a simply portrayal
of the life and suffering of Jesus, Scripture shapes the inward character in Christ's image; "it proposes to connect us
with the Life of God."[24] The atonement on the subjective side,
in sum, is an expressive transaction in which God communicates
himself to man in an especially forceful way. On the other hand,
Bushnell also recognized an objective representation of the
atonement in Scripture, "objective" in the sense that it depicted Christ's work as a transaction between the Son and the

Father having no immediate, subjective impact on mankind.
Christ is represented under the language of Hebrew sacrifice
as an expiation, a propitiation, an offering, a substitute
offered to God--terms which Bushnell called the "altar form"
of the gospel.[25]

    At first glance, said Bushnell, these two approaches to
the atoning work of Christ seem contradictory. His argument
throughout his works on the atonement, however, was that they
are not really so.

> I design to show that, if the first or sub-
> jective view of Christ, that in which I state
> the end and aim of Christ's work, is true, that
> end or aim could not be effectively realized
> without the second, or objective view, in
> which his whole work is conceived in the altar
> form, and held forth to the objective embrace
> and worship and repose of faith.[26]

Objective atonement can be reconciled with subjective at-one-
ment, that is, if the former can be seen as a vehicle for the
latter, expressing and communicating divine consciousness just
as images serve as vehicles of mind in expressive language.

    Bushnell sought to demonstrate the practical consistency
of these two modes of expression by depicting the objective,
altar form of the atonement as God's "art:"

> a power moving upon man, through [the aesthetic]
> department of his nature, both to regenerate
> his degraded perception of excellence, and also
> to communicate in that way, the fulness and
> beauty of God.[27]

The artfulness of the Scriptures is apparent in two connections,
said Bushnell. First, just as all artists and all genuinely
original minds find that they must stretch the resources of
language and, in a sense, create a new language to express
their insights, so we find God preparing a new "language" for
what he intends to express in Christ through his providential
control of the events recorded in the Old Testament histories.
The meaning of Christ's life and death is so novel, said Bushnell, that no figure in natural language could adequately suggest it. Therefore God, the Author of nature and history, gave
the Jews a religion in which a new language and a corresponding
set of sentiments was prepared "to serve as metaphors of the
new salvation when it should come."[28] For example, ritual
sacrifice was instituted to teach man how painstaking self-

purification and selfless worship could produce the sense of release from sin. So, when Christ was put to death on earth, the complex associations of the concept of "sacrifice," schooled into human culture through the ancient rite, gave a meaning and impressiveness to his death that it could not otherwise have had.[29] Mankind had no analogies in natural experience by which to make the kind of release from sin effected by Christ intelligible and moving. Therefore God instituted the necessary forms for thought through the providential manipulation of history. He instituted rites and "altar forms" as "types" of Christ--i.e. as the vehicles of which Christ and the divine life he expressed were the content. In themselves, the rites only "foreshadow" Christ. But without them, the redemptive significance of God in Christ could never have been communicated. They are "the DIVINE FORM of Christianity . . . substantial to it, or consubstantial with it."[30] Accordingly, God, like any great artist, cannot be translated. His genius comes down to us through the mark he has left on the language and culture of the race. One cannot change what is special in his "language" without losing the self-communication thus artfully prepared. We are led into the author's meaning only by attending to it, never by trying to explain it away.

A second sense in which art was presumed to facilitate the growth of character gave Bushnell an additional rationale for retaining the altar form of Scripture. As we noted in the previous chapter, Bushnell saw the problem of understanding unusual expressions, fresh metaphors, and "difficult writing" in general, as a problem of spiritual culture. An expression which goes over one's head requires one to transcend one's self in order to comprehend it, to grow beyond one's limits. What is more, he held, the greatest art also has an educative power to nurture the reader in the very qualities of character necessary to interpret it. It transforms its audience into the author's image through "the wondrous art by which some men are able to propitiate and assist the generative understanding of others, so as to draw them readily into higher realizations of truth."[31]

In Bushnell's opinion, a great deal of the power of Christianity to regenerate man's "degraded perception" depends on its

being a work of art in this sense. The very forms in which
Scripture communicates must somehow have power to open mankind
to communion with God. To show how the objective language of
Scripture can do this, he pointed out several ways in which
objective representations in general serve as means of
spiritual culture. First, he noted our "mental instinct" to
throw subjective impressions into objective representations.
We say "it is sweet" instead of "I have a sensation of sweet-
ness;" and we say "time is swift" instead of "our internal
states and successions transpire rapidly."[32] Similarly in religion: though the "truths" of religion are all subjective
impressions and inward states, mankind has always held these
truths under objective forms. The reason, he said, is simply
that the objective statement is punchier, more impressive, and
therefore more practical as a tool for communicating the subjective fact. "If we had none but subjective language, we
should even die of inanity."[33] Second, objective language can
serve as a means of spiritual culture simply by facilitating
self-forgetfulness. As Bushnell wrote in "Unconscious Influence,"
the most powerful influences on human identity are those that
work in an "unconscious," "implicit," and "latent" fashion.
Thus, he held here that the Scriptures employ artistic indirection as a vital part of their accommodation to human needs.

> [Man] wants a place where he can give himself
> away, without meeting any suggestive that shall
> carry him back into himself--an altar form whose
> art is so transcendent that all art is concealed,
> and no occuring thought of working on himself
> propels him backward on his old center. And
> here it is that the objective view of Christ
> holds a connection so profound, with all that
> is freest, most unselfish and most elevated in
> Christian experience.[34]

What mankind "wants," that is, is an object of faith, something
to be open and receptive to. Spiritual culture gets hopelessly
bogged down when it is approached as simple self-culture, he
held. Working constantly on ourselves, we only become more
preoccupied with self, and actually lose receptivity to inspirations from without.[35] But by giving ourselves to outside influences, new possibilities are opened.[36] Therefore, said
Bushnell, the Scriptures give mankind objective forms--and
plenty of them--suited to supply the soul's need for "some

objective power to engage his affection and be a higher nature, present, by which to elevate and assimilate his own."[37]

To sum up, the gospel is God's artful strategy for renewing a race that could not receive his self-communication without a special preparation. God prepares the historical forms of Scripture as vehicles of meaning--vehicles sufficiently impressive and sufficiently cryptic to engage our faith[38]--and so insinuates himself into our degraded perceptions to educate us in spite of ourselves. Persons are moved by representations of the divine on the level of self and history, but the "Divine Art hid in it, transforms their inner life, in the immediate, absolute manner of art."[39] This is the particular skill of the artist as educator. God the archetypal Author and the archetypal educator, simply exercises this skill to a superlative degree.[40]

Bushnell thus based his case that the objective and subjective elements in the work of redemption are mutually supportive on the assumption that the dynamics of spiritual culture reflect the ways in which we come to understand human expressions. Symbols, human and divine, become effective when we give them willing assent in the form of receptivity or faith, "giving our heart to the expression of integrity in the form."[41] The symbol thus received touches the roots of the will and reveals its meaning in the life-direction it fosters. It imports transforming energies into life that act on persons in and through their receptivity:

> winning faith, it works by the faith it wins;
> and so being trusted in, it makes trust a footing
> of life and character.[42]

Understood on this model, the objective and subjective views of the atonement are wholly complementary. The subjective account of the atonement as a change wrought in human consciousness focuses our active attention on human nature and human needs. The objective, "altar form" of the atonement is equally "true," on the other hand, insofar as it is required to meet the needs the subjective view acknowledges but cannot fulfil on its own. "The two views are not logically equivalent, but they are not the less really so on that account."[43] As in the case of terms in a paradox, the contradictory half-truths unite to drive the mind towards the one truth of experience that gave rise to them. Therefore,

> We must receive them all, objective and sub-
> jective, as they stand in the scripture, and
> use them as an inward ritual, designed to work
> in the heart their own transcendent life-
> giving impressions.[44]

2. Justice and Mercy

Just as Bushnell believed that a theory of the atonement
based on the analogy of expressive communication could accom-
modate both orthodox "objective" language and the Unitarian
aim of at-one-ment, so he believed that his understanding of
divine-human relations suggested a way to resolve the ancient
tension between justice and mercy--law and gospel--in the
Christian redemptive scheme. He allowed that justice and mercy
represented contradictory elements in the Christian understanding of God. But through his theory of language, he believed
he could show that such contradictory statements and acts can
be understood "comprehensively" as expressions of a single
intention. As a general rule for the interpretation of "difficult" writing, Bushnell held that the interpreter should
attempt to discover the underlying unity of the author's expressions before resorting to the conclusion that the author
was "at war" with himself. Given the tension between God's
justice and his mercy, then, Bushnell understood his task to be
to show how these two "expressions" of God were united under a
single controlling purpose. The theological problem, as he
saw it, was not to solve a puzzle but to show that, at base,
there was no puzzle to be solved.

Bushnell discussed two ways in which justice and mercy work
together, both of which reflect his understanding of the atonement as a process in which the divine life is communicated to
mankind through symbolic expressions. On the one hand, he saw
them working separately over time to restore human receptivity
to the divine. On the other, he saw them working in "radical
union," as complimentary vehicles of the divine character. We
will look at each approach in turn.

First, said Bushnell, God works progressively on mankind
over time because fallen man requires training in order to become redeemable. In the fall, mankind lost the receptive

sensibility by means of which God's redemptive self-communication could be embraced. Sin vitiates the sympathy between man
and God. And where there is no ground of sympathy between
communicating parties, there can be no receptivity, no communication.

> It is the misery and shame of bad minds under
> sin, that excellence and beauty, powerful as they
> still are over the sentiments of their higher
> nature not yet extirpated, are no longer suf-
> ficient, by themselves, to recover and restore
> the broken homage of their fall. They move on
> a point, too far above the plane of motivity
> occupied by sin, to control and subdue it.[45]

God's dilemma, then, is that if he wants to get through to man,
he must find a way sufficiently "artful" to "create the very
homage by which he is to be received."[46]

God will not simply force himself on man, said Bushnell,
because he has too much respect for freedom as an essential
quality of all moral nature. Therefore, God must appeal to
mankind by stealth. He must somehow use the forms of sinful
human experience to drive persons beyond themselves. This is
where retributive justice comes in. The message of divine
justice--that sin will be punished and virtue rewarded--grabs
man on the "plane of motivity" where he lives. Through guilt
and fear, it reawakens the buried and abused moral sense,
which is the ground of the possibility of human communication
with God.

Bushnell most frequently illustrated this process by reference to Christ's peculiar skills as a teacher. Christ's work
is an archetype of the problem of communicating the incommunicable:

> the world itself was a dead receptivity, and
> it was to be the glory of [Christ's] power,
> that he could open a receptivity where there
> was none.[47]

A principal reason for Christ's success in carrying through this
paradoxical mission, said Bushnell, is the strictness with
which he upholds the penal law. Christ was practical enough
to realize that fallen man will not be moved by a simple display of God's beauty and goodness--an appeal to man's higher
loves.

> A beginning has to be made, he clearly sees,
> with sin, at its own level; the level of guilty

apprehension, fear, selfishly interested forecast of the future.[48]

Therefore, Christ showed no scruples about playing on man's self-interest by "warnings and appeals of terror." For example, Christ taught a doctrine of eternal punishment without feeling any modern sentimental compunctions. But Christ's assertion of God's inexorable justice was never intended as an end in itself. He taught grotesqueries in order to startle mankind into receptivity.

> By this appalling law-work he breaks their security, startles their negligence, rouses their guiltiness into a ferment, and calls out the question, what shall we do?[49]

Thus, by means of ideas designed to grab what is lowest in man, Christ sought to awaken the sense of sin and right--the moral sense--which will prepare the ground for man's more direct appreciation and appropriation of God's excellence. "There must be law, conviction, judgement, fear taking hold of natures dead to love, and by this necessary first effect, preparing the way for love."[50]

Bushnell also illustrated the propaedeutic relations between justice and mercy by means of more homely examples of ethical training. Everywhere, he said, we find that a "two-factor method" is what works best "in almost every sort of training wanted for the advancement of our human state."[51]

In the home, children must first pass through a painful discipline of repression and restraint in order to reach the point where they will freely and spontaneously recognize that the parental law is essential to their own happiness.[52] In school, drill ideally gives way to the free love of learning. Likewise in the army and the civil state, repressive discipline is designed to result in a spontaneous harmony, in which the law fulfils the highest desires of every member.[53] Thus, in every case where training aims at producing high qualities of character, it begins with character at its lowest point. We pass from effort to inspiration, from work to play, from discipline to spontaneity. "A transition is to be made from principle enforced by statute to principle beheld by its own attractions and accepted in love for its own sake."[54] It is not always clear how the transition is made, but experience teaches that somehow

the miracle occurs. And it is clear that the drill contributes
to the end that transcends it. Thus, the practical earthly
teacher, like God himself, has always begun his work by enfor-
cing a discipline and appealing to self-interested motives,
"even when his object is to consumate a character wholly super-
ior to their active sway."[55]

By means of these illustrations, Bushnell ushered in his
main point: a similar rationale can account for the relations
of law and gospel over time depicted in the Old and New Testa-
ments. The Old Testament tells the story of a people under the
reign of penal law, an age when habits of obedience and moral
rigor were being schooled into the Jewish race to prepare it
to receive what Christ communicates. Because the ancient Jews
were a primitive people, said Bushnell, their training had to
begin at a low level.

> Beginning at a point where men's ideas are low
> and their spiritual apprehensions coarse, it
> must take hold of them at the first, in such a
> way as they are capable of being taken hold of.[56]

"[C]ondenscending to the lowness of barbarous minds," God edu-
cates them to receive the larger idea.[57] Like the vocabulary
of ritual terms that the Old Testament history prepares, however, the Old Testament law is not an end in itself. "The law,
by itself, makes nothing in us answer to its own high intentions,
and is never expected, simply as law, to become a footing of
salvation."[58] The law is fulfilled only in the transition from
legality to Christian freedom made possible by Christ's communication of God. But it is equally true that without the law
to prepare mankind the latter communication could never have
been made.[59] The Old Testament and the New--law and gospel--are
thus interdependent stages on the way to the realization of
God's one redemptive purpose.

> Without some such grip of law and justice on the
> soul, no grace-power of God could ever win it
> back; and without the grace-power felt in its
> blessed attractions, no mere law and justice
> power could beget any thing closer to God than
> a compelled obedience . . . . There was in fact
> an antecedent necessity of their conjoined
> working that, in due qualifying of each other,
> they may complement what would otherwise be a
> fault in each.[60]

Law without mercy is vicious; mercy without justice is vapid.
But together, they are the Way.

Considerations like the above led Bushnell to speculate
that while justice and mercy are practically distinct, they must
also be joined in the "radical union" of the controlling purpose behind them.[61] Law and gospel may be distinct with respect
to man. The one inspires fear, the other love. The one works
by repression, the other by attraction. But from God's standpoint, the two express a single intention. They have a common
origin in God's love and a common end or office: "to restore
and establish the everlasting, impersonal law"--the moral law
which is man's own proper principle of identity.[62] Thus, what
man experiences as a contradiction is coherent and simultaneous
in God. The relations of justice and mercy, if fact, are similar to the relations of nature and the supernatural: "however
distinct in idea the two systems . . . may be to us, they are
yet, in some higher view, one system to Him."[63] This, then,
would explain the puzzling fact that Christ insists on the continued sway of the penal law at the same time as he works to
communicate mercy. Retributive justice continues to hold the
world under laws of moral cause and effect, just as the natural
order of the world continues along side the new supernatural
order of grace. Justice and mercy co-operate not only in the
long run of time, but in the life of every individual.

The ultimate reason why God's intentions are expressed in
this double fashion is that there is a certain duplicity inherent in all moral life. The life of mind, in Bushnell's view,
is inevitably divided between the inward and the outward, the
private and the communal, supernatural freedoms and the natural
web of cause and effect. God seeks to redeem the whole man,
not to save one aspect of his experience at the expense of others.
Therefore, he works according to two principles: right and
love. The law of right is a goad to man in his privacy. Love
is the same law framed with regard to the mind's relations to
other beings. Love, in short, is the law of right in community,
communion, and communication.[64] The relations between the two
are superficially ironic. Community and privacy, like nature
and supernatural, seem to be contradictory interests. But
Bushnell's theory of the atonement is designed to show that all

such contraries have been comprehended and reconciled in God's
will and in the expressive processes by which God's will is
implemented. In God's expressive, redemptive economy, self-
realization and "complete society" are one. The contraries that
tear our lives in two, rightly viewed, become the co-operative
means to our redemption.

Bushnell therefore frequently represented the relations
of justice and mercy under images that suggest their simulta-
neity. For instance, he compared justice and mercy to the
co-operative action of centrifugal and centripetal forces in
physics. Neither ever occurs in nature without the other.
Taken singly, in fact, either concept of force is an illusion,
a misleading half-truth. But together, they define the course
of nature.[65] Similarly, Bushnell compared justice and mercy
to two gravitational fields whose combined effects define man's
proper course:

> we spend out lives between them, seeking our
> orbit under them, as the orbs of heaven seek
> theirs, between the systematically contrasting
> forces by which they are swayed.[66]

Untimately there is no before and after in the relations of
law and gospel, then, just as there is no before and after in
the "eternal" life of God. Rather, justice and mercy are co-
operative factors in the world's life to the end.

God's nature is thus a complex and apparently paradoxical
moral unity. There is mercy in his justice from the beginning,
or, as Bushnell wrote in *The Vicarious Sacrifice*, "there is a
cross in God before the wood is seen upon Calvary."[67] Likewise,
there is a quality of strictness in his mercy that can never
pass away--no more than centrifugal force can ever exist without
its contrary. God's nature is therefore perplexing but, as
Bushnell was at pains to show, it reveals its integrity in the
practical work of redemption. Together, justice and mercy conspire to nurture a Christlike character in mankind. The contradictory formulas conspire to drive man's mind to the infinite.

Bushnell went on to translate this vision of the harmony
of divine justice and mercy back into a formula for the fulfilment of human life. The understanding of God, based on analogies
of human communicative processes, reaches its end in the model
it provides for human moral growth. Just as God's nature is a

blend of justice and mercy, he held, so human life is inevitably
lived between the poles of history and transcendence--community
and freedom--and finds its norms in a proper adjustment to
both. Human experience, that is, is inevitably "mixed." The
universe, designed for the training of character, reflects
that duplicity in a blend of harmony and dissension, ecstasy
and tragedy. Harmony without tragedy would lose its piquancy;
tragedy without ecstasy would be cruel and futile. A harmonious, normative character must include contraries, then--shocks
of movement, growth, and feeling--"even as the kosmos of matter
rests in the periolous equilibrium and lively play of antagonis-
tic forces."[68] Without this lively interaction of contraries,
the world--like language stripped of figures--would lose its
"tonic efficacy" and become "insipid."[69] The redemptive process thus works by the ambiguities of our experience, and redeemed life, as a fruit of growth, will continue to reflect
them.

For Bushnell, in sum, redeemed consciousness comprehends
all the contrary impulses of life in history. History and transcendence, community and privacy, justice and mercy, atonement
and at-one-ment--all make claims on human allegiance that cannot be sustained at the expense of any of the others. As Bushnell had discovered long before, human self-realization does
not carry persons outside of community, but consists in their
discovery of the identity of self and common humanity. Just
so, God does not erect the structure of the law only to take
it away in the end. Redemption is not freedom from the law,
but freedom within the law. The end partakes of the form of
the training, just as the training is designed to be appropriate to the end.

> [God's] beginning will go through to his end,
> and the law and law-sanctions, never abated or
> brought off, will be working faithfully on, with
> all the gracious powers and tender motivities
> in Christ--part and parcel with them, in the
> one comprehensive purpose; even as the lightnings
> and the dews take part together in the growth
> of the world.[70]

3. The Moral Power of Love

A final theme in Bushnell's works on the atonement is the need for a common ground of intersubjective likeness between man and God in order for the atonement, as a communication of divine character, to be effective. Bushnell often said that sinful man has lost his primary likeness to God; the world has become a "dead receptivity." On the other hand, Bushnell's theory of communication stipulated that the possibility of divine-human communication of any sort presupposes that the divine and human natures share a common stock of spiritual or moral experience by virtue of which their expressions are mutually intelligible. Bushnell accordingly looked for something common to God and fallen man that could serve as a foothold for a salvation that works across moral distance "in the immediate, absolute manner of art."[71]

Bushnell's first step was to argue that the absence of any such common footing would entail that all of our talk about God is nonsense, a conclusion he considered self-evidently false. A God who is not "good" or "just" in the same sense in which we apply those terms to ourselves, he said, would not be properly "good" or "just" at all.

> What can we think, or know, of a goodness over
> and above all standards of good? We might as well
> talk of extensions beyond space, or truths
> beyond the true.[72]

Therefore, said Bushnell, if the terms we apply to God are informative, they must refer to human and divine natures univocally.[73] This law of interpretation raises a strong presumption, then, that if we can be said to understand anything of God at all, we must share a common moral nature with him. "Goodness, holy virtue, is the same in all worlds and beings, measured by the same universal and eternal standards; else it is nothing to us."[74] In Forgiveness and Law, he went so far as to argue that anything true of man's moral experience must also be true of God's. He celebrated

> the grand analogy or almost identity that subsists
> between our moral nature and that of God; so
> that our moral pathologies and those of God make
> faithful answer to each other, and he is brought
> so close to us that almost anything that occurs
> in the workings or exigencies of our moral in-
> stincts may even be expected of his.[75]

Bushnell seldom stretched the point this far, but he was seldom far from the point: communication without common experience would be impossible.

Once the supposition of a common ground between God and man is established, the next question is, what is that common point on which the redemptive transaction pivots? In previous chapters, we have noted Bushnell's use of "character" in this connection. Character, in its normative sense, is the image of the divine moral nature in man, the hallmark of the creator. It is at once the goal of human self-realization and the index of redemption. Character, indeed, is the meaning and end of the Christian religion as Bushnell understood it. In his writings on the atonement, Bushnell appropriated a term from orthodox theology to play a similar role in his thinking. What the human and divine natures have in common, he said, is their capacity for "vicarious love." "Vicarious," in Bushnell's usage, shows few traces of its orthodox origins. Traditional theology held Christ's sacrifice to be vicarious in the sense that Christ takes on the sins of the world and, suffering them, pays the penalty for them in mankind's place. All Bushnell took over from the tradition was the implication that vicarious love involves identification with another in suffering; and even this he reduced to emotional identification or sympathy. Christ "bears our sins," he said, only in the sense of being "profoundly identified with us in our fallen state and burdened in feeling with our evils."[76] Christ suffers for mankind, that is, precisely as a mother suffers for her child or a friend suffers for a friend.

Vicarious love, thus defined, serves to bridge the gap between God and fallen man in two senses. First, Bushnell claimed, it is a property common to human and divine natures; "vicarious sacrifice is the common property of holy virtue in all minds, created or uncreated."[77] Persons are capable of natural love; Scripture defines God as loving in essence. And insofar as both are capable of love, both are capable of vicarious love, for

> love is a principle essentially vicarious in
> its own nature, identifying the subject with
> others, so as to suffer their adversities and
> pains, and taking on itself the burden of their
> evils.[78]

A bridgehead between divine and human natures is therefore assured. Second, vicarious love, again by definition, involves not only the possibility of a bridge, but an active power to bridge the gap in fact. Vicarious love is actively relational and powerfully effective. We naturally love a friend who suffers for our sake, Bushnell claimed. Where the suffering is great, the example of a friend may even have a power to shake us out of our selfish complacency and inspire similarly self-sacrificing motives in us. Likewise in the case of divine-human relations: we love Christ because he first loved us; and we are able to love him because in his own vicarious love he gave us the tragic shock we required to awaken our deadened sensibilities:

> what to our slow feeling, is even eternal good-
> ness, till we see it tragically moved? Nay, it
> was even necessary, if transgressors were to have
> their dull heart opened to this goodness, that
> they should see it presented and gibbeted by them-
> selves. Thus, and therefore, he dies, raising
> by his death at our hands, those terrible con-
> victions that will rend our bosom open to his
> love--dies for love's sake into love in us
> So he will become the power of God unto salva-
> tion, gathering you in, as it were, with all your
> disorders into the infolding, new-creating
> sympathy of his own character in good[79]

Vicarious love, in other words, can stimulate the very sensibility by which it is to be received. It draws out our own capacity for vicarious love by a directly attractive power.

> Vicarious love in him answered by vicarious love
> in us, tiny and weak though it be, as an insect
> life fluttering responsively to the sun--this
> is the only footing of grace, in which Christ
> is truly received, and according to his gracious
> power.[80]

Bushnell's definition of all love as essentially vicarious in this sense must certainly be regarded as prescriptive rather than descriptive, even though Bushnell meant it descriptively. Nevertheless, we will not quarrel, for the conceit has its own peculiar cogency in the context of Bushnell's theological romance. In it, Bushnell's vision of the Christian redemptive economy reached its peak of concentration and refinement. Vicarious love is at once the mark of the divine in man and the power by which the divine possibility of existence can be realized.

>What we call [Christ's] redemption of mankind
must bring them to the common standard. Executed
by vicarious sacrifice in himself, it must also
be issued in vicarious sacrifice in them.[81]

The work of Christ is to make men Christlike; and in this work,
Christ's nature is both the end and the means. He works by
love for love, through community for community. What Bushnell
has caught here, we might say, is a vision of the perfect symmetry of the moral universe. There is no disjunction between
effort and attainment, means and ends, because both are made
of the same stuff. Spontaneous human loves serve divine ends;
divine purposes fulfil the deepest longings of the human heart.
Human love reveals the divine; divine love makes the human
possible. Divine nature and human norms are mutually defined,
mutually realized.

Bushnell's comments on the nature of Christ's redemptive
power harmonize with this vision of moral symmetry. Christ's
power, he said, is identical with his nature, and is exercised
by means of his likeness to man. To show how this could be so,
Bushnell drew a distinction between what he called God's
"attribute power" and his "moral power." When we conceive of
God's qualities in the abstract, said Bushnell, we attribute
him with -inconceivable greatness: infinity, omnipotence, and
omniscience. Under these conceptions, we can understand well
enough how God is a sovereign power over the world. But these
attributes are so impersonal--"thin and cold"--that they stand
in the way of our understanding God as a power "within" us,
appealing to our wills and shaping our characters. Conceiving
of God as an "attribute power," that is, "we very nearly think
away, or annihilate, all that creates an effective impress on
our sentiment and character."[82] But a God who makes no impression cannot be a redeemer, for without impression, there is no
communication. Therefore, said Bushnell, God makes himself
less abstract for our sakes. He represents himself in Christ
in order to gain a foothold in human sensibilities--a foothold
for the salvation that works by impression.

By becoming a character like man, in other words, God gets
a kind of power that only character can exert. Bushnell called
this power "influence" or "moral power." It is a power of
attraction as opposed to a power of coercion, the natural power

of human identity to "beget" itself in others.

> It enters into human thought and knowledge as
> a vital force; and since it is perfect, a vital
> force that cannot die or cease to work.[83]

As we have noted before, Bushnell used a concept of moral power
as early as 1833, in the sermon "Duty Not Measured by Our Own
Ability." Likewise, "influence" was a pivotal concept in
several of his works on Christian nurture and in the sermon
"Unconscious Influence." But it was not until he wrote *The
Vicarious Sacrifice* that Bushnell gave these ideas a full-dress
theological development. While this concept of moral power had
always implied the likeness of the communicating parties, now it
served to underline the likeness of man and God in Christ.

Christ is a moral power for two reasons: first, because he
embodies God's own qualities, he has the potential power of attraction that goodness, truth, and beauty exert "by nature" in
Bushnell's universe; second, because Christ is a human person,
he brings the divine character close enough to humanity for it
to become impressive. Confronted with Christ, mankind feels a
shock of recognition for the nature he has lost and yet retains
in a painfully atrophied form. Christ's moral power, then,
consists in his ability to force the world to recognize itself
in him. He works wholly by what he is:

> not by action, but by a quality of being, or by
> the worth, and beauty, and divine greatness of
> a character . . . effective thus, in simply
> being what it is.[84]

"[H]e will be the regenerator of souls not by action upon them,
but by what he is to sight"--or we would say, by what he is as
a symbolic expression of divine character.[85]

Christ's moral power thus works on the world primarily by
"assimilation, or a certain divine contagion."[86] But there is
another, less direct way in which Christ exerts a shaping influence over mankind. In Christ, Bushnell repeatedly stressed,
the divine life has entered into the currents of history. His
influence--his "divine contagion"--has become part of the world's
influence, carried by everyone and everything he has touched.
Thus, because Christ brought the divine life into history, now
man's own contact with history is potentially redemptive. Man
can get the form of a divine character simply by taking from
the world what Christ has lived into it. This aspect of Christ's

relation to the world is summed up, said Bushnell, under the
idea of Christ as a "second Adam" to the race.

> Adam is our head physiologically, Christ is our
> head by the head influences he inaugurates, by
> the authority, sympathy, beauty, of his suffering
> goodness--a power that propagates across all the
> lines of generation, as effectively as if it
> traveled by descent--a new regenerative power
> incarnated into the race as such. . . .[87]

The reality of this influence, in turn, is proved by what Bushnell took to be the self-evident improvement or Christianization
of Western society.

> [The divine life] penetrates more and more vis-
> ibly our sentiments, opinions, laws, sciences,
> inventions, modes of commerce, modes of society,
> advancing, as it were, by the slow measured step
> of centuries, to a complete dominion over the
> race. . . . Not that Christ grows better, but
> that he is more and more completely apprehended,
> as he becomes more evidently incarnated among men,
> and obtains a fitter representation to thought,
> in the thoughts and works of his people.[88]

Bushnell had his quarrels with modernity. But for both tem-
peramental and theological reasons, he always leaned toward
the position that the spirit of the age, *mutatis mutandis*, is
the spirit of God. That God's life entered the world in Christ,
he argued, is what makes Christ's incarnation different from
a mere theophany. A theophany--for instance, the burning bush--
is transient; but in Christ God intruded himself on the world
in such a way that his life can never be gotten out of it "any
more than if it were a new diffusive element in the world's
atmosphere."[89]

To further clarify this concept of the moral power of
character and vicarious love, Bushnell distinguished it from
"example." He insisted that the expressive Christ does more
than illustrate a model of Christian charity to be imitated.
Rather, as an expression, Christ is a "vehicle of God to the
soul, that is able to copy God into it."[90] Precisely as an expression, he is the dynamic power of regeneration itself--both
means and end. The entire gospel, in fact, like every other
vehicle of divine revelation, is a power "operating simply by
the expression of God, and being only what is expressed by the
shining tokens of love and sacrifice."[91] Because the concepts
of "example" and "imitation" resemble this grand gospel scheme

of expressive communication, they are highly suggestive, but
also terribly thin, said Bushnell.[92] They comprehend the form
of the gospel as an image of God, but fail to grasp its power--
the power of an expression to ingenerate itself in the mind of
a receptive and faithful interpreter, and even to beget or call
forth the attentiveness necessary to its own reception.

The symmetry or reciprocity of Bushnell's moral universe
has a final interesting theological consequence: the concepts
of God and man become, to a degree, interchangeable in Bushnell's
thought. On the one hand, it is a properly divine identity
and power that circulates, from Christ, throughout Christian
society. On the other hand, that identity is also properly
human; it is humanity in its highest and most characteristic
form. This ambiguity has its roots in Bushnell's now familiar
"law of expression:" everything a person is capable of understanding he is also capable of becoming. Every possibility of
human experience, sacred or secular, is a properly human possibility. If a person can experience the divine life through
the interpretation of divine self-expression, then, it must be
because he has the seeds of a divine possibility in him from
the start. Thus, Bushnell even found it proper to say:

> Redemption, life, resurrection--all are, in
> a sense, being and to be, by man. When we say
> *humanity* there is enclosed, and, as it were,
> closeted in it, all the inspiration, all the
> light, all the life-impulse of the divine man,
> and so, all the supernatural, resurgent powers
> of a complete salvation.[93]

Of course, Bushnell did not mean that all powers of salvation
are equally at man's beck and call. On the contrary, because
humanity is lost, some powers--such as those that relate man
to God in Christ--can only be called out by a divine nature or
self-presentation. But the power of the divine image, insofar
as it can be received and reconstructed in the human mind, is
also a power of the mind. The expression and what it inspires
are one. Thus, Christ's love, insofar as mankind responds to
it, is as properly human as divine, and nonetheless divine for
being realized in man. Bushnell sums up the point in a paraphrase of the gospel of Luke (7:40-47):

> [Christ's] forgiving much is going to produce
> a loving much, and of course, the same kind of
> loving which is operated and expressed in the
> forgiveness.[94]

Christ's love calls out man's love, and the love thus evoked
is common to both. What Christ gives to man, in short, is man's
own possibilities. Fallen man stands at the beginning of a course
of growth; Christ at the end. But if the end were not also
in the beginning, the circle could never be drawn.

4. Symbolism and Growth

Throughout this chapter, we have stressed the ways in which
Bushnell's interpretation of the atonement drew upon his theory
of interpersonal communication. In earlier chapters, however,
we indicated how the theory of communication itself reflected
themes in Bushnell's personal history and represented an
attempt to comprehend the various strands of his experience
in a single, inclusive vision. It is fitting in conclusion,
then, to attempt to draw some connections between Bushnell's
theory of the atonement, as the capstone of his theology, and
the personal interests that gave rise to his intellectual
project.

In his doctrine of the atonement, Bushnell discovered the
ultimate congruence of the contrary imperatives that shaped
his career from the beginning. Early on, he had discovered
a power to "be" in receptivity to his Christian heritage. By
giving himself over to his inbred allegiance to Christian
symbolism, he found that the past held a power to integrate
and intensify present spiritual life. The personal growth he
achieved through this insight served him ever after as a model
of redemption and a touchstone for the experience of God. On
the other hand, Bushnell was personally acquainted with the
restless energies in mankind that hamper the realization of
"complete society"--the integration of the individual with the
Christian community. Persons are moved, first of all, by their
own projects of self-realization. Fallen mankind lives in tension with community, in alienation from the life of God, in a
moral state that is inevitably "mixed." Bushnell not only felt
these contrary impulses personally; he saw them reflected in
the theological debates of his age. The orthodox party stood
for the authority of the past; the Unitarians for the brash
energies of self-realization. Neither party alone, however,
held the full secret of a Christian character as Bushnell

understood it. He came to feel, therefore, that the main problem of personal life and theology alike was to find some way to
harmonize these two sides of human nature: the need to integrate one's life with the past and the demand for self-realization.

His understanding of Christian redemption as a process of
expressive communication solves this problem elegantly. In communication of all kinds, he held, the tensions between the subjective interest of self-realization and the need to draw on
the energies of tradition are included and harmonized. Communication makes use of expressive symbols, words or acts composed of an objective, tradition-bound vehicle and a subjective
content. Through the medium of a common language, the inward
life of minds is made public. And through the imaginative interpretation of expressive forms--understood as a process in which
the subjective meaning of a symbol is supplied out of the recipient's own repertoire of thought and feeling--the inward
experience expressed is reproduced in the mind of the interpreter. Expressive symbols, so conceived, are powers that
produce a common intersubjective identity. What is encountered
in expressions at once calls out the recipient's own possibilities of experience and integrates him with the community.

This theory of communication, in turn, gave Bushnell a
way to interpret the Christian redemptive economy as an educative scheme embracing both tradition and personal freedom.
Divine character and normative human character are one, he
held. The forms of the Christian religion--understood as expressions of the divine mind--are therefore effective means of
human self-realization. When we attend to God's self-expression
in Scripture, nature, and Christ, our own normative selfhood
is called out. By being receptive to tradition, we are transformed into God's image, "from glory to glory." And in becoming
like God, we become more fully ourselves.

Bushnell's reinterpretation of Christian doctrine in the
light of his theory of communication thus provided him with a
key to the puzzle of his life. By portraying the Christian
redemptive economy as an affair of expressive communication,
Bushnell assured himself that his own divided allegiances were
comprehended and mutually justified in a manner similar to that

in which content and vehicle co-operate in an expressive symbol. As the symbol integrates form and content, so the claims of the past and the impulse of self-realization are integrated in the Christian self. The "truth" of Christian consciousness is confirmed by its harmony with the expression of God in tradition. And the validity of the tradition, in turn, is practically confirmed by its power to express and propagate the divine mind in history, a power that operates through the social forces that shape personal growth. Atonement is thus at-one-ment on both personal and communal levels for the Christian self. As a person who has attained the condition of a symbol, the Christian is one whose life is assured of meaning.

NOTES

CHAPTER V

[1]For Bushnell's principal discussions of the trinity and
the incarnation see *God in Christ* (1849; rpt. New York: AMS
Press, 1972), pp. 121-81; *Christ in Theology* (Hartford:
Brown & Parsons, 1851), pp. 90-211; "The Christian Trinity,
A Practical Truth," in *Building Eras in Religion* (New York:
Charles Scribner's Sons, 1910), and "Our Relation to Christ in
the Future Life," in *Sermons on Living Subjects* (New York:
Charles Scribner's Sons, 1890). Two helpful modern discussions
of Bushnell's doctrine of the trinity are Fred Kirschenmann,
"Horace Bushnell: Orthodox or Sabellian?" *Church History*,
XXXIII (March 1964), pp. 49-59; and Chapter VI of Donald Crosby,
Horace Bushnell's Theory of Language (The Hague: Mouton, 1975).

[2]See especially Charles Hodge, "Bushnell's Discourses,"
Biblical Repertory and Princeton Review, XXI (April 1849), pp.
259-98; Enoch Pond, *Review of Dr. Bushnell's "God in Christ"*
(Bangor: 1849).

[3]Cheney, *Life and Letters of Horace Bushnell* (1880; rpt.
New York: Arno Press, Inc., 1969), p. 252. This work will be
cited hereafter as *LL*.
For vivid documentary evidence of Bushnell's feelings of
exclusion, see his letters to Leonard Bacon for the years 1849
and 1850. MSS Yale University Library.
For survey accounts of the controversy aroused by *God in
Christ* see H. Shelton Smith, *Horace Bushnell* (New York: Oxford
University Press, 1965), pp. 152-59; and Edwin Pond Parker,
The Hartford Central Association and the Bushnell Controversy
(Hartford: Case, Lockwood & Brainard, 1896).

[4]A notable exception was Henry Goodwin, a young Hartford
church member in whom Bushnell placed great confidence. See
Bushnell's letters to Goodwin in *LL*, and Goodwin's own treatise
on language, "Thoughts, Words, and Things," *Bibliotheca Sacra*,
VI (May 1849), pp. 271-300.

[5]*LL*, p. 251.

[6]*Ibid.*

[7]*Ibid.*, p. 265. There is little information available on
Bushnell's ailment. It is tempting to assume that Bushnell's
problems were chiefly psychosomatic, if only because his syn-
drome is so similar to the complaints common among Victorian
American men of letters. See Stow Persons, *The Decline of
American Gentility* (New York: Columbia University Press, 1973),
pp. 285-92.

[8]Bushnell, "The Dissolving of Doubts," *Sermons on Living
Subjects*, pp. 168-72.

[9]*LL*, p. 451.

[10]Bushnell, *Forgiveness and Law* (New York: Scribner, Armstrong & Co., 1874), p. 10.

[11]The role of the war in Bushnell's thoughts on the redemptive meaning of suffering is evidenced in "Our Obligations to the Dead," (1865), in *Building Eras*. The influence of the war here should not be overestimated, however. Similar ideas can be found in a much earlier sermon of Bushnell's on "The Power of God in Self-Sacrifice," in *Sermons for the New Life* (New York: Charles Scribner, 1858).

[12]Bushnell, *Forgiveness and Law*, p. 16.

[13]See *ibid.*, p. 12.

[14]*The Vicarious Sacrifice* was first published in one volume in 1866. In the Centenary Edition (New York: Charles Scribner's Sons, 1907), it appears in two volumes. Of these, the first is the original version in its entirety. The second volume is actually a reprint of *Forgiveness and Law*. All subsequent references to *Vicarious Sacrifice* will be to volume I of the 1907 edition.

[15]We make this point about continuity in Bushnell's work before going on to a close analysis of the works in order to clear the air of a current misinterpretation of Bushnell's later years. For example, Barbara Cross holds that Bushnell's thought underwent a "sharp reversal" soon after the publication of *The Vicarious Sacrifice*. His early work, it is said, represents a worldly and relatively easy-going compromise with popular taste, epitomized by his assumption that the aesthetic sensibility can receive Christian truth. Bushnell's superficial confidence was supposedly blasted, however, by Henry James, Sr.'s review of *The Vicarious Sacrifice* in the *North American Review* (CII [April 1866], pp. 556-71. James' authorship of the review is reported in Fredric Young, *The Philosophy of Henry James, Sr.* [New York: Bookman Associates, 1951], and is insisted upon by William Clebsch, *American Religious Thought* [Chicago: University of Chicago Press, 1973], pp. 121, 193.) James pointed out that the vicarious ideal Bushnell took for the norm of human love was not what men usually meant by love. This revelation is supposed to have so unhinged Bushnell that he began to assert the absolute difference of human and divine loves in his sermons while contradicting himself brazenly in his published works. (The one sermon cited by Cross as evidence is "God Reigns for the Largest Love," MS Yale Divinity School Library.) So Cross claims, "it is impossible to unite all the centrifugal messages inspiring the last decades of Bushnell's life." (Cross, *Horace Bushnell* [Chicago: University of Chicago Press, 1958], pp. 147-54.)

We submit that this analysis is a better measure of confusion in the minds of the commentators than in Bushnell's. It has been the burden of this thesis to show that from the very beginning of his career, Bushnell sustained a dynamic tension between human interests and divine ideals, such that divine nature and normative human nature become mutually interpreting categories. There should be a strong presumption against the claim, then, that he found it unsettling when James averred that his idea of the human was colored by his idea of the divine. The evidence Cross brings forward to illustrate Bushnell's presumed change of heart includes nothing that Bushnell had not said and assimilated into the main currents of his thought twenty or thirty years before. Therefore, on the principle that it is always better interpretive practice to assume continuity rather than discontinuity in a person's thought where there is no strong evidence to the contrary, we reject the suggestion that Henry James, Sr.'s article had any significant impact on the course of Bushnell's thought.

[16]For a good survey of thought on the atonement in New England in this period, see Dorus Paul Rudisill, *The Doctrine of the Atonement in Jonathan Edwards and His Successors* (New York: Poseidon Books, 1971).

[17]See Conrad Wright, *The Beginnings of Unitarianism in America* (Boston: Starr King Press, 1955), esp. ch. 7, pp. 161-84.

[18]Channing, *Works* (Boston: American Unitarian Association, 1897), p. 380.

[19]*God in Christ*, p. 190. Bushnell found the Grotian theory somewhat preferable to the satisfaction theory. He heartily concurred with the principle that "the value of Christ's life and death is measured by what is therein expressed." He believed, however, that Christ's expression is not intended to make a point about God so much as to work a change in man. If Christ suffers only to demonstrate his own divine virtue as the Grotian theory held, "he expresses nothing but ostentation." *Ibid.*, pp. 37-39.

[20]*Ibid.*, p. 269.

[21]*Ibid.*, p. 273. Reviewers of Bushnell's works on the atonement were—and continue to be--struck by echoes of Unitarian thinkers like Channing and Noah Worcester in Bushnell. See James Freeman Clarke, "Bushnell on Vicarious Sacrifice," *Christian Examiner*, LXXX (May 1866), pp. 372-73; Ann Douglas, *Feminization* (New York: Alfred A. Knopf, 1977), pp. 124, 127.

[22]*God in Christ*, p. 203.

[23]*Ibid.*

[24]*Ibid.*, p. 204.

[25]*Ibid.*, p. 190.

[26]*Ibid.*, p. 192.

[27]*Ibid.*, p. 204.

[28]*Building Eras*, p. 254.

[29]To make this point, Bushnell needed to argue (quite implausibly) that expiatory sacrifice, designed to appease the

wrath of a god, is a degeneration from the root-form of sacrifice, which is free of all magical overtones. The significance
of sacrifice, he held, is not its power to appease a god, but
its power to beget awe and moral fervor in the mind of the cele-
brant. See *Christ in Theology*, pp. 242ff; *The Vicarious Sacrifice*, pp. 454ff.

[30] *God in Christ*, p. 258.

[31] *Ibid.*, p. 88.

[32] *Christ in Theology*, pp. 248-49; *God in Christ*,
pp. 246-47.

[33] *Christ in Theology*, p. 248.

[34] *God in Christ*, pp. 264-65.

[35] See "Self-Examination Examined," in *Sermons on Living
Subjects*, p. 239; *God in Christ*, p. 264.

[36] This self-giving is the heart of faith, on Bushnell's account. "Faith," said Bushnell, is an act of trust in which one
person submits himself to the influence of another. "[I]t is
being trusting itself to being, and so becoming other and different, by a relation wholly transactional." A good illustration, he believed, is the relation between a patient and a
physician. It is not enough to be aware of a physician's
powers in the abstract. The patient will never improve until
he submits himself to the physician's care. Similarly in the
case of art or Scripture: to get the benefit of what is expressed, one must submit one's mind to the personal force in
the expression, just as one would submit to the influence of a
medicine in order to be healed. Without such faith, there can
be no growth. With it, the mind is open to be assimilated
into sympathy with the mind expressed, or in the case of
Scripture, into a practical union with God. See Bushnell, "The
Reason of Faith," *Sermons for the New Life*, pp. 94, 97; *Vicarious Sacrifice*, p. 435.

[37] *God in Christ*, p. 212.

[38] On the practical benefits of the mysterious in history, see
"Of Oblivion" in *Moral Uses of Dark Things* (New York: Charles
Scribner's Sons, 1910), p. 83: "Let the blank spaces be large
enough to give the imagination play. . . . Only so could a real
gospel be written. What we call our gospel is so written, and
no such life as that of Christ could be otherwise given to the
world. A full-written, circumstantial biography would be a
mortal suffocation of his power."

[39] *God in Christ*, p. 267.

[40] Recognition of how faithful reception of operative truths
can bring persons into practical communion with God's self-
communication is the genuine meaning behind the doctrine of
justification by faith, Bushnell believed. He argued that
justification is, in essence, a wholly subjective or "moral"

affair. God justifies men by communicating his life to them, representing himself in Christ.

> God is just, as being righteous, and justifies, simply as communicating his own character and becoming a righteousness upon us (*Vicarious Sacrifice*, p. 408).

Faith figures into the communicative process as receptivity to the forms of God's self-expression, and a willingness to be transformed into the image they convey (*ibid.*, p. 415). God's art captures our hearts and imaginations, and so, "winning faith, it works by the faith it wins; and so being trusted in, it makes trust a footing of life and character" (*ibid.*, p. 404). Faith is justifying, in short, because it opens the door to the operative power of the expression, to bear the soul "up out of its thralldom and weak self-endeavor" (*ibid.*).

Bushnell gave a similar treatment to the doctrine of the sanctifying power of the Holy Spirit. This, too, is explained in terms of God's communicative work. In brief, the Holy Spirit can be understood as the subjective aspect of what Christ presents objectively. The Spirit, working through faith, is God communicating himself through "the attitude of mind induced by the resting of a soul on an objective and vicarious mercy . . ." (*God in Christ*, p. 265). Christ's work prepares objective "energizing powers" of impression in his life; the Spirit is the agent that realizes that power of impression in man.

> Christ is a power to the soul before its thought, and by that which is given to thought in his person. The Spirit is a power back of thought, opening thought as a receptivity towards him, and, in that manner, setting the subject under the impression of Christ's life, and death, and character (*Vicarious Sacrifice*, p. 157).

Justification and sanctification are thus in essence one thing. Both refer to stages in the process by which God communicates his life to man. They remain distinct as stages, but they are continuous, as the work of the Spirit continues the work of Christ (*ibid.*, pp. 440-41).

[41.]*God in Christ*, p. 255.

[42]*Vicarious Sacrifice*, p. 404. On these grounds, Bushnell distinguished both art and religious faith from philosophy. As an approach to the problem of existence, says Bushnell, philosophy amounts to nothing but self-culture. It sticks resolutely to the resources of reflective action--self-reflection--rather than seeking energies from without. Religion and art, by contrast, operate by inviting man to become absorbed in the transforming power of something other than the soul's own circumstances.

> No man is in the Christian state till he gets by, and, in one sense, beyond reflective action. And precisely here is the fundamental necessity of an objective form or forms of art, in the Christian scheme (*God in Christ*, p. 163).

Just as man cannot "lift himself by his own shoulders," he cannot advance spiritually without objective helps. Art-forms provide those helps. As an "objective grace," they give man an opportunity to go beyond his own powers into the sphere of influence exerted by another mind through symbols.

If Bushnell can thus distinguish faith from philosophy, however, he has a little more trouble distinguishing religion from art. While he believes that the analogy between religion and poetry is an appropriate one, he also wants to be able to say that religion is something more than poetry. Poetry and art remain on the level of human capacity: they "cannot quite create a soul under the ribs of death" (ibid., p. 88). Christainity, on the other hand, is radically regenerative. It transmits a power that wholly transcends human capacity. Thus Bushnell insisted that receptive faith is different from a merely aesthetic attraction to a beautiful and moving spectacle. Taking delight in Christian symbols, in other words, is not the same thing as being Christian. Faith requires the extra step of a "practical embrace" of God, a voluntary submission of the will to be "new charactered" in the gospel. We may respond to a work of art and not be changed by it; but in the case of Christian faith, understanding always involves the tranformation of the recipient. Bushnell thus pointed towards a way of distinguishing art and religion in terms of their effects. See Bushnell, "Religious Nature and Religious Character," in *Sermons on Living Subjects*, pp. 129-47.

Bushnell's distinction between religion and art led Barbara Cross to think that Bushnell eventually repudiated his earlier analogy between faith and artistic receptivity. (See n. 15 above.) She assumed Bushnell's meaning to be that while art attracts its audience, the Christian truth is fundamentally repulsive to the natural man, and therefore that the gospel requires a special effort of self-overcoming to be received. Cross is mistaken, however. Bushnell believed that both art and faith presuppose a fundamental likeness between the communicating parties. The difference between them is simply that whereas it is part of our definition of faith that it have a transforming effect on believers, we do not necessarily expect the same of art.

43 *God in Christ*, p. 257.

44 *Christ in Theology*, p. 266.

45 *Vicarious Sacrifice*, p. 322.

46 *Ibid.*, p. 220.

47 *Ibid.*, pp. 219-20.

48 *Ibid.*, p. 324.

49 *Ibid.*, p. 351.

50 *Ibid.*, p. 401.

[51]*Forgiveness and Law*, p. 130.

[52]Bushnell used the example of a grown son's spontaneous obedience to his mother's will, which is a striking parallel to his own willingness to conform to his mother's desires rather than go West to practice law. Compare the following with Chapter I above: "The boy who, at eight years of age, was tearing himself against every point of maternal restriction, will finally, at thirty, obey every softest wish of his mother as if it were an edict, and will even catch it by anticipation before it is expressed" (*Forgiveness and Law*, p. 122).

[53]*Ibid.*, pp. 120-29.

[54]*Ibid.*, p. 130.

[55]*Vicarious Sacrifice*, p. 325.

[56]*Ibid.*, pp. 63-64.

[57]*Ibid.*, p. 67.

[58]*Forgiveness and Law*, p. 99.

[59]*Vicarious Sacrifice*, pp. 65-67.

[60]*Ibid.*, p. 273.

[61]*Ibid.*, p. 289.

[62]*Ibid.*, pp. 291, 272.

[63]*Christ in Theology*, p. 279.

[64]*Vicarious Sacrifice*, p. 306.

[65]*Ibid.*, pp. 272-274.

[66]*Christ in Theology*, p. 279

[67]*Vicarious Sacrifice*, p. 73.

[68]*Ibid.*, p. 363.

[69]*Ibid.*, pp. 361-63. Bushnell thus ridicules thinkers among the naturalists and the Unitarians who can imagine no value in a world order that is not perfectly one and at rest. Likewise, Bushnell is disturbed by the Bible's fleeting intimations that God may someday swallow up the dynamic community of beings and "become all in all," reducing the world to a flat unity. See *Vicarious Sacrifice*, p. 363; *God in Christ*, p. 177.

[70]*Forgiveness and Law*, p. 176.

[71]*God in Christ*, p. 267.

[72]*Vicarious Sacrifice*, p. 57.

[73] *Forgiveness and Law*, p. 13.

[74] *Vicarious Sacrifice*, p. 57.

[75] *Forgiveness and Law*, p. 35.

[76] *Vicarious Sacrifice*, p. 41.

[77] *Ibid.*, p. 59.

[78] *Ibid.*, p. 42. Henry James, Sr., argues quite plausibly that Bushnell, in his haste to find a common ground between human nature and the supposed moral nature of God, has misrepresented human love. Vicarious love, on Bushnell's account, is love for what is inherently unlovely--indentification with another's sin as sin. But, says James, such a love is "unnatural." Instinctive human love "always responds to a real or seeming worth in its object." Even in the apparently altruistic behavior of mothers and patriots, love never embraces what is abhorrent and obviously evil. "How then," asked James, "shall Christ be conceived to love the sinner, in any natural, unforced, unsophisticated sense of the word *love*?" If Christ's love is like ours, that is, it cannot be "vicarious" in Bushnell's sense of that word. But if Christ's love is unlike ours, it cannot be a ground of sympathy between man and God. See Henry James, Sr., *North American Review*, CII (April 1866), pp. 561-62.
    Bushnell never replied directly to this charge, but we imagine his response would have been something like that suggested in n. 15 above.

[79] Bushnell, "Salvation for the Lost Condition," in *Christ and His Salvation* (New York: Scribners, 1865), p. 89.

[80] *Vicarious Sacrifice*, p. 124.

[81] *Ibid.*, p. 105.

[82] *Ibid.*, p. 187.

[83] *God in Christ*, p. 206.

[84] *Vicarious Sacrifice*, p. 168.

[85] *Ibid.*, p. 174.

[86] *Forgiveness and Law*, p. 153.

[87] Bushnell, *Christ and His Salvation*, p. 279.

[88] *Vicarious Sacrifice*, pp. 211-12.

[89] *Ibid.*, p. 221.

[90] *Ibid.*, p. 170.

[91] *Ibid.*, p. 24.

[92] *Ibid.*

[93]Bushnell, "Salvation by Man," in *Christ and His Salvation*, p. 271.

[94]Bushnell, "God Reigns for the Largest Love," MS Yale Divinity School Library.

INDEX

"Abiding spirit," 41-42, 57, 62-63, 79-80.
Abrams, M.H., xvi, 31, 32.
Adam, 88-89, 93.
Ahlstrom, Sydney, xv, 59.
Alison, Joseph, 32.
America, eschatological significance of, 7-8, 9-10, 13, 29,
    93.
Analogy, 17-21, 24, 44-45, 47-48, 110, 116, 157 (see also
    Nature; Symbolism).
Arminianism, 10, 11.
Atonement, xiv, 48, 90, 106, 119, 139-66:
    Grotian theory, 143-44, 169;
    Satisfaction theory, 143, 169;
    Subjective and objective aspects, 143, 145-50;
    Unitarian theory, 144.
Auerbach, Erich, 28.
Augustine, 1.

Baird, R.D., xv.
Baldwin, James Mark, 53.
Becker, Ernest, 64.
Beecher, Lyman, 67.
Bercovitch, Sacvan, 6, 7, 10, 41, 42.
Bible (see Scripture).
Biblical quotations:
    Luke 7:40-47, 163;
    Romans 5:14, 7;
    II Cor. 3:18, 6, 101, 102;
    Galatians 4:19, 101;
    Philippians 2:6-11, 101.
Billings, M.K., 33.
Brumm, Ursula, 6.
Bushnell, Horace
    Biography:
        Early life, 1-5;
        Influence of mother, 1, 2;
        Problem of vocation, 2, 5, 27;
        Experience as a tutor at Yale College, 2-3, 5, 17,
            22, 50, 57;
        Conversion of 1831, 3-4, 16, 39, 40;
        At Yale Divinity School, 4, 35-40;
        Early ministry, 5, 40-42;
        Christian nurture controversy, 97;
        Experience of 1848, 99-100, 101, 103, 139;
        Accusation of heresy in 1849, viii, 140;
        Isolation and depression, 140-41, 167;
        Inspirations in later life, 141.
    Intellectual influences, xii-xiii, 16-17, 22-25, 34, 60,
        63, 100, 104-05.
    Reputation, vii-ix.

BIBLIOGRAPHY OF WORKS CITED

Abrams, M.H. *The Mirror and the Lamp: Romantic Theory and the Critical Tradition.* New York: Oxford University Press, 1953.

_____. *Natural Supernaturalism: Tradition and Revolution in Romantic Literature.* New York: W.W. Norton & Co., Inc., 1971.

Ahlstrom, Sydney E. "The Scottish Philosophy and American Theology." *Church History,* XXIV (1955), pp. 257-72.

_____, ed. *Theology in America: The Major Protestant Voices from Puritanism to Neo-Orthodoxy.* Indianapolis: The Bobbs-Merrill Co., Inc., 1967.

Auerbach, Erich. *Scenes from the Drama of European Literature.* New York: Meridian Books, 1959.

Baird, Robert Dahlen. "Religion is Life: An Inquiry into the Dominating Motif in the Theology of Horace Bushnell." Diss. University of Iowa 1964.

Bartlett, Irving H. "The Romantic Theology of Horace Bushnell." Diss. Brown University 1952.

Becker, Ernest. *The Structure of Evil: An Essay on the Unification of the Science of Man.* New York: George Braziller, 1968.

Beecher, Lyman. *The Autobiography of Lyman Beecher.* Ed. Barbara M. Cross. 2 vols. Cambridge: The Belknap Press of Harvard University Press, 1961.

Bercovitch, Sacvan. *The Puritan Origins of the American Self.* New Haven: Yale University Press, 1975.

_____, ed. *Typology and Early American Literature.* Amherst: University of Massachusetts Press, 1972.

Billings, Mildred Kitto. "The Theology of Horace Bushnell Considered in Relation to that of Samuel Taylor Coleridge." Diss. University of Chicago 1960.

Blau, Joseph. L., ed. *American Philosophical Addresses, 1700-1900.* New York: Columbia University Press, 1946.

Brumm, Ursula. *American Thought and Religious Typology.* New Brunswick, N.J.: Rutgers University Press, 1970.

Bushnell, Horace. *Building Eras in Religion.* New York: Charles Scribner's Sons, 1910.

183

_____. *Christ and His Salvation: In Sermons Variously Related Thereto.* New York: Charles Scribner & Co., 1865.

_____. "Christian Comprehensiveness." *The New Englander*, VI (January 1848), pp. 81-111.

_____. *Christian Nurture.* New Haven: Yale University Press, 1967.

_____. *Christ in Theology.* Hartford: Brown & Parsons, 1851.

_____. "Christ the Form of the Soul." MS Yale Divinity School Library.

_____. "Discourse on the Moral Tendencies and Results of Human History, Delivered before the Society of Alumni, in Yale College." Hartford: J.W. Judd, 1843.

_____. *Forgiveness and Law, Grounded in Principles Interpreted by Human Analogies.* New York: Scribner, Armstrong & Co., 1874.

_____. *God in Christ: Three Discourses Delivered at New Haven, Cambridge, and Andover, with a Preliminary Dissertation on Language.* Hartford, 1849; rpt. New York: AMS Press, 1972.

_____. "God Reigns for the Largest Love." MS Yale Divinity School Library.

_____. Letters to Leonard Bacon. MSS Yale University Library.

_____. Letter to James Freeman Clarke. Hartford, August 30, 1847. MS the Houghton Library of Harvard University.

_____. *Moral Uses of Dark Things.* New York: Charles Scribner's Sons, 1910.

_____. ["Natural Science and Moral Philosophy."] MS Yale Divinity School Library.

_____. *Nature and the Supernatural as Together Constituting the One System of God.* 3rd edition, 1858; rpt. New York: AMS Press, 1973.

_____. "Our Gospel a Gift to the Imagination." *Hours at Home*, X (December 1869), pp. 159-72.

_____. "Pure Love." MS Yale Divinity School Library.

_____. "Revelation." MS Yale Divinity School Library.

_____. *Sermons for the New Life.* New York: Charles Scribner, 1858.

_____. *Sermons on Living Subjects.* New York: Charles Scribner's Sons, 1890.

_____. *The Spirit in Man.* New York: Charles Scribner's Sons, 1910.

_____. "Twentieth Anniversary: A Commemorative Discourse Delivered to the North Church of Hartford, May 22, 1853." Hartford: Elihu Geer, 1853.

_____. *The Vicarious Sacrifice Grounded in Principles Interpreted by Human Analogies.* New York: Charles Scribner's Sons, 1907.

_____. *Views of Christian Nurture and of Subjects Adjacent Thereto.* Hartford, 1847; rpt Delmar, N.Y.: Scholars' Facsimiles & Reprints, 1975.

_____. *Work and Play.* New York: Charles Scribner's Sons, 1903.

Bushnell Centenary: Minutes of the General Association of Connecticut at the 193rd Annual Meeting Held in Hartford, June 17, 18, 1902. Hartford: Hartford Press, The Case, Lockwood & Brainard Co., 1902.

Calvin, John. *Institutes of the Christian Religion.* Trans. John Allen. 6th American edition. 2 vols. Philadelphia: Presbyterian Board of Christian Education, 1928.

Carse, James. *Jonathan Edwards and the Visibility of God.* New York: Charles Scribner's Sons, 1967.

Channing, William Ellery. *The Works of William Ellery Channing, D.D.* Boston: American Unitarian Association, 1897.

Charvat, William. *The Origins of American Critical Thought 1810-1835.* Philadelphia: University of Pennsylvania Press, 1936.

Cheney, Mary Bushnell, *Life and Letters of Horace Bushnell.* New York, 1880; rpt. New York: Arno Press, Inc., 1969.

Coleridge, Samuel Taylor. *Aids to Reflection.* 4th London edition, 1840; rpt. Port Washington, N.Y.: Kennikat Press, 1971.

Clarke, James Freeman. "Bushnell on Vicarious Sacrifice." *Christian Examiner,* LXXX (May 1866), pp. 360-77.

Clebsch, William A. *American Religious Thought: A History.* Chicago: University of Chicago·Press, 1973.

Collingwood, R.G. *An Autobiography.* London: Oxford University Press, 1939.

Crosby, Donald A. *Horace Bushnell's Theory of Language in the Context of Other Nineteenth Century Philosophies of Language.* The Hague: Mouton, 1975.

Cross, Barbara M. *Horace Bushnell: Minister to a Changing America.* Chicago: University of Chicago Press, 1958.

Davis, Merrell R. "Emerson's 'Reason' and the Scottish Philosophers." *New England Quarterly*, 17 (1944), pp. 209-26.

Delattre, Roland. *Beauty and Sensibility in the Thought of Jonathan Edwards: An Essay in Aesthetics and Theological Ethics*. New Haven: Yale University Press, 1968.

Douglas, Ann. *The Feminization of American Culture*. New York: Alfred A. Knopf, 1977.

Edwards, Jonathan. *Freedom of the Will*. Ed. Paul Ramsey. New Haven: Yale University Press, 1957.

_____. *Images or Shadows of Divine Things by Jonathan Edwards*. Ed. Perry Miller. New Haven: Yale University Press, 1948.

_____. *Religious Affections*. Ed. John E. Smith. New Haven: Yale University Press, 1959.

_____. *The Works of President Jonathan Edwards*. 10 vols. London 1817; rpt. New York: Burt Franklin, 1968.

Emerson, Ralph Waldo. *The Complete Works of Ralph Waldo Emerson*. Centenary Edition. Boston & New York: Houghton, Mifflin and Co., 1903.

_____. *The Journals of Ralph Waldo Emerson*. Eds. Edward Waldo Emerson and Waldo Emerson Forbes. 10 vols. Boston & New York: Houghton, 1909-1914.

Faust, Clarence H., and Johnson, Thomas H., eds. *Jonathan Edwards: Representative Selections with Introduction, Bibliography and Notes*. American Century Series edition. New York: Hill and Wang, 1962.

Feidelson, Charles, Jr. *Symbolism and American Literature*. Chicago: University of Chicago Press, 1953.

Foard, Lawrence Clinton. "The Copernican Revolution in Theology: Studies of the Critical· and Romantic Elements in the Theory of Religious Language Proposed by Horace Bushnell." Diss. Temple University 1970.

Foster, Frank Hugh. *A Genetic History of the New England Theology*. Chicago: University of Chicago Press, 1907.

Gibbs, Josiah Willard, Sr. *Philological Studies: with English Illustrations*. New Haven: Durie & Peck, 1857.

Goodwin, Henry M. "Thoughts, Words, and Things." *Bibliotheca Sacra*, VI (May 1849), pp. 271-300.

Grave. S.A. *The Scottish Philosophy of Common Sense*. Oxford: Oxford University Press, 1960.

Harris, Victor. "Allegory to Analogy in the Interpretation of Scripture," *Philological Quarterly*, XLV (January 1966), pp. 1-23.

Haroutunian, Joseph. *Piety Versus Moralism: The Passing of the New England Theology.* New York: Henry Holt & Co., 1932.

Hillis, Frederick Whiley, and Bloom, Harold, eds. *From Sensibility to Romanticism: Essays Presented to Frederick A. Pottle.* New York: Oxford University Press, 1965.

Hodge, Charles. "Bushnell's Discourses." *Biblical Repertory and Princeton Review,* XXI (April 1849), pp. 259-98.

_____. "Bushnell on Christian Nurture." *Biblical Repertory and Princeton Review,* XIX (1847), pp. 502-39.

_____. *The Way of Life.* Philadelphia: American Sunday School Union, 1841.

Hodges, Herbert Arthur, *Wilhelm Dilthey: An Introduction.* New York: Oxford University Press, 1944.

Howell, John Edmund. "A Study of the Theological Method of Horace Bushnell and its Application to his Cardinal Doctrines." Diss. Duke University 1963.

James, Henry, Sr. "Review of *The Vicarious Sacrifice.*" *North American Review,* CII (April 1866), pp. 556-71.

James, William. "Review of Bushnell's *Women's Sufferage* and J.S. Mill's *The Subjection of Women.*" *North American Review,* CIX (October 1869), pp. 556-65.

_____. *The Varieties of Religious Experience.* New York: Collier Books, 1961.

Johnson, Alexander Bryan. *A Treatise on Language.* Ed. David Rynin. Berkeley: University of California Press, 1959.

Johnson, William. *Nature and the Supernatural in the Theology of Horace Bushnell.* Lund: cwk Gleerup, 1963.

Keller, Charles Roy. *The Second Great Awakening in Connecticut.* New Haven: Yale University Press, 1942.

Keller, Karl. *The Example of Edward Taylor.* Amherst: The University of Massachusetts Press, 1975.

Kirby, William. *On the Power, Wisdom and Goodness of God, as Manifested in the Creation of Animals and in Their History, Habits and Instincts.* Philadelphia: Carey, Lea & Blanchard, 1836.

Kirschenmann, Fred. "Horace Bushnell: Orthodox or Sabellian?" *Church History,* XXXII (March 1964), pp. 49-59.

Knights, L.C. *Further Explorations.* London: Chatto, 1965.

Lewis, R.W.B. *The American Adam: Innocence, Tragedy, and Tradition in the Nineteenth Century.* Chicago: University of Chicago Press, 1955.

Lovejoy, Arthur O. *The Great Chain of Being: A Study in the History of an Idea.* Cambridge: Harvard University Press, 1936.

Marx, Leo. *The Machine in the Garden: Technology and the Pastoral Idea in America.* London: Oxford University Press, 1964.

Mather, Samuel. *Figures and Types of the Old Testament Opened and Explained.* 2nd. London edition, 1705; rpt. New York: Johnson Reprint Corporation, 1969.

Mead, Sidney. *Nathaniel William Taylor, 1786-1858: A Connecticut Liberal.* Chicago: University of Chicago Press, 1942.

Meyer, D.H. *The Instructed Conscience: The Shaping of the American National Ethic.* Philadelphia: University of Pennsylvania Press, 1972.

Miller, Perry. *Errand into the Wilderness.* Cambridge: The Belknap Press of Harvard University Press, 1956.

_____. *Jonathan Edwards.* New York: W. Sloane Associates, 1949.

_____. *The Life of the Mind in America: From the Revolution to the Civil War.* New York: Harcourt, Brace and World, 1965.

_____. *The New England Mind: From Colony to Province.* Cambridge: Harvard University Press, 1953.

_____. *The New England Mind: The Seventeenth Century.* New York: The Macmillian Company, 1939.

Morell, John Daniel. *The Philosophy of Religion.* New York: D. Appleton & Co., 1849.

Nevin, John Williamson. "Educational Religion." *The Weekly Messenger of the German Reformed Church,* XII, New Series, June 23, June 30, July 7, and July 14, 1847.

Olshewsky, Thomas, ed. *Problems in the Philosophy of Language.* New York: Holt, Reinhart and Winston, Inc., 1969.

Parker, Edwin Pond. *The Hartford Central Association and the Bushnell Controversy: An Historical Address Given before the Hartford Central Association.* Hartford: Case, Lockwood & Brainard, 1896.

Persons, Stow. *The Decline of American Gentility.* New York: Columbia University Press, 1973.

Pettit, Norman. *The Heart Prepared: Grace and Conversion in Puritan Spiritual Life.* New Haven: Yale University Press, 1966.

Pond, Enoch. *Review of Dr. Bushnell's "God in Christ."* Bangor, Me.: 1849.

Porter, Noah. "Horace Bushnell: A Memorial Sermon Preached in the Chapel of Yale College, Sunday, March 26th, 1876." *The New Englander*, XXXVI (1877), pp. 157-69.

Reid, Thomas. *The Works of Thomas Reid, D.D., F.R.S., with an Account of His Life and Writings by Dugald Stewart.* 3 vols. New York: E. Duyakinak, Collins and Hanney, and R. and W.A. Bartow, 1822.

Rudisill, Dorus Paul. *The Doctrine of the Atonement in Jonathan Edwards and His Successors.* New York: Poseidon Books, 1971.

Schleiermacher, Friedrich. *On Religion: Speeches to its Cultured Despisers.* New York: Harper & Row, 1958.

_____. "On the Discrepancy Between the Sabellian and Athanasian Method of Representing the Doctrine of the Trinity." Trans. with notes by Moses Stuart. *Biblical Repository and Quarterly Review*, V (April 1835), pp. 265-353; and VI (July 1835), pp. 1-116.

Schneider, Herbert W. *A History of American Philosophy.* New York: Columbia University Press, 1946.

Singleton, Gregory H. "Protestant Voluntary Organizations and the Shaping of Victorian America." *American Quarterly*, XXVII (December 1975), pp. 549-560.

Smith, Henry Nash. "Emerson's Problem of Vocation: A Note on 'The American Scholar'." *New England Quarterly*, (March 1939), pp. 52-67.

Smith, H. Shelton, ed. *Horace Bushnell.* A Library of Protestant Thought. New York: Oxford University Press, 1965.

_____. *Changing Conceptions of Original Sin: A Study in American Theology Since 1750.* New York: Charles Scribner's Sons, 1955.

Stephens, Wallace. *Opus Posthumous.* Ed. Samuel French Morse. New York: Alfred A. Knopf, 1957.

Stewart, Dugald. *Collected Works.* Ed. Sir William Hamilton. 7 vols. Edinburgh: T. & T. Clark, 1877.

Taylor, Edward. *The Poems of Edward Taylor.* Ed. Donald E. Stanford. New Haven: Yale University Press, 1960.

Taylor, Nathaniel William. *Essays, Lectures, Etc., Upon Select Topics in Revealed Theology.* New York: Clark, Austin and Smith, 1859.

_____. *Lectures on the Moral Government of God.* 2 vols. New York: Clark, Austin and Smith, 1859.

_____. *Practical Sermons.* New York: Clark, Austin and Smith, 1859.

Tyler, Bennet. *Letters to the Rev. Horace Bushnell, D.D. Containing Strictures on his Book Entitled "Views of Christian Nurture and of Subjects Adjacent Thereto."* Hartford: Brown & Parsons, 1848.

Wheelwright, Philip. *The Burning Fountain: A Study in the Language of Symbolism.* Bloomington: Indiana University Press, 1968.

Williams, Roger. *Complete Writings.* 7 vols. New York: Russell & Russell, 1963.

Wright, Conrad. *The Beginnings of Unitarianism in America.* Boston: Starr King Press, 1955.

Young, Fredric. *The Philosophy of Henry James, Sr.* New York: Bookman Associates, 1951.